Fodor's Inside

Nashville

Mar 30th

CONTENTS

ABOUT THIS GUIDE

Inside Nashville is Music City like you've never seen it. Written entirely by locals, it includes features on the city's dives, honky-tonks, and food havens, and plenty of insider tips. The result is a curated compilation infused with authentic Southern flavor, accompanied by easy-to-use maps. Whether you're visiting Nashville for the first time or a seasoned traveler looking to explore a new neighborhood, this is the guide for you. We've handpicked the top things to do and rated the sights, shopping, dining, and nightlife in the city's most dynamic, up-and-coming neighborhoods. Truly exceptional experiences in all categories are marked with a ★.

Restaurants, bars, and cafés are a huge part of Nashville's appeal, of course, and you'll find plenty to savor in its diverse neighborhoods. We cover cuisines in all price points, and everything from enduring institutions and groundbreaking chefs. We cover hotels in the Experience section at the front of this guide.

#FODORSONTHEGO

We've highlighted fun neighborhood facts throughout this guide. As you explore Nashville, we invite you to use **#FodorsOnTheGo** to share your favorite discoveries with us.

Use the $ to $$$$ price charts below to estimate meal and room costs. We list adult prices for sights; ask about discounts when purchasing tickets. Nashville is constantly changing. All prices, opening times, and other details in this guide were accurate at press time. Always confirm information when it matters, especially when making a detour to a specific place.

Visit Fodors.com for expanded restaurant and hotel reviews, additional recommendations, news, and features.

WHAT IT COSTS: Restaurants			
$	$$	$$$	$$$$
Under $13	$13-$24	$25-$35	Over $35

Prices are the average cost of a main course at dinner or, if dinner is not served, at lunch.

WHAT IT COSTS: Hotels			
$	$$	$$$	$$$$
Under $300	$300-$449	$450-$600	Over $600

Prices are the lowest cost of a standard double room in high season.

1 | # Experience Nashville

WELCOME TO NASHVILLE

Nashville's history often focuses on the more recent past: the story of country music as told through the Grand Ole Opry radio show, the birth of the careers of Dolly Parton and Patsy Cline, and the recording studios where the ghost of Elvis hovers over the piano. But it's worth digging a little deeper and looking out even further to learn about the Civil War history of Franklin, Tennessee, or the rail yards and mills of the Gulch and Wedgewood-Houston, which have been repurposed as gallery spaces. Musicians still flock to Nashville in hopes of stardom, and recording studios can be found by the dozen in Berry Hill, but the music coming out of the city is not limited to country—exports include funk, soul, and hip-hop. Large-scale housing and business developments continue to rapidly change the city's landscape, yet each neighborhood maintains its own identity and local-favorite staples. Throughout the city you'll find innovative food and Southern classics, secret speakeasies with craft cocktails, and local dives. Sample international cuisine by traveling up Nolensville Pike from Bell Road to Thompson Lane, or Charlotte Pike, west of White Bridge. Most of the neighborhoods covered in this book are small, walkable, and close to another. Here's a rundown of the areas we cover in detail. The numbers refer to chapter numbers.

---

2. DOWNTOWN

Lower Broadway, aka Honky Tonk Highway, is a must for first-time visitors; surrounding the area are art galleries, world-class museums, and the symphony.

3. GERMANTOWN

This booming historic neighborhood of classic row houses is filled with some of the best dining in Nashville. Come here for a ball game at First Tennessee Park. New to the area is the Tennessee State Museum, which should not be missed.

4. HILLSBORO VILLAGE

Accessible by bus from Downtown, this bikeable, walkable neighborhood is home to students of Belmont and Vanderbilt universities. Come here for dives, down-home restaurant staples, and to visit the historic Belcourt Theatre.

5. EAST NASHVILLE

Trendy East Nashville is comprised of several smaller neighborhoods, all with excellent options for dining, nature, and nights out. Go dancing at a locals-loved watering hole and rest your head at the hip Urban Cowboy B&B.

6. 12 SOUTH

Street fairs and a strip lined with cafes, restaurants, and shops (some owned by celebrities) make up the scenery of this highly walkable neighborhood.

7. WEDGEWOOD-HOUSTON

Things are changing rapidly for this neighborhood, where high-end restaurants and craft distilleries mingle with railroad tracks and warehouses, and a 1930s hosiery mill.

8. MELROSE AND BERRY HILL

If you want to see where Nashville's countless musicians record, go to the microneighborhood of Berry Hill. To the northwest is the eclectic yet suburban Melrose neighborhood, known especially for 8th Avenue, which has antiques and vintage stores.

9. SYLVAN PARK AND THE NATIONS

You'll find the most activity in these west Nashville neighborhoods on Charlotte and 51st avenues. Residential Sylvan Park has bungalows and Victorian homes, whereas The Nations has modern dwellings. Come here for shopping and green spaces.

10. THE GULCH

This now ritzy area was once a rail yard before services shut down in the late '70s. It was revitalized starting in the early 2000s, and today it's filled with rooftop bars, music venues, and impressive dining options.

11. MIDTOWN AND EDGEHILL

Tucked between downtown Nashville and the suburban enclaves of Green Hills and Belle Meade, Midtown is close to attractions like the Grand Ole Opry and Printer's Alley yet has lots of local shops and a neighborhood feel.

12. FRANKLIN, TENNESSEE

Twenty miles south of Nashville is this small town with a complex history; Franklin was devastated at the end of the Civil War and its plantation economy collapsed when slavery was abolished. Victorian houses and a quaint downtown are remnants of old Tennessee.

13. GREATER NASHVILLE

Well beyond the city center are Nashville's forests and the Harpeth River, which you can explore by canoe or on foot. On the outskirts of town discover cultural and historical landmarks, and eclectic gems and eateries with authentic international cuisine.

TOP EXPERIENCES IN NASHVILLE

LIVE MUSIC

Music City isn't just a place for country heads: **Marathon Music Works**, a 14,000-square-foot venue just outside of downtown, hosts an eclectic mix of performances throughout the year. **Cannery Ballroom** has a similar vibe but a more intimate feel. Midtown's **Exit/In**, where the Red Hot Chili Peppers once had Thanksgiving dinner after a late-night set, features punk, rock, and hip-hop performances.

ON THE GREEN

Take a midday stroll in **Centennial Park**, where you can lounge in front of Lake Watauga, or wander the sunken garden. The **Warner Parks** (Percy and Edwin) are also nearby; enjoy their 3,200 acres of rolling hills, meadows, and forests. **Cheekwood Botanical Gardens** offers a similar respite, with nearly a dozen individual gardens throughout, and a sculpture trail. In the southern part of the city is **Radnor Lake State Park**, a nature preserve with more than 5 miles of hiking trails, some of which are accessible to pets, bicycles, and all-terrain wheelchairs.

SHOPPING

For local goods, head to the **Nashville Flea Market**, which is open at the Fairgrounds every fourth weekend of the month; there you can buy anything from jewelry and leather products to health and beauty goods. **Nashville Farmers' Market** is a great place for home-baked goodies. If thrifting is your thing, check out **Southern Thrift**, which has locations in west and south Nashville, and **Smack**, a vintage clothing store in the heart of midtown. You can also head to **GasLamp Antiques** for clothing, books, and—you guessed it—lamps.

ON THE SCREEN

Nashville is home to several movie theaters, but none are quite like **The Belcourt**, a newly renovated, nonprofit film center that features some of today's most avant-garde films. If you're up for an excursion, take a drive down to Watertown, Tennessee (approximately 40 minutes outside the city), for the **Stardust Drive-in**, which plays movies on weekend nights, rain or shine, and offers seasonal double features.

ON THE STAGE

For live performances, visit the **Tennessee Performing Arts Center** (TPAC), home to productions by the Nashville Ballet, the Nashville Opera, and the Nashville Repertory Theatre. The **Schermerhorn Symphony Center** is another excellent venue for live musical performances, and offers annual free days of music. The **CMA Music Festival**, a four-day event in June, also offers free day concerts by a wide range of country music performers.

TREATS AND EATS

If you're looking for something cool, try **Las Paletas**, a gourmet "ice pop" shop that serves cream- and fruit-based treats in traditional Mexican flavors; or **Bobbie's Dairy Dip**, a patio-style eatery that serves dipped cones, milk shakes, and banana splits along with other drive-in fare like hamburgers and hot dogs. If you're on the hunt for baked desserts, check out **Five Daughters Bakery**, home of the croissant-style Hundred Layer Doughnut, and **Vegan Vee Gluten Free Bakery**, which serves doughnuts, cakes, and their legendary jumbo cookie sandwiches.

FESTIVALS

Nashville is the home of festivals year-round, but few are as popular as the late-summer **Tomato Art Festival**, where attendees can sample entries in the Bloody Mary Contest, and experience the best in Nashville food truck cuisine. In the fall, the **Southern Festival of Books** draws writers and book lovers from around the world, and **Shakespeare in the Park** offers free live productions of the bard's most popular plays in the Centennial Park amphitheater. The annual **African Street Festival** is another fall favorite, where artists gather to celebrate African and African American culture.

THE ART SCENE

For exhibits by some of the newest and most provocative artists, visit the **Frist Center for the Visual Arts**. If you're looking for smaller exhibits, check out **Fisk University Galleries**, which are home to world-class artwork from the past two centuries, including permanent collections by Elizabeth Catlett and Georgia O'Keeffe. The new **Tennessee State Museum** is a must-see for an historical overview of the mid-South.

SOUTHERN COMFORTS

For some of the best drinks in the city, visit the mixologists at **Patterson House**, or drink and dine at Union Common, which has live jazz performances on Sundays. **Tavern** 's 2-for-1 weekend brunch specials are not to be missed, nor is **Pinewood Social**, where you can enjoy a cocktail along with a game of pool, a karaoke performance, or a few rounds of bowling. You can also take a tour of **Tennessee Brew Works**, followed by dinner and live music in their taproom.

GREAT FOR KIDS

The **Nashville Zoo** houses both native and exotic species, as well as a working farm and a petting zoo; or, spend the day at the **Adventure Science Center**, which has more than 150 interactive exhibits, a planetarium, and a 75-foot-tall Adventure Tower with breathtaking views of the city. **Nashville Children's Theatre** is another excellent place for a family outing. It has hosted adaptations of Broadway productions as well as original plays by its troupe of performers.

COOLEST PLACES TO STAY

There are plenty of stylish lodging options in Nashville; choose from rooftop hangouts, unique dining options, and gorgeous interiors.

UNION STATION HOTEL

This gorgeous building is more than 100 years old and once housed one of the South's most bustling train stations. With a 65-foot barrel-vaulted lobby ceiling, huge stone fireplaces, stained-glass windows, crystal chandeliers, and even their own blend of Jack Daniel's whiskey, a stay here includes a unique peek into local history. The rooms were recently renovated, and each sports a modern look. $ *Rooms from: $209 ✉ 1001 Broadway, Downtown ☎ 615/726–1001 🌐 unionstationhotelnashville.com 🛏 125 rooms 🍽 No meals.*

URBAN COWBOY B&B

This intimate, revamped Victorian bed-and-breakfast in the famously hip East Nashville neighborhood provides refuge from the crowds. Each room has a claw-foot tub and bold patterns and textures. The on-site bar hosts live music and is a hit with the locals. $ *Rooms from: $250 ✉ 1603 Woodland St., East Nashville ☎ 347/840–0525 🌐 urbancowboy.com/nashville 🛏 8 rooms 🍽 No meals.*

THE GERMANTOWN INN

Situated in a gorgeous late-1800s brick home that was recently renovated, this six-room inn is the epitome of cozy and upscale. The Germantown neighborhood is a real gem for foodies, and the inn is close to some of the best restaurants in town like City House, 5th and Taylor, Monell's, and Rolf and Daughters. $ *Rooms from: $230 ✉ 1218 6th Ave. N., Germantown ☎ 615/581–1218 🌐 germantowninn.com 🛏 10 rooms 🍽 Free breakfast.*

NOELLE HOTEL

Simple, modern rooms with art deco touches can be found at Noelle. Perch atop the roof for a drink at Rare Bird, head back in time to the 1930s and have a cocktail in the Trade Room, or have a leisurely meal at the main restaurant, which offers upscale American tavern food. They also offer a complimentary morning coffee delivery. $ *Rooms from: $270 ✉ 200 4th Ave. N, Downtown ☎ 615/649–5000 🌐 noelle-nashville.com 🛏 224 rooms 🍽 No meals.*

THOMPSON HOTEL

Award-winning for its architecture, this luxury boutique hotel is one of the best spots to stay in the city. A grab-and-go coffee shop and an upscale seafood restaurant are on the first floor, but the trendy rooftop bar known as the L.A. Jackson is where this hotel really shines. [$] *Rooms from: $315 ✉ 401 11th Ave. S, The Gulch ☎ 615/262–6000 🌐 thompsonhotels.com 🛏 224 rooms 🍽 No meals.*

THE FAIRLANE

Just a stone's throw away from the iconic Batman building and three blocks from the hustle and bustle of the honky-tonks sits this new boutique hotel resplendent with '70s retro-modern flair. Floor-to-ceiling windows provide natural light in each room and views of the Nashville skyline. [$] *Rooms from: $269 ✉ 401 Union St., Downtown ☎ 615/933–2186 🌐 fairlanehotel.com/the-fairlane 🛏 81 rooms 🍽 No meals.*

THE INN AT OPRYLAND

About 20 minutes from the center of the city, the Inn at Opryland took the place of the Opryland amusement park. An opulent and innovative 1977 building with stunning atriums and extensive indoor gardens, the hotel has retained some of the amusement park kitsch (for example, you can take a boat ride down their indoor river). On-site are numerous bars, restaurants, spas, retailers, and more. [$] *Rooms from: $129 ✉ 2401 Music Valley Dr., Opryland ☎ 615/889–1000 🌐 marriott.com 🛏 303 rooms 🍽 No meals.*

OMNI NASHVILLE HOTEL

Right next to the expansive new convention center, the modern Omni hotel has stellar views, luxe modern interior filled with wood and marble, a restaurant with a seriously good (and seriously Southern) biscuit bar, and a coffee shop serving locally roasted Bongo Java coffee. The city's largest music venues and sports arenas are all within walking distance. [$] *Rooms from: $221 ✉ 250 5th Ave. S, Downtown ☎ 800/444–6664 🌐 omnihotels.com 🛏 800 rooms 🍽 No meals.*

21C MUSEUM HOTEL

Perhaps one of Nashville's most avant garde hotels, this pick boasts a specially curated collection of modern art in common spaces and funky, eclectic rooms. The on-site restaurant, Gray & Dudley, offers hearty comfort food, and the clean and sparse interior showcases a rotating exhibition. The museum portions of the hotel are free and open to the public every day of the year, and you can get a special guided docent tour on Wednesday and Friday at 5 pm. [$] *Rooms from: $227 ✉ 221 2nd Ave. N., Downtown ☎ 615/610–6400 🌐 21cmuseumhotels.com/nashville 🛏 124 rooms 🍽 No meals.*

STRICTLY FOR TOURISTS

First time in Nashville? Don't skip the Broadway honky-tonks, historic music sites, and architectural gems that make the city a true destination.

CENTENNIAL PARK AND THE PARTHENON

Nashville's most popular park, this is a haven for sunbathers, dog walkers, and kite fliers. In the warmest months you can watch Shakespeare in the park, or stop by the band shell for live music, weekly swing-dancing nights, food trucks, festivals like Musicians' Corner, and more. The crown jewel of this green space, though, is the replica of the Parthenon, built in 1897. It's worth the small price of admission to see the permanent collection of art inside along with the 42-foot-tall gold statue of the goddess Athena. *West End*

THE GRAND OLE OPRY

Although the Opry moved from its original home at the Ryman Auditorium in 1974, it retains its charm with magical musical performances. The historic weekly country and bluegrass program lives on in this spacious building that also hosts its fair share of touring acts from around the country. They offer daily tours so you can take a peek backstage. *Opryland Dr.*

THE COUNTRY MUSIC HALL OF FAME

Detailed rotating exhibits that explore the legacies of artists and musical movements—like the outlaw country of the '70s—give visitors a reason to keep coming back, but the expansive permanent collection of country music relics prove Nashville's lasting reign as Music City. *Downtown*

MUSIC ROW

While many historic buildings and studios have sadly been razed in recent years to make way for condos and high-rises, you can still peer into Nashville's past in this area between the Edgehill and Midtown neighborhoods. See where iconic records were born and take a few tours of studios like the famous Ocean Way or RCA Studio B, where Elvis Presley, Dolly Parton, and Willie Nelson recorded classics. *Music Row*

HONKY-TONKS ON BROADWAY

Follow the neon lights to find an array of Nashville's lively honky-tonks that line the once-infamous and now just plain famous downtown street. Start at Robert's Western World for a fried bologna sandwich and a cold beer and hear live country classics—nothing recorded past 1980! Work your way down to Tootsie's Orchid Lounge where the crowd gets a little more rowdy, then listen to bands at the three-story Nudie's Honky Tonk, where Nudie Cohn's legendary rhinestone suits adorn the walls. *Lower Broad*

THE BLUEBIRD CAFE

Located a little further off the beaten path in the Green Hills neighborhood is this intimate listening room that's a rite of passage for any serious songwriter trying to cut their teeth in the city. Line up early for your chosen showtime to secure a seat. You're likely to hear a top-notch song well before it hits the charts as many writers for big labels workshop here. Talking during performances is strictly prohibited, so avoid this spot if you're traveling with a rambunctious group. *Green Hills*

CHEEKWOOD ESTATE & GARDENS

Tucked away near the rolling hills of old horse farms and plantations is this art-lover's oasis. The lush botanicals, verdant trees, shimmering ponds, and scattered sculptures lend a whimsical quality to this space where rotating exhibits from renowned artists like Dale Chihuly can be found. In the historic mansion you can find a small permanent collection with pieces from Andy Warhol and Robert Rauschenberg. If you're visiting during fall or winter, don't miss their special holiday festivities or exquisite Christmas lights. *West Meade*

MUSICIANS HALL OF FAME AND MUSEUM

Located inside the Municipal Auditorium is another powerful testament to the musical legacy of the city. You'll find special exhibits on the GRAMMY Awards, Motown, Stax, Muscle Shoals, and more, and, of course, some Nashville pioneers. Beyond big-name acts, you'll also learn about the lesser-known session musicians who played on some of the most popular recordings in history. *Downtown*

FREE THINGS TO DO

Tourism is one of Nashville's most lucrative industries, but that doesn't mean you have to spend a ton of money to have a great time. Here's where the locals go for fun at no cost.

JEFFERSON STREET ART CRAWL

Every fourth Saturday of the month, the historically black community of north Nashville hosts the Jefferson Street Art Crawl, an event where art lovers can browse galleries that showcase African American art, attend public showings of up-and-coming artists, and even visit One Drop Ink, a tattoo lounge that offers discounted rates for piercings and other body art during the crawl. The Music City Blue Circuit also offers free shuttle service between destinations.

LIVE MUSIC AT THE FRIST

Every Thursday and Friday evening you can lounge in the Frist's café while listening to live music. Admission to the café is free, though food and drinks are not. Parking is $5.

BIG BAND DANCES IN METRO PARKS

Summer months bring lots of activities to Nashville's parks, and Big Band Dances is one of them. They take place on Saturday nights, and attendees are encouraged to bring blankets and lawn chairs, as well as a few bucks for food truck goodies, since part of the concession proceeds help sponsor the event. If you're not the most confident about your moves, group dance lessons are offered from 7 to 7:30 pm, shortly before the dance begins.

WARNER PARK NATURE CENTER EVENTS

If you want to get down and dirty and learn about birds, insects, and trees, consider attending one of the Nature Center's free summer events. There's a lot to choose from, but some standouts are the annual **Insects of the Night**, where you can dress up as your favorite insect, play games, and participate in night hikes; and **Friday iSpy**, where naturalists help park goers learn about soil, pollinating plants, snakes, and salamanders.

JAZZ ON THE CUMBERLAND

From May until November, this concert series is held monthly on Sundays in Cumberland Park from 5:30 to 8 pm. The concert itself is free, but drivers must pay $5 to park in nearby lots. Food trucks and other concessions are also on hand, though no alcoholic beverages are allowed.

FOURTH OF JULY IN NASHVILLE

Nashville is a great place to celebrate Independence Day, as there's no shortage of festivities. Downtown events typically begin at noon with a string of free concerts, culminating with a Nashville Symphony performance in the Ascend Amphitheater during the nighttime fireworks display.

TITANS' SUMMER PRACTICE

If you're a sports fan on a budget, you can still snag an opportunity to see some live action on the field; the Tennessee Titans' practice sessions at St. Thomas Sports Park are free for fans from July until August.

OKTOBERFEST IN NASHVILLE

This German street fair and fall festival includes a dachshund derby, a 5k "Bier Run," a beer slide, and live German music, all set in Nashville's Germantown neighborhood, just north of downtown. Admission to the four-day event is free, and offers free and kid-friendly activities throughout, though VIP tickets are available. VIP access includes beer and whiskey tastings, an all-you-can-eat buffet, and private (and air-conditioned) bathrooms.

ARRINGTON VINEYARDS

If you've got a little gas to burn, consider visiting Arrington Vineyards, a 75-acre winery approximately 40 miles south of the city. Parking and admission are free, and visitors are encouraged to bring along blankets, chairs, and food to enjoy with Arrington's world-class wines. (You can also have food delivered to you by Simply Living Life, which has a special catering menu for vineyard guests.) Wine tastings, small concessions, and private events are also available for a fee.

KIDSVILLE

Every Saturday between 11 and noon, musicians, storytellers, and educators host a free event for children at the Parthenon in Centennial Park. Events include live music (of course), interactive games, as well as fitness, literacy, and nutrition programs. If you're looking for other free kid-friendly outings, please note that several parks and museums—including Cheekwood, The Frist, Belmont Mansion, and Belle Meade Plantation—are free for kids.

WHERE TO DRINK

Can a city famous for its music also be known for its drinks? Nashville is making a case for it.

BROADWAY STAPLES

Much of Nashville's boozy reputation is tied to Broadway, where the classic honky-tonks and huge party bars have perfected the pairing of live music and a constant flow of libations. Broadway itself boasts a variety of offerings, accommodating country music fans of all ages. The giant three-story **Honky Tonk Central** is a favorite of bachelorette parties and young travelers, whereas the legendary **Tootsie's Orchid Lounge** draws country music fans, two-steppers, and history buffs.

Should hunger strike while boot-scooting down the **Honky Tonk Highway**, **Robert's Western World** has you covered with the Recession Special: a hot dog, bag of chips, and beer. For more munchies, **Acme Feed & Seed** is a favorite of locals and travelers alike, offering tasty Southern fare, strong cocktails, and even sushi, on multiple floors. Their rooftop claims one of the best views of the famous strip, with a panorama of the Cumberland River on one side and a bird's-eye view of the neon on the other.

LOCALS-ONLY

Locals don't often make it down to Broadway; their preferred nightlife spot can be found in midtown. The side-by-side **Winners & Losers** is the cornerstone of Demonbreun, offering college-bar-style drink specials and—being just a stone's throw from Music Row—a glimpse at a famous face or two. Roadhouse-style **Red Door Saloon** is just down the block, and **Kung Fu Saloon** offers quirky outdoor seating options and games of both the arcade and yard variety.

CRAFT COCKTAILS

The breakneck pace on Broadway is half the fun, with bartenders often filling two beers at once from the tap. Those looking for a slower experience, however, will be glad to know Nashville has a booming craft cocktail scene. The **Patterson House** is the city's richest source for classic cocktails, mixing up Prohibition-era recipes alongside a house menu of contemporary cocktails. East Nashville's **The Fox Bar & Cocktail Club** offers carefully curated classics (including a martini with melted beeswax dripped into local spirits) in an intimate hideaway, and just up the road, **Rosemary** features playful and seasonal creations in a converted house with backyard seating. However, not all cocktails in Nashville are served in intimate lounges. **Old Glory** and **Bastion** are great examples of converted industrial spaces whose creative cocktail menus are as cool as their design. **Greenhouse Bar**, as the name suggests, serves their drinks and food in a converted greenhouse.

FRITO PIES AND DIVES

In search of a shot-and-a-beer special? **Duke's** has it covered with the Federale and Patriot, alongside a deli serving bodega-style sandwiches. Up the street at **Dino's**, their shot-and-a-pony combo pairs well with a Frito Pie.

While Dino's calls itself Nashville's oldest dive bar, fellow beer-and-burger stronghold **Brown's Diner** holds Nashville's oldest beer license and has been in continuous operation since 1927. That's not the only dive of distinction, either: **Rosie's Twin Kegs** exhibits Nashville's oldest operating shuffleboard along with its offerings of cheap beer and karaoke. If you're celebrating a birthday, be sure to stop by **The Villager** for their traditional birthday offering: a dog bowl of beer.

BREWERIES AND DISTILLERIES

Great beer and liquor aren't just served in Nashville, they're also made here. Local breweries like **Yazoo**, **Jackalope**, **Black Abbey**, and **Little Harpeth Brewing** have tastings, tours, and taprooms. **Corsair Distillery** crafts whiskey and gin in small batches, serving tastings and hosting tours of their facilities in Marathon Village.

DRINKS WITH A SIDE OF ENTERTAINMENT

Nearly every bar on Broadway features country cover bands or concerts by local artists. Beyond Broadway, **Belcourt Taps** frequently hosts writer's rounds in their welcoming setting, as do **The Listening Room** and **The Sutler**. Bluegrass mecca **The Station Inn** is a must for any music fan, and for those who like to two step to country music, the dance floor at **The Nashville Palace** is the biggest and best in town. Classic dive **Springwater Supper Club & Lounge** hosts rock shows in one room and has pool tables and darts in the other.

BARS WITH A VIEW

For a final toast to all of the drinking experiences Nashville has to offer, head to one of the city's rooftop cocktail bars like **L.A. Jackson** or **Rare Bird** and raise a glass while enjoying some of the best views of Music City.

WHAT TO WATCH AND READ BEFORE YOU VISIT

Nashville is the city of reinvention, welcoming the indefinable and the new. It's known as Music City, but also inspired and fostered art in the form of literature and film. Here's what to read, watch, and listen to as you explore every facet of this town.

READ

Nashville: Scenes from the New American South, written by best-selling author Ann Patchett with photography by Heidi Ross, challenges everything you think you know about the South. This is not about Nashville's past but its explosive present. **Insider Tip:** Get a signed copy at Parnassus Books, Patchett's independent bookstore located in Nashville's Green Hills just south of downtown.

Lorraine: The Girl Who Sang the Storm Away should come with its own sound track. Written by Ketch Secor, founder of bluegrass band Old Crow Medicine Show, it's the story of girl growing up with her grandfather in Tennessee, for whom music provides both comfort and identity. It's beautifully illustrated by famous Nashville artist Higgins Bond.

For authentic Southern recipes you can take home, peruse cookbooks by Nashville's notable country stars, including Tammy Wynette (***The Tammy Wynette Southern Cookbook***) and Dolly Parton (***Dolly's Dixie Fixin's Cookbook***). Still hungry? Check out Caroline Randall Williams' cookbook ***Soul Food Love***, which she co-wrote with her mother, Alice Randall, a Vanderbilt University writer-in-residence and the author of *The Wind Done Gone,* an alternative account of Margaret Mitchell's *Gone with the Wind* from the perspective of one of Scarlett O'Hara's slaves, for something more contemporary.

For a tale with more grit, crack open Brian Allison's ***Murder & Mayhem*** in Nashville, which looks into the colorful history of a section of the city called Smoky Row, the site of mysterious and macabre activity in the 1930s, or ***Strong Inside: Perry Wallace and the Collision of Race and Sports in the South*** by Andrew Maraniss, which tells the true story of the first black Southeastern Conference basketball player and Vanderbilt University student, and his experiences, struggles, and triumphs in the 1960s.

WATCH

A Word on Words: This Emmy-nominated show filmed in Nashville features famous authors discussing their prestigious works at local spots around town in three-minute segments—but it's more fun than it sounds. Think Celeste Ng in firefighter gear discussing her novel *Little Fires Everywhere*, and Margaret Atwood (author of *The Handmaid's Tale*) discussing her 2015 novel *The Heart Goes Last* from a local jail.

The Thing Called Love: This 1993 film follows songwriter Miranda Presley (Samantha Mathis) as she leaves New York to seek stardom in Nashville. There's marriage and mayhem and guitars and drunken brawls ... everything you need to get in the country spirit. Much of the film is set in the iconic Bluebird Café where so many country stars got their start. It also stars River Phoenix and Sandra Bullock.

Heartworn Highways: This two-part documentary from 1976 follows iconic singer-songwriters like Guy Clark and Steve Young during their rise to fame. Its sequel, ***Heartworn Highways Revisted***, picks up 40 years in the future, and features modern artists like Jonny Fritz and Langhorne Slim as they pursue the same dream as their predecessors.

SIDE TRIP: A GUIDE TO MUSIC VALLEY

There's more to Music Valley than just tour buses full of retired couples in cowboy boots. Right off of Briley Parkway, between I-65 and I-40, there's a long strip of land inside the Cumberland River's first narrow loop on the northeast side of town. This is Music Valley—the old slice of farmland where the Grand Ole Opry settled down for good in 1974. The Opry's relocation to this sparse site set off a chain reaction of development in the following years—first a theme park (Opryland, which closed in 1997), then a resort, then a monolithic mall, and a hundred little shops, restaurants, and attractions in between. It's true that most of these things were built to accommodate the Opry's tourism runoff, and that much of Music Valley still accommodates this crowd today. But there's an earnestness to Music Valley's offerings that you won't find on Lower Broadway or Music Row, where country music is a loud, expensive, neon caricature of itself. Music Valley has resisted the influence of new Nashville trends the way that classic country has resisted the influence of pop. Frankly, this isn't the part of town you come to if you want to wait in line to take an Instagram picture in front of a hip mural. This is where you come if you want to listen to real country music while you take a minute to slow down, stop trying to impress everyone, and eat a fried bologna sandwich, probably next to a retired couple in cowboy boots.

SIGHTS

Gaylord Opryland Resort. Technically the Gaylord Opryland Resort is a hotel and convention center, but it's worth a visit even if you aren't staying the night. For one thing, there are 9 acres of gardens inside, all laced with walking paths, fountains, and rivers. These gardens feature more than 50,000 tropical plants, contained within a soaring glass ceiling that lets the sun shine through during the day and reflects a thousand warm twinkle lights at night (particularly at Christmas). Even the locals can't resist an occasional walk through the immaculately tended branches and waterfalls of the Cascade Atrium—especially when you consider that you can do it with a beer, cocktail, or cup of gelato in hand. There are almost 20 restaurants to choose from if you get hungry, and plenty of kitschy shops if you're in the market for souvenirs. To avoid the hefty parking fee, it's recommended that you park next door at the mall and walk over.

Two Rivers Park. This 374-acre park along the Cumberland River has more recreational activities than any other park in Nashville. To name just a few, there's a skate park, golf course, and small water park called Wave Country, featuring a wave pool and several slides. The Two Rivers Dog Park is one of the largest in the city, and there's a walking track around the perimeter so you can jog or walk while your dog frolics. The Stones River Greenway is a 10.2-mile paved trail that runs straight through Two Rivers Park, ending in the Cumberland River Pedestrian Bridge that leads east across the river to Shelby Bottoms Park. In addition to the natural sights provided by leafy green Tennessee, you may pass a beautiful Italianate mansion on your walk. That's Two Rivers Mansion, an 1859 plantation home that's now used as a private venue for weddings and events.

Willie Nelson and Friends Museum and General Store. All the Nashville classics are amassed here at the Willie Nelson and Friends Museum and General Store: fringe leather goods, zebra print flasks, cowboy hats, fudge, Goo Goo Clusters, and Donald Trump voodoo dolls. At the back of the general store, buy a ticket and go through the door on your right into the 5,000-square-foot museum. There you'll find instruments, awards, photos, costumes, and other Willie Nelson memorabilia on display. However, even if you're not a huge Willie Nelson fan, the "and Friends" part of the "Willie Nelson and Friends Museum" may entice you. There are also memorabilia from the likes of Patsy Cline, Dolly Parton, Porter Wagoner, and 27 other country music superstars.

RESTAURANTS

Caney Fork River Valley Grille. This is truly the only place in Nashville you can find gator chili, wild elk sliders, or a venison sausage Philly. Though the Caney Fork River Valley Grille is best known for their ribs and catfish, their wild game menu is a must-try for those with a taste for adventure. There's live music every Friday and Saturday against a backdrop of taxidermy possums, bears, deer, wolves, bobcats, and much more. The indoor catfish pond is especially scenic, if you prefer a livelier view during dinner.

Cock of the Walk. This catfish surf 'n' turf restaurant has been turning out Nashville's favorite fried fillets for 36 years. From the rustic wood-paneled walls, to the rows of rocking chairs, to the shrine of signed head shots from country music legends, Cock of the Walk tackles traditional Tennessee cooking in a laid-back family atmosphere. Beyond the obvious steak, catfish, and shrimp mains, they also offer several standout sides like coleslaw, hush puppies, and pickled onions.

Scoreboard Bar and Grill. Good drink specials, hot chicken, and chill karaoke characterize this sports bar and restaurant. There's a rustic/modern dissonance here, with old-timey features like log-cabin-style booths and a cigarette vending machine right next to more updated fixtures like pool tables, televisions, and a virtual golfing game. This is a great pick for sports fans especially, with plenty of indoor and outdoor seating and a menu full of game-day essentials like burgers, wings, and nachos.

Sukho Thai. If you need a break from the nonstop glitter and grit that characterizes most of Music Valley, consider having a tranquil meal at Sukho Thai. Despite the fact that it's next door to a go-kart track, this place is quite elegant. The carved wooden details, romantic lighting, and peaceful music are calming after a day of honky-tonking, and dishes like the basil lamb will not disappoint.

BARS AND NIGHTLIFE

The Nashville Palace. If you're a classic country music fan who laments the day country-pop was ever invented, get yourself to the Nashville Palace as quickly you can. This bar and venue is a country music legend and one of the few places in town that showcases classic country exclusively. They have live music from open to close, and you can order a fried bologna sandwich whenever your heart desires. In the back is a huge dance floor where they have special events and concerts (usually ticketed), but it isn't uncommon to see a little line dancing or two-stepping on the smaller dance floor in the front room either.

PERFORMING ARTS

The General Jackson Showboat. *The General Jackson Showboat* is a Victorian-style riverboat that cruises down the Cumberland River up to twice a day. On board, there's a two-story theater that showcases a couple of flashy, choreographed, cheesy but fun contemporary country productions—the "Taste of Tennessee" show, which plays during the midday cruise, and the "Music City Nights" show, which takes place as the sun is setting. Each show comes with a meal, and after the show, you can roam the different decks outside, including a rooftop bar from which you can enjoy views of the sparkling downtown Nashville skyline.

The Grand Ole Opry. The Grand Ole Opry is the most famous country music show in the world—in fact, it's the show that made country music famous. They've been broadcasting their concerts every week since 1925, making it the longest-running radio broadcast in the United States, and there isn't a country, bluegrass, or Americana icon who hasn't performed here. The Opry has been in its current location since 1974, and as such it's the epicenter around which the rest of Music Valley has rippled out over the years. Even if you aren't a huge fan of country music, it's definitely worth a visit for the spectacle of it all. And if attending a live show isn't enough to scratch the big-hair, sparkly jacket, fiddle-sawing itch, you can take a backstage tour seven days a week to hear more about the history, stars, and stories that make the Grand Ole Opry truly grand.

Nashville Nightlife Dinner Theater. The Nashville Nightlife Dinner Theater is a perfect antidote for when ultra-cool New Nashville starts to take itself too seriously. This place is just unpretentious, good-hearted, country music fun. Join 300 of your closest friends for a buffet-style dinner and an hour and a half of some of Nashville's most seasoned musicians putting on the best country music variety show in town. The band performs country music through the ages, from Hank Williams to Toby Keith, and you better believe there's fruit cobbler for dessert.

Texas Troubadour Theater. The Texas Troubadour Theater, named for honky-tonk legend Ernest "Texas Troubadour" Tubb, is home to the famous Ernest Tubb Midnite Jamboree—the second-longest-running radio show in U.S. history, after the Grand Ole Opry. Though Ernest Tubb himself has since passed on, the Midnite Jamboree still records every Saturday night at 10 pm, and you can be part of the live audience for free. They host a variety of other musical shows throughout the week as well. The theater itself is fashioned to look like the Ryman Auditorium, complete with lofty ceilings and church pews. But the Texas Troubadour's pews have cushions, which might actually make it a step above the Ryman.

SHOPPING

Dashwood Vintage and Flora. This amazingly curated boutique specializes in the two things essential to every fashionable home: mid-century furniture and beautiful plants. The offerings here are more vintage than antique—couches, chairs, lamps, tables, and other one-of-a-kind statements pieces from the '50s, '60s, and '70s, all perfectly preserved and irresistibly cool. There are some new items for sale, too, all of which are ethically produced (either American made or, if they're imported, fair trade). And yes—for any literary buffs who were wondering, the name is in fact a reference to Jane Austen's *Sense and Sensibility*.

Jae's Gem Mine. For something really down to earth, visit Jae's Gem Mine to learn about the minerals, fossils, and gemstones native to Tennessee and beyond. Their mission is more scientific than metaphysical, though they do sell crystals—as well as gems, minerals, fossils, and even gold. In addition to retail, they're a full-service rock shop, offering everything from lapidary services (cutting and polishing stones), to geode cracking, to rockhounding classes and trips that take you into nature to find geological treasures of your own. While you're there, be sure to say hello to the shop dog, whose name is (obviously) Rocky.

Mercantile 615. Half mixed market, half wood shop—the old and new meet in unexpected ways at Mercantile 615. A combination of antique, vintage, repurposed, and new items are arranged into simulated mini-rooms throughout the store, so you can see each unique piece of art and furniture displayed in its proper glory. In the workshop area, there's an ever-changing roster of classes for those with idle hands: knitting, macramé, furniture painting, hand lettering, watercolor, and more.

Music Valley Antiques and Marketplace. A treasure trove of brass, porcelain, and wood awaits you in this sunny antiques store. Music Valley Antiques and Marketplace combines the selective inventory of a high-end vintage boutique with the prices of a dig-until-you-hit-the-bottom flea market. With books, art, records, clothes, furniture, dishes, vintage toys, exquisite tea sets, and (of course) instruments from over 30 vendors, you're sure to find at least one thing you didn't know you couldn't live without.

Opry Mills. Opry Mills is the be-all end-all of malls in Tennessee. In fact, it's so gigantic that it has its own exit off of Briley Parkway. There are over 200 stores inside, both outlet and retail, covering every corner of the shopping landscape: shoes, clothes, sporting goods, hunting gear, handbags, and multiple vendors who sell nothing but cowboy boots. And the brands cover just as wide a spectrum, from Coach to Rue21. When you've reached your shopping limit, catch a movie at the Regal Cinema 20 and IMAX Theater and enjoy a bottle of Nashville craft beer. For food, Chuy's Tex-Mex is the best pick for both flavor and value, and the Aquarium Restaurant is an excellent choice if you're willing to shell out a little more for the dreamy experience of dining surrounded by a 200,000-gallon ocean aquarium.

The Tacky Turtle. This vintage/modern marketplace mash-up is full of surprises—from the moment you walk inside, take a free fortune cookie, and see Ernest Tubb's tour bus taking up the right quadrant of the store. (It isn't just for show! You can take a self-guided tour of the honky-tonk legend's mode of transportation for free.) The shop is divided into booths, similar to an antiques store, and each booth features either new items created by local artists and artisans or carefully selected vintage items. From handmade jewelry and decor to perfectly preserved 1950s box hats and fur muffs, everybody's taste is covered. In classic Music Valley fashion, you can expect rhinestones and pallet wood to feature prominently.

2 | # Downtown

GO FOR

Live music

Nightlife center

Quality dining

Sightseeing ★★★★☆ | Shopping ★★★☆☆ | Dining ★★★★★ | Nightlife ★★★★★

Downtown is home to most of the things that make Nashville one of the top tourist destinations in the country. The crown jewel of downtown entertainment is Lower Broadway, located right in the middle of downtown. This stretch of road is called the Honky Tonk Highway, where live country and rock music pour out of nearly every window while beer flows out of every tap. While there is so much of Nashville to explore, spending a night on Broadway captures the essence of the city and is a great choice for short stays. Surrounding Broadway is a growing fine-arts scene with multiple galleries and plenty of restaurants cooking up Southern food. Just a few blocks away are world-class museums and the symphony.
—by Chloe Stillwell and Laura Pochodylo

Sights

The Arts Company
One of the most established galleries in downtown Nashville, The Arts Company features fine-art photography, sculptures, contemporary paintings, and more. The Arts Company premieres new exhibits each month as part of the Nashville Art Crawl. ✉ *215 5th Ave. N, Downtown* ☎ *615/254–2040* 🌐 *www.theartscompany.com* ⏲ *Closed Sun. and Mon.*

Barbershop Harmony Society Museum
Giving sightseers and music historians a break from the city's extensive country music history, the Barbershop Harmony Society works to promote and preserve the history of another kind of American musical art, the barbershop quartet, which has ties to both African American improvisation and European harmony traditions. A quick stop compared to the other music museums in the area, the best feature is the front atrium, which was engineered with a dome that provides perfect acoustics for quartets to practice. ✉ *110 7th Ave. N, Downtown* ☎ *615/823–3993* 🌐 *www.barbershop.org* ⏲ *Closed weekends.*

Bicentennial Capitol Mall State Park
Built to celebrate Tennessee's bicentennial, this beautifully landscaped 19-acre park includes a 2,000-seat amphitheater, a scaled map of the state in granite, a World War II memorial, a wall etched with a time line of state events, and fountains representing each of Tennessee's rivers (you'll see both kids and adults splashing in them April–October). The park has a number of picnic tables and there are several dining options at the nearby Farmers Market. ✉ *600 James Robertson Pkwy., Downtown*

615/741–5280 *tnstateparks.com/parks/info/bicentennial-mall* *Free.*

Civil Rights Room at the Nashville Public Library
Nashville's role in the Civil Rights Movement comes alive in this interactive display inside the library's main branch. Explore the ways black Nashvillians protested segregation, challenged racist laws, and contributed to the nationwide fight for equality through the library's time lines, archival materials, and photos. *615 Church St., Downtown* *615/862–5782* *library.nashville.org/research/collection/civil-rights-room* *Open during regulary library hrs.*

★ **Country Music Hall of Fame and Museum**
This tribute to country music's finest is a full city block long, filled with plaques and exhibits highlighting performers from the old-time favorites to the latest generation of stars, a two-story wall with gold and platinum country records, a theater, and Elvis Presley's solid-gold 1960 Cadillac limo. Tours of the historic RCA Studio B recording studio are also run by the museum. Their extensive collection of memorabilia and rotating exhibits make this an essential stop for any music fan or history buff. *222 5th Ave. S, Downtown* *615/416–2001* *countrymusichalloffame.org* *$27.95.*

Cumberland Park
This park on the east bank of the Cumberland River at the foot of the Shelby Street Pedestrian Bridge was designed with kids and families in mind. Sandboxes, a "sprayground" of fountains, an obstacle course, a climbing wall, and trails (one designed to attract butterflies) are among the offerings for kids; there's also a picnic area and 1,200-seat amphitheater. You can also enjoy great views of the river with the Nashville skyline just beyond the bank. *592 S. 1st St., Downtown* *615/862–8508* *www.nashville.gov.*

GETTING HERE

Downtown Nashville is located in the center of the circle that comprises the city. Join the downtown loop from I–40 if entering from the east or west, or I–65 if coming from the north or south to access downtown. If game day or concert traffic has freeways stalled, main streets like West End Avenue or Woodland Street are effective bypasses. Bus routes are at their most abundant and reliable downtown. Because parking is limited and pricey, utilizing a taxi or rideshare service makes the downtown experience easier, as the surrounding areas are walkable.

The Johnny Cash Museum
The legendary Man in Black has a dedicated space in Nashville. Performance costumes, handwritten lyrics, a wall of gold and platinum records—even a limestone wall from the home Cash shared with his beloved June—are among

the items in this museum located between Broadway and the Country Music Hall of Fame and Museum. Interactive exhibits include presentations of Cash's music in formats ranging from 78rpm records to digital downloads. Clips of Cash's many appearances in films and on television are played in a small theater. ✉ *119 3rd Ave. S, Downtown* ☎ *615/256–1777* 🌐 *www.cashmuseum.com* 🎟 *$18.95.*

★ Patsy Cline Museum

Honoring one of Nashville's most iconic former residents, the Patsy Cline Museum features artifacts like stage costumes, home furnishings, records, and more. The Johnny Cash Museum is the Patsy Cline Museum's downstairs neighbor, making this a convenient stop for country music fans (though they are separate museums charging separate admission). ✉ *119 3rd Ave. S, Downtown* ☎ *615/454–4722* 🌐 *www.patsymuseum.com* 🎟 *$18.95.*

Printer's Alley

If you don't know where to find it, you'll almost miss it. Printer's Alley is a historic Nashville landmark reminiscent of a London side street, and is full of watering holes, karaoke bars, and a jazz club. The historic sign will let you know you've made it to the right place. You can have just as much fun chatting outside with the locals as you will entering any of its infamous haunts. ✉ *Downtown* ✣ *Between Church and Union Sts., east of 4th Ave. N.*

Public Square

Mostly known for hosting festivals like Live on the Green or Nashville Pride, Public Square is located in front of the courthouse. Featuring an expansive green space to have a picnic or play ball, statuesque elevator towers that can be climbed for an expansive view, and fountains that children play in during warm months, it's a lovely place to take a break from the hubbub of downtown. ✉ *Union St. at 3rd Ave. N, Downtown.*

Riverfront Park

Though considerably smaller than the Mississippi, the Cumberland River has been as important to Nashville as the Mississippi has been to Memphis. This welcoming green enclave on its banks has an expansive view of the river and Nissan Stadium, where the Tennessee Titans play. The park serves as a popular venue for free summer concerts, block parties, and the annual New Year's Eve and Fourth of July celebrations (Nashville boasts the largest fireworks display in the South). ✉ *100 1st Ave. N, Downtown* ☎ *615/862–8750* 🌐 *www.nashville.gov.*

Ryman Auditorium and Museum

A country music shrine, the Ryman Auditorium and Museum was home to the Grand Ole Opry from 1943 to

1974 and is listed on the National Register of Historic Places. The auditorium seats 2,000 for live performances of classical, jazz, pop, gospel, and, of course, country. Self-guided tours include photo-ops on the legendary stage, and a stroll through the museum, with its photographs and memorabilia of past Ryman Auditorium performances. Visitors may also take the backstage tour of dressing rooms and even record their own version of a legendary song at the in-house recording studio. ✉ *116 5th Ave. N, Downtown* ☎ *615/889–3060* 🌐 *ryman.com* 🎫 *$21.95.*

The Rymer Gallery

This large, multilevel gallery features rotating exhibits of contemporary artwork, plus thought-provoking installations and events. Their diverse curating makes them a stronghold of the monthly Nashville Art Crawl. ✉ *233 5th Ave. N, Downtown* ☎ *615/752–6030* 🌐 *www.therymergallery.com* ⏲ *Closed Sun. and Mon.*

Tennessee State Capitol

The state capitol was designed by noted Philadelphia architect William Strickland (1788–1854), who was so impressed with his Greek Revival creation that he requested—and received—entombment behind one of the building's walls. On the grounds you'll also find the graves of the 11th U.S. president, James K. Polk, and his wife. ✉ *600 Charlotte Ave., Downtown* ☎ *615/741–2692* 🌐 *www.tn.gov* 🎫 *Free* ⏲ *Closed weekends.*

Tinney Contemporary

Helmed by owner Susan Tinney, Tinney Contemporary displays contemporary paintings, photography, drawings, and beyond in a stylish space on 5th Avenue. The gallery offers full-service art consultation from purchasing to installation, and participates in the Nashville Art Crawl on the first Saturday of each month. ✉ *237 5th Ave. N, 1st fl., Downtown* ☎ *615/255–7816* 🌐 *www.tinneycontemporary.com* ⏲ *Closed Sun. and Mon.*

21c Museum Hotel Nashville

Once a wholesale hardware store, this historic building has been converted into a hotel, museum, event space, and rooftop restaurant in a thoughtful art-centric renovation. The multiple gallery spaces are spread throughout the building, and docent-led tours are available on select days. ✉ *221 2nd Ave. N, Downtown* ☎ *615/610–6400* 🌐 *www.21cmuseumhotels.com/nashville.*

Shopping

Boot Country

If it's time to replace or update your dancing boots, Boot Country offers a wide selection of cowboy boots, Western wear, and other wearable Nashville souvenirs. It is conveniently located for boot-scooters on Broadway, and frequently offers promotions for discounts on new boots. ✉ *304 Broadway, Downtown* ☎ *615/259–1691* 🌐 *www.twofreeboots.com.*

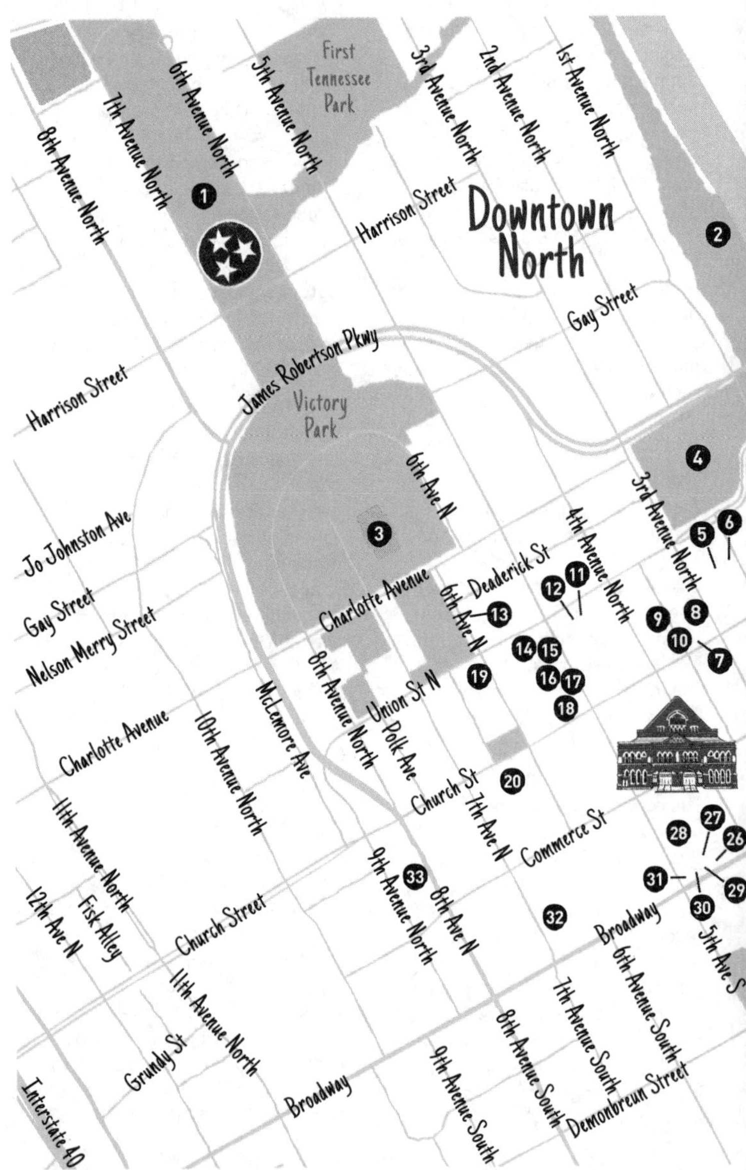

Downtown North
First Tennessee Park
Victory Park
8th Avenue North
7th Avenue North
6th Avenue North
5th Avenue North
3rd Avenue North
2nd Avenue North
1st Avenue North
Harrison Street
Gay Street
James Robertson Pkwy
Harrison Street
6th Ave N
Jo Johnston Ave
Gay Street
Nelson Merry Street
Charlotte Avenue
Deaderick St
4th Avenue North
3rd Avenue North
6th Ave N
8th Avenue North
Union St N
McLemore Ave
Charlotte Avenue
10th Avenue North
Polk Ave
Church St
7th Ave N
Commerce St
11th Avenue North
Fisk Alley
12th Ave N
Church Street
9th Avenue North
8th Ave N
Broadway
6th Avenue South
5th Ave S
11th Avenue North
Grundy St
Broadway
9th Avenue South
8th Avenue South
7th Avenue South
Demonbreun Street
Interstate 40
1
2
3
4
5
6
7
8
9
10
11
12
13
14
15
16
17
18
19
20
26
27
28
29
30
31
32
33

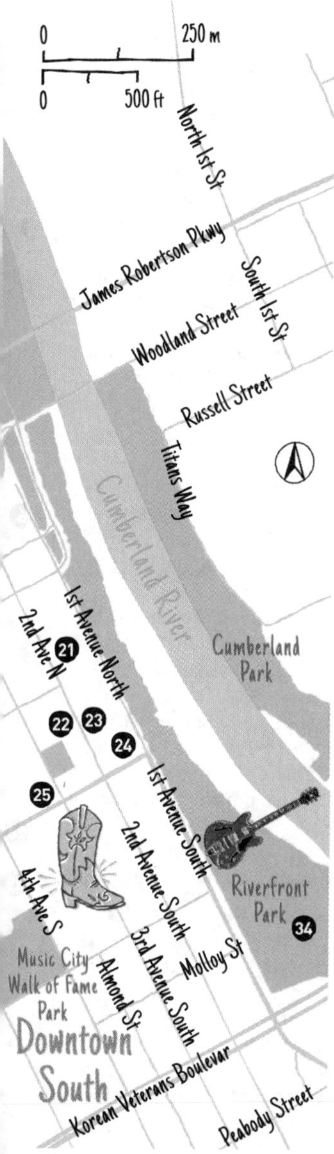

SIGHTS

The Arts Company ... 17
Barbershop Harmony Society Museum ... 32
Bicentennial Capitol Mall State Park ... 1
Civil Rights Room at the Nashville Public Library ... 20
Printers Alley ... 10
Public Square ... 4
Riverfront Park ... 2
Ryman Auditorium and Museum ... 28
The Rymer Gallery ... 15
Tennessee State Capitol ... 3
Tinney Contemporary ... 14
21c Museum Hotel Nashville ... 6

SHOPPING

Boot Country ... 25

COFFEE & QUICK BITES

Mike's Ice Cream ... 22

DINING

Capitol Grille and Oak Bar ... 19
417 Union ... 11
Gray & Dudley ... 5
Koto Sushi Bar ... 12
Puckett's Grocery and Restaurant ... 18
Sea Salt ... 8
The Old Spaghetti Factory ... 21
The Standard At The Smith House ... 33
Woolworth On 5th ... 16

BARS & NIGHTLIFE

Hard Rock Cafe ... 24
Layla's Honky Tonk .. 29
Legends Corner ... 31
Lonnie's Western Room ... 7
Robert's Western World ... 27
Skull's Rainbow Room ... 9
The Stage on Broadway ... 26
Tootsie's Orchid Lounge ... 30
Wildhorse Saloon ... 23

PERFORMING ARTS

CMA Music Festival ... 34
Tennessee Performing Arts Center ... 13

Ernest Tubb Record Shop
When Grand Ole Opry star Ernest Tubb had trouble buying and selling country music records, he took matters into his own hands by opening up his own record store in 1947 on Broadway. It still stands today, with its legendary spinning sign serving as a Nashville landmark, and sells records, CDs, country music memorabilia, and more. ✉ *417 Broadway, Downtown* ☎ *615/255–7503* 🌐 *etrecordshop.com.*

Goo Goo Shop
The Goo Goo Cluster is a legendary Nashville candy confection so good that it deserves to have an entire store dedicated to it. A chocolate-covered cluster of nuts and nougat, every flavor of Goo Goos is available here alongside retro-style Nashville souvenirs. ✉ *116 3rd Ave. S, Downtown* ☎ *615/490–6685* 🌐 *googoo.com.*

Hatch Show Print
Hatch Show Print is home to the legendary letterpress style that has single-handedly created the signature iconography of Nashville through its handmade show posters. Housed within the Country Music Hall of Fame and Museum, the print studio offers art for sale as well as tours demonstrating their unique printing and design process. ✉ *224 5th Ave. S, Downtown* ☎ *615/256–2805* 🌐 *hatchshowprint.com.*

Coffee and Quick Bites

Mike's Ice Cream
$ | American. A downtown Nashville staple for many years, Mike's reminds you of a classic 1950s soda parlor, complete with vintage murals. Featuring classics like perfectly dipped cones and tall sundaes covered in chocolate, it's a great way to end a day walking around downtown. **Known for:** hand-dipped ice cream; extravagant sundaes; old-fashioned sodas. *Average main: $7* ✉ *129 2nd Ave. N, Downtown* ☎ *615/742–6453* 🌐 *mikesicecream.com.*

Dining

Bakersfield
$ | Modern Mexican. One of the better options for a casual meal, Bakersfield specializes in Mexican street food that is authentic and quick. The bar also serves more than 100 types of tequila, so that you can get the full experience. **Known for:** extensive tequila selection; elevated Mexican street-food favorites; handmade tortillas made in-house. *Average main: $10* ✉ *201 3rd Ave. S, Downtown* ☎ *615/522–0970* 🌐 *www.bakersfieldtacos.com.*

★ **Capitol Grille and Oak Bar**
$$$ | Southern. The Capitol Grille, in Downtown's historic Hermitage Hotel, features a farm-to-table menu from their own 245-acre farm a short distance away. Tennessee Black Angus beef and fresh vegetables, along with fresh seafood, are regulars on this

A BRIEF HISTORY OF PRINTER'S ALLEY

When it comes to Nashville nightlife, the Honky Tonk Highway on Lower Broadway gets the lion's share of attention, but it is not the only street downtown designated for good times. Just 2½ blocks north of the neon is Printer's Alley.

Hopping Heyday

Located between Union and Church streets, Printer's Alley was formerly the center of printing presses for publishers, as well as saloons, burlesque shows, and Prohibition-era speakeasies. The area has a history of debauchery dating back to the early 1900s.

Fun-Filled Future

While the mood has changed a bit, tradition hasn't: the Bourbon Street Blues & Boogie Bar upholds the alley's legacy of live jazz music, and Skull's Rainbow Room serves great food in addition to hosting burlesque performances. Karaoke is also a stronghold of Printer's Alley culture, and Ms. Kelli's Karaoke Club is a great spot to sing and dance.

Southern cuisine menu. **Known for:** top-quality, locally sourced meats; weekend brunch; classic, sophisticated surroundings. *Average main: $32* ✉ *231 6th Ave. N, Downtown* ☎ *615/345–7116* 🌐 *www.capitolgrille-nashville.com.*

City Winery

$$ | American. As a restaurant, concert venue, and wine bar, the versatility of City Winery's offerings make it a standout in the city. The Barrel Room restaurant and wine bar within City Winery serves hearty, Southern-inspired fare for brunch and dinner with an extensive wine list. **Known for:** popular concert venue; thoughtful wine selections; trendy brunch. *Average main: $17* ✉ *609 Lafayette St., Downtown* ☎ *615/324–1010* 🌐 *citywinery.com/nashville.*

Dandgure's Cafeteria

$ | Southern. Don't let appearances deceive you: just because this cafeteria doesn't feature white tablecloths or a maître d' does not mean the Southern and soul food is not out-of-this world good. After your first bite of the straightforward no-frills country cooking, it will be no mystery why Anthony Bourdain made a stop here while filming *Parts Unknown*. **Known for:** rich, down-home flavors; traditional meat-and three plates; cafeteria-style service. *Average main: $6* ✉ *538 Lafayette St., Downtown* ☎ *615/256–8501* 🌐 *www.dansnashvillecafe.com* ⏲ *Closed weekends.*

The Diner

$$ | American. Despite its name, this eatery challenges diner conventions by occupying six stories of a downtown building and serving upscale entrées like steaks, oysters, and sushi (yet they still honor diner culture by remaining open

SIGHTS

Country Music Hall of Fame and Museum 20

Cumberland Park 1

The Johnny Cash Museum 10

Patsy Cline Museum...... 9

SHOPPING

Ernest Tubb Record Shop 19

Goo Goo Shop 7

Hatch Show Print 21

DINING

Bakersfield 6

City Winery 30

Dandgure's Cafeteria .. 29

The Diner 5

Hermitage Cafe 24

House of Cards 8

Husk 25

Martin's Bar-B-Que Joint 22

Merchants Restaurant 16

The Southern Steak & Oyster 4

Sun Diner 11

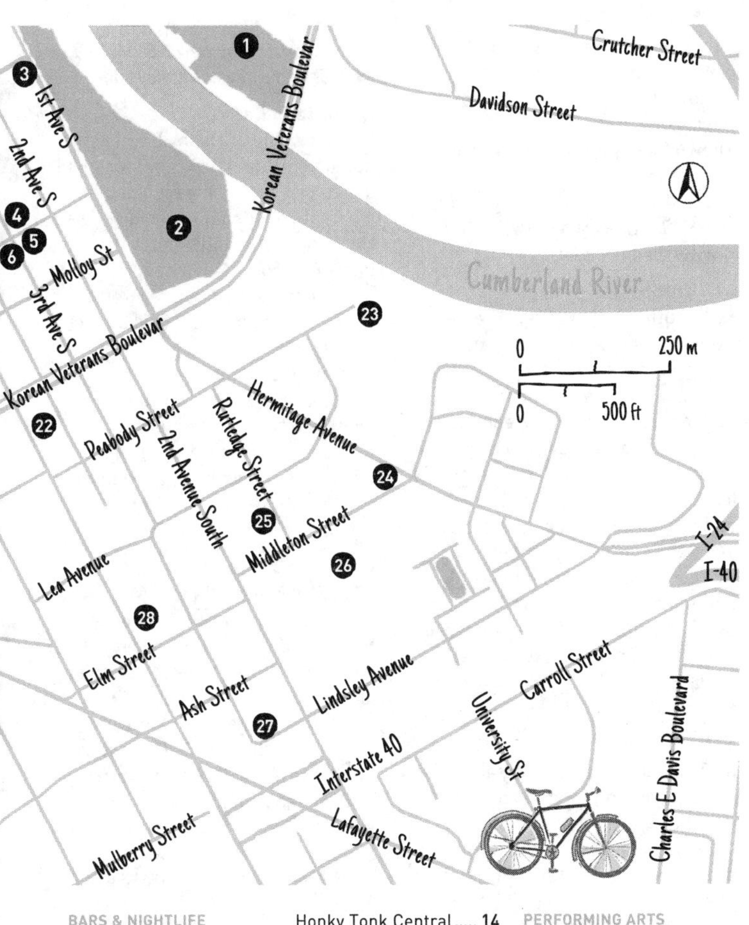

BARS & NIGHTLIFE

Acme Feed & Seed 3

AJs Good Time Bar 18

Ascend Amphitheater.... 2

Broadway Brewhouse 15

The Den Taproom & Brewery 32

Flying Saucer Draught Emporium...... 34

Honky Tonk Central..... 14

The Listening Room Cafe.............................. 28

Nudie's Honky Tonk..... 17

Pinewood Social........... 23

Schermerhorn Symphony Center.......................... 12

Tennessee Brew Works.................. 31

3rd & Lindsley.............. 27

Yazoo Taproom 33

PERFORMING ARTS

Nashville Children's Theatre 26

Nashville Symphony 13

for 24 hours a day). Each luxe level features a different focus like fresh seafood or cocktails, and the rooftop view is one of the best in the city. **Known for:** oyster and sushi bars; first-floor coffee shop; rooftop views. *Average main: $14* ✉ *200 3rd Ave. S, Downtown* ☎ *615/782-7150* 🌐 *www.thediner.com.*

417 Union

$$ | Southern. You wouldn't guess from its understated, antique-looking exterior that the restaurant opens up into a bit of an antebellum relic on the inside. This restaurant envelopes you in rich woodwork common in old Southern homes, featuring fireplaces original to the building, white tablecloths, waiters in white coats, and chandeliers, while also serving traditional Southern cuisine. **Known for:** hearty Southern classics; fresh-squeezed lemonade; friendly service. *Average main: $15* ✉ *417 Union St., Downtown* ☎ *615/401-7241* 🌐 *417union.com.*

Gray & Dudley

$$$ | American. Featuring absurdist art in the dining room, and adjacent galleries with interactive installations, this restaurant in the bottom of the 21c Museum Hotel provides more than a meal, but a one-of-a-kind immersive experience. Featuring rich dishes that modernize Southern cuisine with surprising flavors, it includes a variety of hearth-baked in-house breads. **Known for:** updated Southern-inspired entrées; eclectic artwork; complimentary valet parking. *Average main: $25* ✉ *221 2nd Ave. N, Downtown* ☎ *615/610-6460* 🌐 *www.grayanddudley.com.*

Hermitage Cafe

$ | Diner. One of Nashville's best qualities is that it is known for indulgence just as much as it celebrates the beauty of understated grit. The Hermitage Cafe falls under the latter category, as it's a no-frills hole-in-the-wall diner, favored by the late-night music crowd as the perfect place to get a greasy spoon kind of meal in the wee hours of the morning. **Known for:** late-night hours; classic diner food; no-nonsense aura. *Average main: $8* ✉ *71 Hermitage Ave, Downtown* ☎ *615/254-8871* 🌐 *www.hermitage-cafetn.com* 💳 *No credit cards.*

House of Cards

$$$ | Steakhouse. With a strict dress code and no-phone policy, House of Cards is a must-see for locals and tourists alike looking for an unusual night. The fine-dining meal price comes with a private magic show that rivals Hollywood's infamous Magic Castle. **Known for:** live magic show; speakeasy entrance; cigar menu. *Average main: $35* ✉ *119 3rd Ave. S, lower level, Downtown* ☎ *615/730-8326* 🌐 *www.hocnashville.com.*

★ **Husk**

$$$ | Southern. Southern charm abounds in both decor and flavors at Husk, located in a converted historic home. With seasonal ingredients sourced from in and around Tennessee, the menu at this must-try restaurant staple (with other locations in Charleston and

Savannah) is elevated and dynamic. **Known for:** attentive service; fresh, local ingredients; small dynamic menu. *Average main: $25 ✉ 37 Rutledge St., Downtown ☎ 615/256-6565 🌐 husknashville.com.*

Koto Sushi Bar

$ | Sushi. A bit of a best-kept local secret, Koto is an unassuming small sushi restaurant featuring soothing, traditional Japanese decor. Frequented by downtown business-people at lunch and locals who live in the area or are attending a show at night, the restaurant boasts some of the best sushi in town, and sitting at the sushi bar and asking the chef to surprise you is highly recommended. **Known for:** pork wasabi dumplings; wide array of sushi rolls; intimate, low-key environment. *Average main: $10 ✉ 421 Union St., Downtown ☎ 615/255-8122 🌐 www.koto-sushibar.com ⏲ Closed Sun.*

Martin's Bar-B-Que Joint

$ | Barbecue. Barbecue can be very contentious in the South, as every state has a different variation with cities vying for the best version. Martin's prepares their dry rubs in-house, and offers up authentic Tennessee "Bar-B-Que" that will allow you to at least decide for yourself if Tennessee does it best. **Known for:** whole-hog barbecue; outdoor beer garden; rich Southern desserts. *Average main: $11 ✉ 410 4th Ave. S, Downtown ☎ 615/288-0880.*

Merchants Restaurant

$$ | Contemporary. Housed in the former Merchants Hotel, built in 1892, the restaurant retains many of the hotel's original fireplaces, wainscoting, and custom sconces. There's a casual bar–grill atmosphere and menu on the first floor, while the second floor features formal dining in a room with hardwood floors, brick walls, and ceiling fans. **Known for:** upscale entrées; classic cocktails; sophisticated surroundings. *Average main: $20 ✉ 401 Broadway, Downtown ☎ 615/254-1892 🌐 www.merchantsrestaurant.com.*

The Old Spaghetti Factory

$ | American. Brick walls, hardwood floors, and booths made from converted antique beds create a comfortable, rustic ambience in this converted tobacco warehouse in downtown Nashville. There are stained-glass windows, antique light fixtures, and an authentic Nashville trolley car parked in the dining room, plus an extensive collection of photographs and prints of historic Nashville. **Known for:** three-course meals; family-friendly atmosphere; spumoni ice cream. *Average main: $11.50 ✉ 160 2nd Ave. N, Downtown ☎ 615/224-9010 🌐 www.osf.com.*

Puckett's Grocery and Restaurant

$$ | Southern. If you're walking near 5th and Church downtown, you'll probably pick up the aromas from Puckett's before you see it: Puckett's is an in-town version of the popular Lieper's Fork Puckett's, a Tennessee eatery and music venue. Here you'll find new twists on Southern favorites, including barbecue sliders and "redneck burritos" of pulled pork, baked beans, and slaw, as well as salads. **Known for:** down-home country food; live music; daily specials. *Average main: $19* ✉ *500 Church St., Downtown* ☎ *615/770–2772* 🌐 *www.puckettsgrocery.com.*

Sea Salt

$$$ | Seafood. A fine-dining seafood restaurant, this downtown eatery's menu is inspired by French cuisine, and takes its name from the pink sea salt blocks that decorate each table. A great place for a special occasion, it's located in a beautiful historic building. **Known for:** fresh seafood; weekend brunch; historic atmosphere. *Average main: $30* ✉ *209 3rd Ave. N, Downtown* ☎ *615/891–2221* 🌐 *www.seasaltnashville.com.*

The Southern Steak & Oyster

$$ | American. An energetic addition to Nashville's dining scene, The Southern is an airy restaurant on the ground floor of the Pinnacle building. Its proximity close to a number of major sights, including Bridgestone Arena, lower Broadway, and the Country Music Hall of Fame and Museum means a steady stream of sports fans, locals, and visitors—and live music. **Known for:** seafood with a Southern twist; meat-centric entrées and creative cocktails; indulgent weekend brunch. *Average main: $20* ✉ *150 3rd Ave. S, Downtown* ☎ *615/724–1762* 🌐 *www.thesouthernnashville.com.*

The Standard at the Smith House

$$$$ | American. A beautiful and historic 24-room town house built in the 1840s is the setting for this unique restaurant. The house retains much of the home's original decor, and dinner is served among fireplaces, oak floors, antiques, and paintings. **Known for:** antique decor; exotic game specials; elevated steak-house fare. *Average main: $38* ✉ *167 Rosa L. Parks Blvd., Downtown* ☎ *615/254–1277* 🌐 *www.smithhouse-nashville.com* ⏲ *Closed Sun.*

Sun Diner

$ | Diner. A city that can party all night needs all-night food options, and that's where Sun Diner comes in, serving Southern favorites and breakfast food 24 hours a day. Located steps away from the music of Broadway, the Sun Diner takes its name from legendary rockabilly and country record label Sun Records from Memphis. **Known for:** retro-themed decor; hearty Southern breakfast; convenient location. *Average main: $12* ✉ *105 3rd Ave. S, Downtown* ☎ *615/742–9099* 🌐 *sundinernashville.com.*

Woolworth on 5th

$$ | Southern. A historic site of the civil rights lunch sit-ins of the 1960s, this restaurant was renovated and reopened to preserve and celebrate Nashville's rich history. Featuring traditional Southern lunch fare, unique decor, and weekend brunch events with DJs, this is a can't-miss stop on any trip to downtown Nashville. **Known for:** historical surroundings; live big band and jazz music; straight-ahead

Southern favorites. *Average main: $15* ✉ *221 5th Ave. N, Downtown* ☎ *615/891–1361* 🌐 *woolworthonfifth.com.*

Bars and Nightlife

★ Acme Feed & Seed
This converted old factory has a radio station, bar, and dance hall on the first floor, a sushi bar and venue on the second, a private event space on the fourth, and a DJ hall and bar on the roof. The food menu includes eclectic street food in addition to the sushi. ✉ *101 Broadway, Downtown* ☎ *615/915–0888* 🌐 *theacmenashville.com.*

AJs Good Time Bar
Country star Alan Jackson's Broadway honky-tonk occupies three levels, all dedicated to having a good time. Not every level is the same—while all feature beer and live music, check out the third floor for karaoke and the rooftop level for skyline views. ✉ *421 Broadway, Downtown* ☎ *615/678–4808* 🌐 *www.ajsgoodtimebar.com.*

Ascend Amphitheater
This outdoor amphitheater is nestled into a hill between Broadway and the Cumberland River, making for great skyline views. Ascend Amphitheater regularly hosts popular musical artists and other touring acts, especially during the spring and summer months. ✉ *310 1st Ave. S, Downtown* ☎ *615/999–9000* 🌐 *www.ascendamphitheater.com.*

Broadway Brewhouse
Less of a party scene and more of a place to sit and chat over a pint, Broadway Brewhouse's draft selection is rivaled by few places in town. The owner also started Honky Tonk Central alongside the owner of Tootsie's Orchid Lounge. ✉ *317 Broadway, Downtown* ☎ *615/271–2838* 🌐 *broadwaybrewhouse.net.*

The Den Taproom & Brewery
The Den features the original home of Jackalope Brewing Company, a taproom, and ZolliKoffee café. Snacks are available, and food trucks often frequent their parking lot. ✉ *701 8th Ave. S, Downtown* ☎ *615/873–4313* 🌐 *jackalopebrew.com.*

★ Flying Saucer Draught Emporium
Housed in a portion of the old train station, the unassuming exterior barely hints at the cavernous, wood-paneled interior with ample seating to enjoy your brews and delicious pub food. ✉ *111 10th Ave. S, Suite 310, Downtown* ☎ *615/259–3039* 🌐 *www.beerknurd.com/locations/nashville-flying-saucer.*

Hard Rock Cafe
The Nashville branch of the Hard Rock Cafe is situated at the river end of Broadway and is packed with rock memorabilia from around Nashville and the world. ✉ *100 Broadway, Downtown* ☎ *615/742–9900* 🌐 *www.hardrock.com.*

Honky Tonk Central
From the owner of Tootsie's, the balconies of this three-story club teem with revelers enjoying

great live music, food, and beverages. ✉ *329 Broadway, Downtown* ☎ *615/742–9095* 🌐 *www.honkytonkcentral.com.*

Layla's Honky Tonk
A stronghold in the row of classic honky-tonks on Broadway, Layla's offers an intimate dance floor and live music, often with a bluegrass twist. The best pairing to your beer can be found at the Chicago-style hot dog cart outside the front door. ✉ *418 Broadway, Downtown* ☎ *615/726–2799* 🌐 *www.laylasnashville.com.*

Legends Corner
This no-frills, all-fun honky-tonk is a Broadway watering hole with plenty of live country music and room to dance. Don't miss the star-studded mural on the outside wall featuring Dolly Parton, Willie Nelson, Johnny Cash, Taylor Swift, and Merle Haggard, among others. ✉ *428 Broadway, Downtown* ☎ *615/248–6334* 🌐 *www.legendscorner.com.*

The Listening Room Cafe
One of Nashville's greatest musical traditions is the "writer's round": a group of songwriters performing their compositions one after the other in a round, creating an intimate environment focused on the music. The Listening Room Cafe is one of the premiere places to experience a writer's round in Nashville, and its high-quality, straight-ahead Southern food brunch, lunch, and dinner menus paired with its bar add a tasty twist to the music. ✉ *618 4th Ave. S, Downtown* ☎ *615/259–3600* 🌐 *listeningroomcafe.com.*

Lonnie's Western Room
If you want to sing karaoke in downtown Nashville, this is the place to do it. It's a smoke-filled, carpeted time warp that will make you feel like you've gone back to the '70s. With an extensive catalog of songs to sing, Jell-O shots behind the bar, and an always unpredictable and wild crowd, you're guaranteed to make some kind of memories here. ✉ *308 Church St., Downtown* ☎ *615/613–7500* 🌐 *lonnieswesternroom.com.*

Nudie's Honky Tonk
Inspired by the glitz and glamour of rhinestone-loving Western clothier Nudie's Rodeo Tailors, Nudie's Honky Tonk is home to Nashville's longest bar. This multilevel space features a rooftop bar and is decorated with historic stage costumes designed by Nudie Cohn and worn by artists like Bob Dylan, Johnny Cash, Roy Rogers, and more. ✉ *409 Broadway, Downtown* ☎ *615/942–6307* 🌐 *www.nudieshonkytonk.com.*

★ **Pinewood Social**
Everything you need for a good time at work or play is at Pinewood Social, an all-day hangout featuring a coffee bar, craft cocktails, a bowling alley, private karaoke rooms, bocce ball, and even an outdoor pool. This sceney spot is always bustling because the food is as good as the fun. ✉ *33 Peabody St., Downtown* ☎ *615/751–8111* 🌐 *www.pinewoodsocial.com.*

★ Robert's Western World
If you ask any native Nashvillian (even famous locals), they'll tell you that Robert's is the best honky-tonk in town, with live music and dancing nightly. The two-level bar has been a local staple for decades and is located across from the back artist entry to the Ryman where country legends sneak out to drink on the strip. Peruse the boot collection on the infamous boot wall and enjoy a fried bologna sandwich. ✉ *416b Broadway, Downtown* ☎ *615/244–9552* 🌐 *robertswesternworld.com.*

Schermerhorn Symphony Center
The splendid home of the Nashville Symphony is a modern take on a great European concert hall. In addition to the Symphony, the Schermerhorn hosts many other concerts and boasts an on-site café. ✉ *1 Symphony Pl., Downtown* ☎ *615/687–6500* 🌐 *www.nashvillesymphony.org* 🎫 *Free.*

Skull's Rainbow Room
A reimagined version of a past Printer's Alley staple, Skull's Rainbow Room serves classic entrées like steaks and chops, ready to be washed down with a boozy blend from their classic cocktail list. Taking center stage alongside food and drink at this dimly lit yet swanky lounge is the entertainment, alternating between live jazz and live burlesque performances. ✉ *222 Printer's Alley, Downtown* ☎ *615/810–9631* 🌐 *www.skullsrainbowroom.com.*

The Stage on Broadway
The backdrop for many a movie and music video, The Stage is classic lower Broadway in both looks and entertainment. With live music starting in the early afternoon and its convenient location across from Bridgestone Arena, it's a great stop before or after a game or concert. ✉ *412 Broadway, Downtown* ☎ *615/726–0504* 🌐 *www.thestageonbroadway.com.*

Tennessee Brew Works
The taproom at Tennessee Brew Works allows craft beer fans to enjoy a beer right where it was brewed, and hear live music or watch a sports game in the process. Enjoy seasonally rotating taps as well as a full menu of food that features menu items prepared with the craft brewer's beer. ✉ *809 Ewing Ave., Downtown* ☎ *615/436–0500* 🌐 *www.tnbrew.com.*

3rd & Lindsley
A local favorite, 3rd & Lindsley hosts musical acts from around town and around the world. This no-frills venue has ample room for dancing, and also has a full lunch and dinner menu, in addition to a full bar. For some of the best bets for musical events in town, 3rd & Lindsley is a must. ✉ *818 3rd Ave. S, Downtown* ☎ *615/259–9891* 🌐 *www.3rdandlindsley.com.*

Tootsie's Orchid Lounge
Tootsie's gets its name from its purple walls and exterior, which also features one of the more famous downtown murals of '80s country stars. A multilevel honky-

tonk playground, you can see live music on all of its four floors, including the rooftop. Take note of the neon sign in the back alley for the famous Tootsie's Upstairs, a novelty relic of the '60s and '70s when country legends would go sit in the private room and drink after shows at the Ryman. ✉ *422 Broadway, Downtown* ☎ *615/726–0463* 🌐 *www.tootsies.net*.

Wildhorse Saloon
Live music, barbecue, and dancing—lessons are offered daily—are what makes the spacious Wild Horse Saloon so popular. All ages (under 18 must be accompanied by an adult) are welcome until midnight. ✉ *120 2nd Ave., Downtown* ☎ *615/902–8200* 🌐 *www.wildhorsesaloon.com*.

Yazoo Taproom
Home to one of Nashville's most popular local breweries, the Yazoo Taproom offers pints, flights, and bottles of their beers brewed on-site. Their laid-back indoor-outdoor space houses their brewing operations, and they offer tours to curious beer lovers. ✉ *910 Division St., Downtown* ☎ *615/891–4649* 🌐 *yazoobrew.com*.

 Performing Arts

CMA Music Festival
In the second week of June, the CMA Music Festival hosts big-name country music stars at Nissan Stadium, Riverfront Park, and Bridgestone Arena. Over the long weekend lower Broadway also hosts many free concerts. ✉ *Riverfront Park, Nashville* ☎ *615/244–2840* 🌐 *www.cmaworld.com*.

Nashville Children's Theatre
Performing classic shows for children since the 1930s, this theater company touts the title of the oldest continually running children's theater company. They also host drama workshops. ✉ *25 Middleton St., Downtown* ☎ *615/254–9103 main office, 615/252–4675 box office* 🌐 *www.nashvillechildrenstheatre.org*.

Nashville Symphony
Nashville's Symphony orchestra performs around 140 concerts a year, typically at the Schermerhorn Symphony Center, and often collaborates with visiting artists or other members of the Nashville arts community. ✉ *1 Symphony Pl., Downtown* ☎ *615/687–6400* 🌐 *www.nashvillesymphony.org*.

Tennessee Performing Arts Center *(TPAC)*
This multicultural center with elegant concert halls is the home of the Nashville Ballet, Nashville Opera, Tennessee Repertory Theatre, and various touring performers. The center's Andrew Jackson Hall also hosts touring Broadway shows, and the building also houses the Tennessee State Museum. ✉ *505 Deaderick St., Downtown* ☎ *615/782–4000* 🌐 *www.tpac.org*.

3 | # Germantown

GO FOR

Award-winning restaurants

Historic charm

Close to Downtown

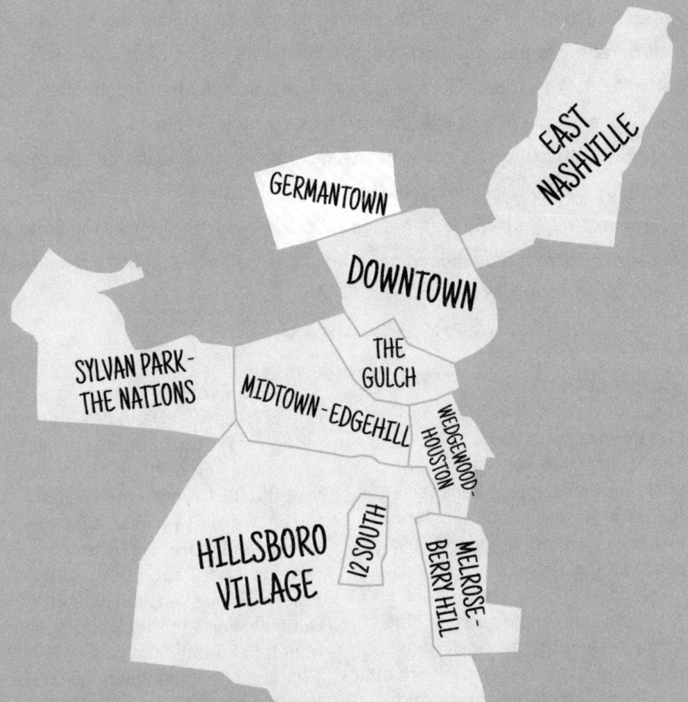

Sightseeing ★★★☆☆ | Shopping ★★★☆☆ | Dining ★★★★★ | Nightlife ★★★★☆

If you're after Nashville's best dining, look no further than Germantown. A historic neighborhood that has seen a boom in development and growth over the last decade, Germantown is home to several of the city's best loved and most acclaimed restaurants, as well as high-end shopping and destinations for sports fans and history buffs alike. The neighborhood itself is a sight to behold, with classic row houses, brick sidewalks, and a tree canopy that makes you forget you're a stone's throw from Downtown. James Beard Award–winning chef Tandy Wilson's restaurant City House is a cornerstone of the neighborhood, beloved for its rustic, Southern take on Italian food. Wilson recently opened a new restaurant, Mop/Broom Mess Hall, just a couple of blocks from City House, where his elevated take on Southern comfort food is not to be missed. Germantown is dotted with local boutiques and coffee shops, making it the ideal destination for a leisurely afternoon after time spent at the nearby, newly reopened Tennessee State Museum or before a Sounds minor league baseball game at First Tennessee Park.—*by Brittney McKenna*

Sights

First Tennessee Park

First Tennessee Park is home to Nashville's triple-A baseball team the Nashville Sounds. Game attendees will enjoy a variety of concessions, including craft cocktails and small bites at outfield bar the Band Box. And if you can't sit through an entire baseball game without getting fidgety, the park also has Ping-Pong tables and a mini-golf course to keep you entertained. ✉ *19 Jr. Gilliam Way, Germantown* ☎ *615/690–4487* 🌐 *www.firsttennesseepark.com.*

★ Fisk University Galleries

One of Nashville's best destinations for fine art is the campus of Fisk University, just north of downtown. Visit the Carl Van Vechten Gallery to see works by Picasso, Cezanne, Renoir, and more. Elsewhere on campus, check out murals by Harlem Renaissance artist Aaron Douglas. For summer visitors, be mindful of limited hours. ✉ *1000 17th Ave. N, Germantown* ☎ *615/329–8720* 🌐 *www.fisk.edu/galleries/the-carl-van-vechten-gallery* ⏲ *Closed Sun.*

NashTrash Tours

Traditional tours are great, but sometimes the best way to explore a new place is through laughter.

NashTrash Tours provides plenty of laughs in its tours of Music City, which showcase the city's sights, sounds, and significant spots through the eyes of two zany sisters. NashTrash offers three different tours, each tailored to different neighborhoods and themes. ✉ *900 Rosa L Parks Blvd., Germantown* ☎ *615/226-7300* 🌐 *www.nashtrash.com*.

★ Nashville Farmers Market
The Nashville Farmers Market is the crown jewel of the Germantown area, bringing the community and surrounding neighborhood together with food, produce, and special events. Visit on a weekday to take advantage of the market's extensive restaurant offerings, which span myriad international cuisines. Come on the weekend for goods from local farmers and artisans. ✉ *900 Rosa L Parks Blvd., Germantown* ☎ *615/880-2001* 🌐 *www.nashvillefarmersmarket.org*.

Tennessee State Museum
In late 2018, the Tennessee State Museum relocated from downtown Nashville to its own building in Germantown, right next to the popular Farmers Market. Visitors to the museum will find thousands of artifacts and pieces of art in the museum's permanent collection, as well as periodic rotating exhibitions, all telling the story of Tennessee and its people. Admission to the museum is always free. ✉ *1000 Rosa Parks Blvd., Germantown* ☎ *615/741-2692* 🌐 *www.tnmuseum.org* ⏲ *Closed Mon.*

GETTING HERE

Germantown is easily accessible via bus. If it's a nice day, bike or walk from Downtown on the Music City Bikeway, which offers scenic views of the Cumberland River. Once in Germantown, points of interest are easily walkable.

Shopping

Abednego
Whether you're buying for yourself or for a friend, Abednego is the perfect spot to buy a gift. The locally owned boutique carries a curated selection of men's and women's clothing, accessories, and grooming and personal care supplies, as well as home decor, candles, and small trinkets. They have a cute selection of greeting cards, too, making it a one-stop gift shop. ✉ *1210 4th Ave. N, Germantown* ☎ *615/712-6028* 🌐 *www.abednegoboutique.com* ⏲ *Closed Mon.*

Alexis+Bolt
Germantown clothing boutique Alexis+Bolt describes its mission as bringing together a mix of "carefully curated goods" for like-minded shoppers to take home and enjoy. Among those goods, which span men's and women's clothing and accessories, you'll find staple brands like Wrangler and Scott & Soda as well as harder-to-find designers like Mink Pink and Project Social. ✉ *506 Monroe St., Germantown* ☎ *615/578-8257* 🌐 *www.alexisandbolt.com* ⏲ *Closed Mon.*

Salemtown
Historic Buena Vista
Fisk Area
Hope Gardens
Owen St
10th Ave N
Buchanan
10th Ave N
Interstate 65
Nassau St
Jenkins St
8th Avenue North
Garfield Street
7th Ave N
6th Ave N
5th Ave N
Hume Street
Arthur Avenue
11th Avenue North
12th Avenue North
Delta Avenue
9th Avenue North
Garfield St
10th Ave N
Arthur Avenue
Cheatham Place
Taylor St
7th Ave N
6th Ave N
Heiman Street
14th Avenue North
Heiman St
Interstate 40
Madison Street
Scovel Street
Rev Dr Enoch Jones Boulevard
Jefferson Street
9th Avenue North
8th Avenue North
Phillips St
Jackson St
Locklayer St
Ireland St
Tredco Dr
Warren Street
11th Avenue North
Morrison Street
12th Avenue North
14th Ave N
Meharry Boulevard
Phillips St
Jackson St
Ireland St
16th Avenue North
Blank Street
17th Avenue North
Herman St
Interstate 40
10th Avenue North
Jo Johnston Ave
Clinton St
0
250 m
0
500 ft
1
2
3
4
5
6
7
8
9
16
17
18
31
35
36
37
38
39
40
41

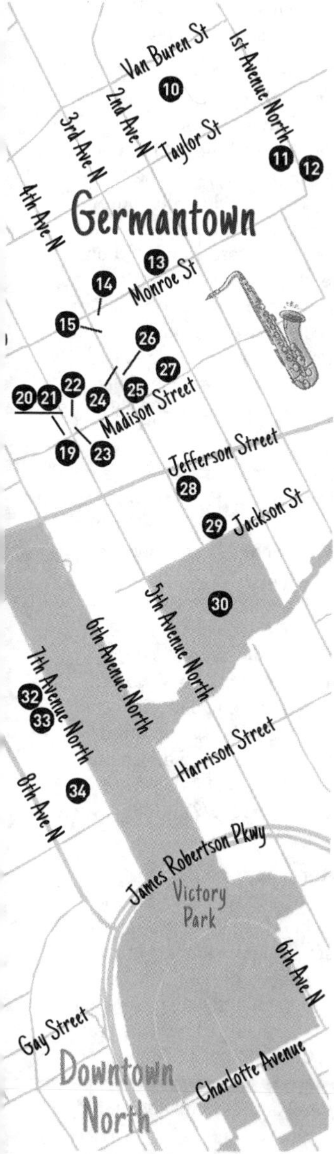

SIGHTS

First Tennessee Park 30
Fisk University Galleries 41
NashTrash Tours 33
Nashville Farmers' Market 32
Tennessee State Museum 31

SHOPPING

Abednego 26
Alexis + Bolt 16
The Bang Candy Company 36
Batch Nashville 34
The Dress Theory 3
Jack Daniel's General Store 37
Nisolo 2
Peter Nappi 12
Wilder 24

COFFEE & QUICK BITES

Barista Parlor Germantown 14
The Christie Cookie Co 27
The Cupcake Collection 18
Red Bicycle Coffee & Crêpes 22
Steadfast Coffee 6
Tempered Café and Chocolate 20

DINING

Big Al's Deli 9
City House 15
5th and Taylor 8
Germantown Café 23
Henrietta Red 25
Monell's Dining and Catering 17
Mop/Broom Mess Hall 13
Rolf and Daughters 5
Silo 19
Slim and Husky's Pizza Beeria 4
Von Elrod's Beer Garden and Sausage House 29

BARS & NIGHTLIFE

Bearded Iris Brewing 10
Corsair Distillers 35
The Green Hour 21
Grinder's Switch Winery 39
Minerva Avenue 1
Neighbors Germantown 28
Nelson's Green Brier Distillery 40

PERFORMING ARTS

The Back Corner 7
Nashville Jazz Workshop 11
Third Coast Comedy Club 38

The Bang Candy Company
If you have a sweet tooth, you can't skip a trip to the Bang Candy Company. Located in the Marathon Village complex, Bang specializes in handmade, creatively flavored marshmallows, but is far more than a one-trick pony. The shop also sells handmade syrups, chocolates and other adventurous confections, as well as "CBD Dream Drops," which blend tasty confections with relaxing CBD oil. ✉ *1300 Clinton St., Suite 127, Marathon Village* ☎ *625 /953–1065* 🌐 *www.bangcandycompany.com* 🕒 *Closed Mon.*

Batch Nashville
While visiting the Nashville Farmers Market, be sure to stop in Batch Nashville, a highly curated shop featuring gifts, snacks, and treats from some of Nashville's (and the greater South's) best-loved creators. From artisanal chocolate bars to locally roasted coffee, the gifts at Batch are sure to please even your most finicky friends. ✉ *900 Rosa L Parks Blvd., Germantown* ☎ *615/913–3912* 🌐 *www.batchusa.com*.

The Dress Theory
For those visiting Nashville in search of the perfect wedding dress, look no further than the Dress Theory. The Dress Theory is one of the city's premier destinations for unique bridal gowns, and carries designers like Flora, Jenny Packham, Truvelle, and Sarah Seven. Hours are by appointment only, meaning you'll have a comfortable, personalized experience. ✉ *915 Buchanan St., Germantown* ☎ *615/440–3953* 🌐 *www.thedresstheory.com* 🕒 *Open by appointment only*.

Jack Daniel's General Store
If you can't make it down to Lynchburg to see the Jack Daniel's distillery in person, visit the famed whiskey maker's Nashville output for all your Jack Daniel's–branded gear needs. Located in Marathon Village, the sizable shop sells shirts, glassware, and accessories galore for you or the whiskey lover in your life. Note that the store does not sell alcohol. ✉ *1310 Clinton St., Suite 101, Marathon Village* ☎ *629/702–2969*.

Nisolo
When Nisolo relocated from its Marathon Village location in 2015, it was one of the first businesses to open in what's now known as the Buchanan Arts District. Now, the stretch of historic Buchanan Street is bustling with galleries and restaurants, with Nisolo, a local pioneer of ethically made leather shoes and goods, its retail anchor. Stop in for handcrafted leather chukkas, messenger bags, and much more. ✉ *1803 9th Ave. N, Germantown* ☎ *615/953–1087* 🌐 *www.nisolo.com*.

★ **Peter Nappi**
Housed in a beautiful, old brick factory building, Peter Nappi's flagship store is a work of art in its own right. Once inside, you'll be greeted by an immaculately designed showroom showcasing handmade leather shoes, boots, bags, and goods. The store carries an array of personal and home accessories, too, but it's

the leather goods, which are made in Italy and shipped to Nashville, that are the stars of the show. *✉ 1308 Adams St., Germantown ☎ 615/248–3310 🌐 www.peternappi.com ⏲ Closed Sun.*

Wilder

As its name might suggest, Germantown boutique Wilder is no ordinary place to buy home furnishings. The brightly lit shop is an Instagramer's dream, as are Wilder's uncommon wares. Stock varies by season, but head to Wilder if you want your dinnerware to be as well designed as your sofa. The store is also an authorized Herman Miller retailer. *✉ 1212 4th Ave. N, Germantown ☎ 615/679–0008 🌐 www.wilderlife.com.*

Coffee and Quick Bites

Barista Parlor

$ | Café. The original East Nashville Barista Parlor was such a hit that the hip shop has since expanded to several locations around town. One of those is in Germantown, conveniently located right next to popular dinner joint City House. **Known for:** ethically sourced ingredients; thoughtfully prepared coffee; hip, trendy atmosphere. *Average main: $5 ✉ 1230 4th Ave. N, Germantown ☎ 615/401–9144 🌐 www.baristaparlor.com.*

The Christie Cookie Co.

$ | Bakery. A trip to Nashville isn't complete without a Christie Cookie (or six). The Nashville-based bakery makes gourmet cookies with real ingredients, with recipes that have earned the brand national recognition. **Known for:** fresh-baked cookies; gifts for sweets lovers; simple coffee drinks. *Average main: $5 ✉ 1205 3rd Ave. N, Germantown ☎ 800/458–2447 🌐 www.christiecookies.com ⏲ Closed Sun.*

The Cupcake Collection

$ | Bakery. Who doesn't love a good cupcake? Germantown bakery The Cupcake Collection is a locally beloved cupcake shop, serving a variety of tasty, creative cupcakes both for advance order and for walk-in pickup at their storefront. **Known for:** homemade cupcakes in a variety of creative flavors. *Average main: $3 ✉ 1213 6th Ave N, Germantown ☎ 615/244–2900 🌐 www.thecupcakecollection.com ⏲ Closed Sat.*

Red Bicycle Coffee and Crepes

$ | Café. There are a lot of coffee shops in Germantown, but only Red Bicycle has an extensive menu of sweet and savory crepes. The neighborhood café also serves a variety of sandwiches, tacos, pastries, and small snacks, all complemented by a menu of seasonally rotating coffee and espresso drinks and served by one of the friendliest staffs in town. **Known for:** sweet and savory crepes; assorted espresso beverages; creative tacos and sandwiches. *Average main: $7 ✉ 1200 5th Ave. N, Germantown ☎ 615/516–1986 🌐 www.redbicyclecoffee.com.*

Steadfast Coffee

$ | Café. Germantown's Steadfast Coffee offers up the usual assortment of espresso drinks and café-style food options, but they also have some tasty menu items you'll be hard-pressed to find anywhere else. Their coffee soda, for example, is an unusual blend of espresso, soda water, and orange peel, and has to be tried to be understood, while their "rested" coffee drinks bring out new flavors in old classics. **Known for:** creative espresso drinks; refreshing coffee soda. *Average main: $5 ✉ 603 Taylor St., Germantown ☎ 615/891–7424 🌐 www.steadfast.coffee.*

★ Tempered Café and Chocolate

$ | Café. Tempered Café is unlike any other café in Nashville, serving an extensive selection of handcrafted chocolates alongside a full menu of espresso drinks, breakfast and lunch plates, and, yes, homemade hot chocolate and drinking chocolate. Tempered also has a full bar, and offers chocolate and beverage pairings that are unlike anything you've ever tried before. **Known for:** creative, handmade chocolates; rich, drinkable chocolate; accompanying bistro and bar menu. *Average main: $5 ✉ 1201 5th Ave. N, Germantown ☎ 615/454–5432 🌐 www.temperednashville.com ⏲ Closed Mon.*

WORTH A TRIP

Just over a mile from Germantown is Marathon Village. Housed in what remains of Marathon Motor Works (which produced automobiles in the early 20th century), Marathon Village features Corsair Distillery, Nelson's Green Brier Distillery, concert venue Marathon Music Works, an American Pickers store, and a number of shops and small businesses. *See The Gulch (Chapter 10) for information on Marathon Music Works.*

Dining

★ Big Al's Deli

$ | Southern. Tucked away in nearby Salemtown is Big Al's Deli, a neighborhood deli in every sense of the word. Owner Alfonso Hamilton serves home-cooked Southern food out of an otherwise nondescript converted house, making for a dining experience that feels like you're right at home. **Known for:** no-frills breakfast and lunch; friendly service; long waits but the food is worth it. *Average main: $6 ✉ 1828 4th Ave. N, Germantown ☎ 615/242–8118 🌐 www.bigalsdeli-andcatering.com ⏲ Closed Sun.*

★ City House

$$ | Southern. James Beard Award–winning chef Tandy Wilson has built a Nashville institution with City House, one of the first restaurants to take hold in Germantown. The menu changes seasonally but always features thoughtful salads, unusually delicious pizzas, and creative protein options, most of which lean heavily on pork. **Known for:** rustic Italian fare; pork- and meat-forward dishes; comfortable, bright atmosphere. *Average main: $17* ✉ *1222 4th Ave. N, Germantown* ☎ *615/736–5838* 🌐 *www.cityhouse-nashville.com* 🕒 *Closed Tues.*

5th and Taylor

$$$ | Modern American. Housed in a large, artsy space, 5th and Taylor is a culinary playground for chef Daniel Lindley to push the boundaries of modern American cuisine. The menu often includes a number of Southern favorites, like tomato pie and beer can chicken, all elevated by Lindley's finesse and knowledge of flavor. **Known for:** elevated dishes with Southern touches; large, sophisticated dining space; extensive cocktail and beverage program. *Average main: $25* ✉ *1411 5th Ave. N, Germantown* ☎ *615/242–4747* 🌐 *www.5thandtaylor.com.*

Germantown Café

$$ | Southern. One of the early restaurants to open in the now-bustling Germantown neighborhood was Germantown Café. Now a pillar of the neighborhood, the popular dining spot serves inventive takes on an eclectic Southern menu, serving up meals for lunch, dinner, and brunch (on the weekends). **Known for:** classic cocktails; elevated Southern fare; great happy hour. *Average main: $20* ✉ *1200 5th Ave. N, Germantown* ☎ *615 /242–3226* 🌐 *www.germantowncafe.com.*

Henrietta Red

$$ | American. New restaurants have popped up all over Nashville in recent years, but few are as promising as Henrietta Red. The project of chef Julia Sullivan and sommelier Allie Poindexter, the hip Germantown spot is a new go-to destination for creative seafood and craft cocktails. **Known for:** oysters; creative cocktails; inventive desserts. *Average main: $20* ✉ *1200 4th Ave. N, Germantown* ☎ *615/490–8042* 🌐 *www.henriettared.com* 🕒 *Closed Mon.*

Monell's Dining and Catering

$$ | Southern. Much of the dining in Germantown is high-end and experimental, making longtime local favorite Monell's Dining and Catering a welcome dose of Southern comfort food, all served family-style. Visit for breakfast, lunch, or dinner to fill up on Southern favorites like skillet-fried chicken and home-style meatloaf. Just be sure to save room for dessert. **Known for:** skillet-fried chicken; home-cooked breakfast; family-style. *Average main: $15* ✉ *1235 6th Ave. N, Germantown* ☎ *615/248–4747* 🌐 *www.monellstn.com.*

Mop/Broom Mess Hall

$$ | Southern. When ahead-of-its-time eatery Kuchnia and Keller shuttered in mid-2018, City House chef Tandy Wilson took over the space, which once housed a mop and broom manufacturer, and converted it to Mop/Broom Mess Hall, his second Nashville concept. Like City House, the dishes at Mop/Broom each have a uniquely Southern bent, though this particular Wilson endeavor runs a bit more casual. **Known for:** elevated casual Southern cuisine; from James Beard Award–winning chef Tandy Wilson; view of behind the scenes if you sit at the kitchen bar. *Average main: $17* ✉ *1300 3rd Ave. N, Germantown* ☎ *615/689–5224* 🌐 *www.mopbroomnashville.com.*

★ Rolf and Daughters

$$ | Eclectic. Chef Philip Krajeck has devised a simple, innovative menu at Rolf and Daughters, a pillar of dining in both the Germantown neighborhood and greater Nashville. Menu staples include assorted seasonal, house-made pastas, like guest favorite garganelli verde, and creative takes on small plates and vegetable salads. **Known for:** innovative seasonal dishes; creative use of ingredients; cozy, neighborhood atmosphere. *Average main: $20* ✉ *700 Taylor St., Germantown* ☎ *615/866–9897* 🌐 *www.rolfanddaughters.com.*

Silo

$$ | Southern. Silo has been a mainstay in Germantown for several years now, thanks in large part to its commitment to serving fresh, seasonal ingredients with a Southern point of view. While hot chicken runs rampant in Nashville, Silo's take on the local favorite is worth trying, as is their weekend brunch, which makes them one of the neighborhood's few fine-dining establishments to offer brunch service. **Known for:** elevated hot chicken; Southern-inspired brunch; diverse beverage program. *Average main: $23* ✉ *1121 5th Ave. N, Germantown* ☎ *615/750–2912* 🌐 *www.silotn.com.*

★ Slim and Husky's Pizza Beeria

$ | Pizza. Slim and Husky's Pizza Beeria was one of the first new restaurants to open in the burgeoning Buchanan Arts District neighborhood. Owned and operated by neighborhood residents, Slim and Husky's serves a variety of freshly made pizzas, and also offers the option to design your own. **Known for:** tasty build-your-own pizza; homemade cinnamon rolls; hip-hop–inspired atmosphere. *Average main: $10* ✉ *911 Buchanan St., Germantown* ☎ *615/647–7017* 🌐 *www.slimandhuskys.com* ⏲ *Closed Sun.*

Von Elrod's Beer Garden and Sausage House

$$ | German. Von Elrod's Beer Garden and Sausage House was a welcome addition to the Germantown neighborhood when it opened in 2017. Housed in a large, group-friendly space, the restaurant offers a casual alternative to the neighborhood's more-elevated offerings, serving house-made sausages and sides alongside a truly extensive beer menu. **Known for:** house-made sausage; extensive beer list; large outdoor space. *Average main: $14* ✉ *1004 4th Ave. N, Germantown* ☎ *615/866–1620* 🌐 *www.vonelrods.com.*

Bars and Nightlife

Bearded Iris Brewing
Believe it or not, Germantown used to be one of Nashville's industrial hubs. You can see what remains of the neighborhood's old factories and warehouses on its eastern outskirts, where Bearded Iris Brewing lies. Housed in one of these old warehouses, Bearded Iris brews a variety of old-world-style beers that appeal to beer snobs and newbies alike and serves brews in a swanky-comfy setting that combines the best of old and new Germantown. ✉ *101 Van Buren St., Germantown* ☎ *615/928-7988* 🌐 *www.beardedirisbrewing.com.*

★ **Corsair Distillery**
A highlight of Marathon Village is Corsair Distillery, a microdistillery and brewpub offering eclectic, locally made spirits and beer. Visitors can tour the facility—which is housed in a century-old automobile factory—and try full- and sample-size offerings of Corsair spirits in the distillery's taproom. ✉ *1200 Clinton St., Suite 110, Marathon Village* ☎ *615/200-0320* 🌐 *www.corsairdistillery.com.*

★ **The Green Hour**
Located inside Tempered Café and Chocolate (and only open Thursday through Saturday), The Green Hour is one of Germantown's best-kept secrets. It's the only bar in town that specializes in serving a wide variety of absinthe in traditional absinthe drips, making each drink ordered its own experiential treat. And if absinthe isn't your thing, the bar also serves a variety of classic cocktails and a small selection of beer. ✉ *1201 5th Ave. N, Germantown* ☎ *615/454-5432* 🌐 *www.tempered-nashville.com* ☞ *Closed Sun.–Wed.*

BACK IN THE DAY

One of the largest structures in Germantown is Werthan Lofts, a popular condo building that once housed a burlap bag mill, originally built in 1872. Trips through Germantown will yield similarly repurposed buildings, showing the area to be one of Nashville's best-preserved neighborhoods.

Grinder's Switch Winery
While there are a couple of spirits distilleries on the Marathon Village property, Grinder's Switch Winery ought to please the wine lover in your group. Try various wines from Grinder's Switch's middle-Tennessee vineyard in a casual but sophisticated setting. While you're there, pick up a curated local gift or craft in the winery's attached shop. ✉ *1310 Clinton St., Suite 125, Marathon Village* ☎ *615/679-0646* 🌐 *www.gswinery.com.*

Minerva Avenue
Drawing on the popularity of neighborhood pizza-and-beer joint Slim and Husky's, Minerva Avenue is the first true bar to open in the burgeoning Buchanan Arts District. The bar has an easygoing-meets-speakeasy vibe, with a phone out front to alert the host to grant you entrance to the cozy patio. Grab a fresh, locally sourced sandwich and wash it down with a boozy slushie

or a signature cocktail, all of which are named after lines from famous movies. ✉ *1000 Buchanan St., Germantown* ☎ *615/499–4369* 🌐 *www.minervaavenue.com.*

Neighbors Germantown
Neighbors has long been a popular bar in the west Nashville neighborhood Sylvan Park, and in 2018 Germantown got its own outpost of the friendly watering hole. Located in close proximity to Germantown restaurants and to First Tennessee Park, Neighbors is a great spot to pre-game before a Sounds game, toast to a good meal, or post up to watch the Nashville Predators. ✉ *313 Jefferson St., Germantown* ☎ *615/873–1954* 🌐 *www.neighborsnashville.com.*

Nelson's Green Brier Distillery
It wouldn't be a trip to Tennessee without some Tennessee whiskey. Nelson's Green Brier Distillery is home to Belle Meade Bourbon, a local favorite that has grown to national prominence. While on-site, you can tour the distillery, taste spirits, and shop the distillery's gift shop, which carries bottles, glassware, and other booze-centric gifts. ✉ *1414 Clinton St, Germantown* ☎ *615/913–8800* 🌐 *www.greenbrierdistillery.com.*

Performing Arts

The Back Corner
Tucked behind popular Germantown restaurant 5th and Taylor is the Back Corner, a venue, bar, and nightclub operated by the same hospitality group. Most nights at the Back Corner boast some form of entertainment, be it a writer's round from local songsmiths, a themed DJ set, or shows from local and touring musical acts. The Back Corner offers table reservations. Check the calendar before visiting in case of private parties or ticket events. ✉ *1413 5th Ave. N, Germantown* ☎ *615/821–6048* 🌐 *www.thebackcorner.com.*

Nashville Jazz Workshop
If jazz is your thing, be sure to check the calendar of the Nashville Jazz Workshop, which offers classes, performances, and various special events throughout the year. There are typically a couple of events taking place each day, with proceeds benefiting the nonprofit Workshop's mission of keeping jazz in Music City. ✉ *1319 Adams St., Germantown* ☎ *615/242–5299* 🌐 *www.nashvillejazz.org.*

Third Coast Comedy Club
If you're looking for laughs while you're in Music City, look no further than Third Coast Comedy Club. Nestled inside the Marathon Village complex, the local favorite plays host to sketch, improv, and stand-up shows most nights of the week. And if you're interested in brushing up on your own comedy chops, Third Coast also offers classes and workshops (check availability before visiting). ✉ *1310 Clinton St., Suite 121, Marathon Village* ☎ *615/745–1009* 🌐 *www.thirdcoastcomedy.club.*

4 | Hillsboro Village

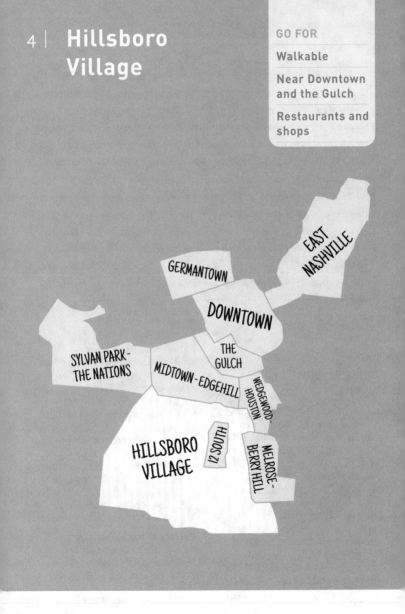

GO FOR

Walkable

Near Downtown and the Gulch

Restaurants and shops

Sightseeing ★★★☆☆ | Shopping ★★★★☆ | Dining ★★★★☆ | Nightlife ★★☆☆☆

Hillsboro Village is one of Nashville's quaintest neighborhoods, playing host to some of the city's more exciting new fast-casual dining options and serving as stomping grounds for both Belmont University and Vanderbilt students. Vintage Nashville mainstays like Pancake Pantry—a must-visit for breakfast lovers—and the historic Belcourt Theatre anchor the neighborhood in the city's history, while new establishments like the brick-and-mortar Grilled Cheeserie Melt Shop (an offshoot of the popular food truck) and Austin transplant Hopdoddy Burger Bar bring new flavor to the area. One could easily spend an entire day in Hillsboro Village: breakfast at Pancake Pantry, a couple of hours browsing shops like UAL and Pangaea, coffee and pastries at Fido, an afternoon matinee at the Belcourt, dinner at Hopdoddy, and a nightcap and darts at longtime local dive the Villager Tavern. Hillsboro Village is also a quick, pedestrian-friendly walk to Belmont Boulevard, which houses a similar strip of like-minded shops and dining options.—*by Brittney McKenna*

Sights

Belmont Mansion
This 1850s Italian-style villa was the home of Adelicia Acklen, Nashville's answer to Scarlett O'Hara, who married "once for money, once for love, and once for the hell of it." On Belmont University's campus, it's a gem right down to its sweeping staircase designed for grand entrances and cast-iron gazebos perfect for romance. Recent renovations have restored Acklen's bedroom to its original splendor, including a detailed reproduction of the wallpaper. The last tour of the day starts at 3:30 pm. ✉ *1900 Belmont Blvd., Belmont* ☎ *615/460–5459* 🌐 *www.belmontmansion.com* 🎫 *$15.*

Fannie Mae Dees Park
While Hillsboro Village itself offers plenty of charming outdoor walking space, the nearby Fannie Mae Dee's Park is the perfect place to stop for a picnic with your Fido goodies. Take the little ones to play on the playground, and check out the large dragon statue. Kids can play on it, but, with its bright colors and funky design, it's just as fun for adults who love a good photo op. ✉ *2400 Blakemore Ave., Hillsboro Village* ☎ *615/862–8400* 🌐 *www.nashville.gov.*

Gallery of Iconic Guitars
Guitars are a dime a dozen in Nashville, but the axes on display at the Gallery of Iconic Guitars on Belmont University's campus are truly one-of-a-kind. From vintage instruments to guitars owned by

legendary musicians, the guitars in Belmont's collection live up to their "iconic" name. The gallery sits within the heart of Belmont University, internationally renowned for its various music programs. ✉ *1907 Belmont Blvd., Hillsboro Village* ☎ *615/460–6984* 🌐 *www.thegigatbelmont.com* 🎟 *$5.*

 Shopping

A Thousand Faces
Whether you're looking for a gift for a loved one or for yourself, A Thousand Faces is sure to have something to tickle your fancy. Check out the cute, curated shop for jewelry, art, accessories, and more. ✉ *1720 21st Ave. S, Hillsboro Village* ☎ *615/298–3304* 🌐 *athousandfaces.com.*

★ **Billy Reid**
"Lived-in luxury" clothing brand Billy Reid is based in Florence, Alabama, but lucky for Tennesseans the store has an outpost in Nashville, too. Visit Billy Reid at the Hill Center at Green Hills for stylish, comfortable pieces that will seamlessly integrate into any wardrobe. ✉ *4015 Hillsboro Pike, Suite 104, Hillsboro Village* ☎ *615/292–2111* 🌐 *www.billyreid.com.*

Davis Cookware and Cutlery Shop
Locally owned cookware shops are growing increasingly rare, as retailers like Amazon and big-box stores grow in prominence. That makes Davis Cookware and Cutlery Shop all the more special. Come for the staff's expertise on knives and kitchen knickknacks, stay to marvel at the gorgeous copper espresso machine parked in the shop's front window. ✉ *1717 21st Ave. S, Hillsboro Village* ☎ *615/298–4728* 🌐 *www.daviscoffeeclub.com* ⏲ *Closed Sun.*

Friedman's Army Navy Store
Friedman's Army Navy Store is far more than surplus, and has been a Hillsboro Village institution since opening in 1972. The store offers plenty of surplus gear, plus camping supplies, outdoor equipment, and all you could possibly need for a last-minute fishing trip at one of Nashville's many beloved watering holes. ✉ *2101 21st Ave. S, Hillsboro Village* ☎ *615/297–3343* 🌐 *www.friedmansarmynavyoutdoorstore.com* ⏲ *Closed Sun.*

GETTING HERE

Hillsboro Village is close to downtown and accessible via bus. It's also an easy neighborhood to bike to and boasts a nearby B-cycle station if you need to rent some wheels. Once you've arrived in or near Hillsboro Village, the area's businesses and attractions are all within easy and safe walking or biking distance.

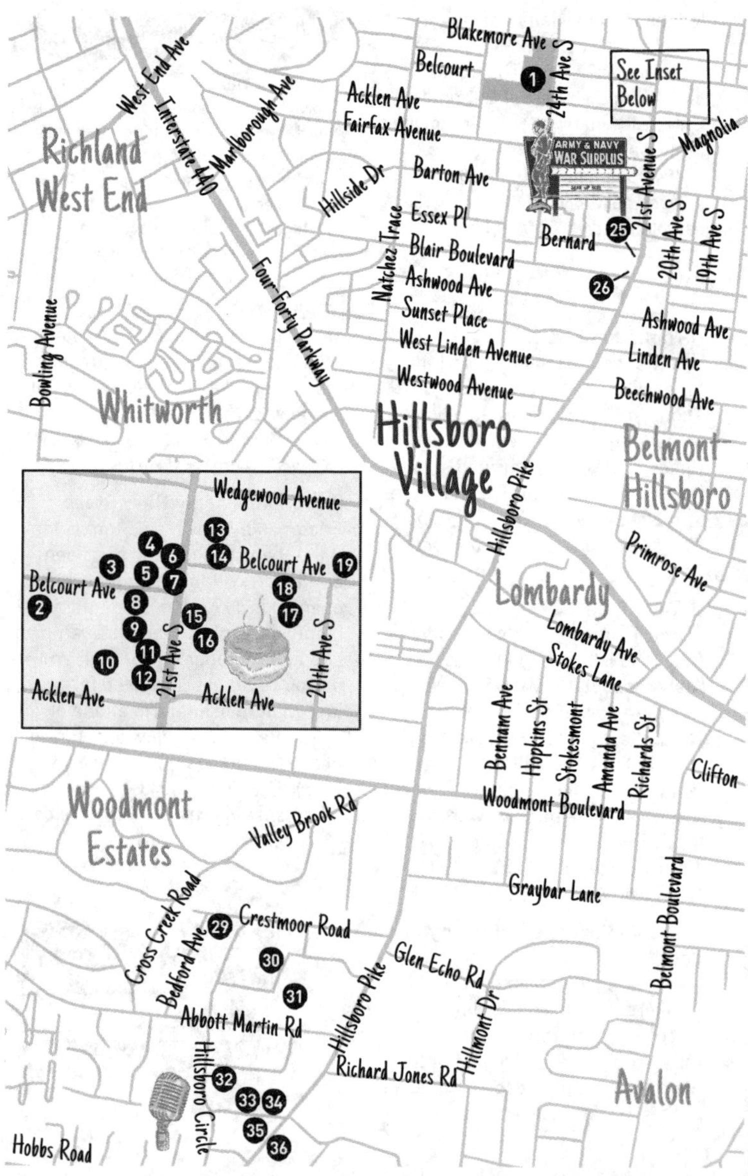

Blakemore Ave S
Belcourt
24th Ave S
See Inset Below
Acklen Ave
Fairfax Avenue
West End Ave
Interstate 440
Marlborough Ave
Richland West End
ARMY & NAVY WAR SURPLUS
Magnolia
Barton Ave
Hillside Dr
Essex Pl
21st Avenue S
20th Ave S
19th Ave S
Natchez Trace
Blair Boulevard
Bernard
Ashwood Ave
Sunset Place
Four-Forty Parkway
West Linden Avenue
Westwood Avenue
Ashwood Ave
Linden Ave
Beechwood Ave
Bowling Avenue
Whitworth
Hillsboro Village
Belmont Hillsboro
Hillsboro Pike
Wedgewood Avenue
Belcourt Ave
Belcourt Ave
21st Ave S
20th Ave S
Acklen Ave
Acklen Ave
Primrose Ave
Lombardy
Lombardy Ave
Stokes Lane
Benham Ave
Hopkins St
Stokesmont
Amanda Ave
Richards St
Clifton
Woodmont Boulevard
Woodmont Estates
Valley Brook Rd
Graybar Lane
Belmont Boulevard
Cross Creek Road
Bedford Ave
Crestmoor Road
Glen Echo Rd
Hillsboro Pike
Hillmont Dr
Abbott Martin Rd
Richard Jones Rd
Hillsboro Circle
Avalon
Hobbs Road

SIGHTS

Belmont Mansion.....20
Fannie Mae Dees Park.....1
Gallery of Iconic Guitars.....21

SHOPPING

A Thousand Faces.....13
Billy Reid.....34
Davis Cookware and Cutlery Shop.....6
Friedman's Army Navy Store.....25
H. Audrey.....35
Hey Rooster General Store.....4
Hill Center at Green Hills.....33
Local Honey.....23
The Mall at Green Hills.....3
Native + Nomad.....10
Pangaea.....5
Posh Boutique.....8
United Apparel Liquidators.....16

COFFEE & QUICK BITES

Bongo Java.....22
Fido.....15
Revelator Coffee.....12

DINING

Biscuit Love.....17
Brown's Diner.....26
Cabana.....19
Copper Kettle Café.....28
Etc. restaurant.....29
The Grilled Cheeserie.....18
Hopdoddy Burger Bar.....9
Martin's Bar-B-Que Joint.....27
McDougal's Chicken Fingers and Wings.....2
Pancake Pantry.....14
Proper Bagel.....24
Table 3 Restaurant and Market.....30

BARS & NIGHTLIFE

Double Dogs.....11
Joe's Place.....32
The Villager Tavern.....7

PERFORMING ARTS

Belcourt Theatre.....3
The Bluebird Cafe.....36

★ H. Audrey

Nashville's Holly Williams (the granddaughter of Hank Williams) is a fixture of the local boutique scene, and H. Audrey is one of her beloved outposts. Stop in at the shop's location at the Hill Center at Green Hills for a thoughtfully curated selection of women's clothing and accessories, all presented in a beautifully styled space. ✉ *4027 Hillsboro Pike, Hillsboro Village* ☎ *615/760–5701* 🌐 *www.haudrey.com*.

Hey Rooster General Store

In 2017, beloved Nashville bookshop BookMan/BookWoman sadly shut its doors. The silver lining is that Hey Rooster General Store came to take its place. Hey Rooster is the perfect spot for grabbing a taste of Nashville to take home, and, with its trinkets and tasty items, makes for a great spot to grab a gift for your vacation dog-sitter, too. ✉ *1711 21st Ave. S, Hillsboro Village* 🌐 *www.heyrooster.com*.

Hill Center at Green Hills

The Hill Center at Green Hills is a relaxing spot for an afternoon of shopping, made easily accessible by ample parking and a pedestrian-friendly layout. Major retailers include Whole Foods, Anthropologie, and West Elm, while local spots include Posh and H. Audrey. There are several fast-casual restaurants in the complex, like Zoe's Kitchen and Pei Wei. ✉ *4015 Hillsboro Pike, Hillsboro Village* ☎ *615/252–8101* 🌐 *www.hillcentergreenhills.com*.

WORTH A TRIP

Both Vanderbilt and Belmont, which are each a short walk from Hillsboro Village, boast visit-worthy campuses. Vanderbilt's campus is an arboretum, and makes for especially lovely walks in the fall. Belmont offers tours of its historic Belmont Mansion and is also home to the Gallery of Iconic Guitars, which features one of the city's most extensive collections of rare and unusual guitars.

Local Honey

Local Honey is one of the city's more unusual gems, as the beloved vintage shop is also home to well-regarded hair salon. If you want to get your hair done, you'll need an appointment, but anyone is welcome to stop in and browse the store's highly curated selection of vintage clothing, shoes, and accessories. ✉ *2009 Belmont Blvd., Hillsboro Village* ☎ *615/915–1354* 🌐 *www.lhnashville.com*.

The Mall at Green Hills

If a day at the mall is what the doctor ordered, look no further than the Mall at Green Hills. Located close to Downtown and Hillsboro Village, the Mall at Green Hills is the perfect one-stop shop for high-end clothing, accessories, home furnishings, and more. Don't miss the brand-new Restoration Hardware, which features four stories of decor as well as several restaurants. ✉ *2126 Abbott Martin Rd., Hillsboro Village* ☎ *615/298–5478* 🌐 *www.shopgreenhills.com*.

Native + Nomad
As you stroll through Hillsboro Village, be sure to stop in Native + Nomad, one of the neighborhood's newer locally owned clothing boutiques. You'll find a number of Nashville clothing and accessory designers represented on the shop's racks, as well as nationally beloved brands. The shop sells Nashville-themed souvenirs, too, making it a good spot to scope out gifts. ✉ *1813 21st Ave. S, Hillsboro Village* ☎ *615/840–7409* 🌐 *shopnativeand-nomad.com.*

★ **Pangaea**
Hillsboro Village has changed a lot in the last few years, but longtime clothing and accessories store Pangaea fortunately still remains. The shop carries a small, curated selection of women's clothes, as well as a bevy of funky home decor items, quirky jewelry pieces, and clever greeting cards, all sourced from makers and artisans around the world. ✉ *1721 21st Ave. S, Hillsboro Village* ☎ *615/269–9665* 🌐 *www.pangaeanashville.com.*

Posh Boutique
The name says it all. Posh Boutique, which also has an outpost in nearby Green Hills, is one of the city's best spots to buy luxurious designer clothing. Posh carries clothing for both men and women, and boasts designers like Botkier and Sanctuary. Stop in to find an outfit for those last-minute dinner reservations you snagged at the nearby Catbird Seat. ✉ *1801 21st Ave. S, Hillsboro Village* ☎ *615/383–9840* 🌐 *www.poshonline.com.*

United Apparel Liquidators
If you're looking to score a killer deal on designer clothing, look no further than United Apparel Liquidators (UAL for short). The small Southern chain has two Nashville locations, with Hillsboro Village's being smaller. It still has an excellent selection, though, with up to 90% off retail prices for brands like Marc Jacobs and Theory (stock varies seasonally). ✉ *1814 21st Ave. S, Hillsboro Village* ☎ *615/540–0211* 🌐 *www.shopual.com.*

Coffee and Quick Bites

Bongo Java
$ | American. The Belmont Boulevard location of Bongo Java is a popular hangout for Belmont students. Accordingly, its food menu is more college-centric (think breakfast sandwiches) than Fido's, though in recent years the local coffee favorite has expanded its menu (and remodeled its building) to suit the needs of the rapidly growing neighborhood. **Known for:** ethically sourced coffee; inventive espresso drinks; all-day breakfast. *Average main: $5* ✉ *2007 Belmont Blvd., Hillsboro Village* ☎ *615/385–5282* 🌐 *www.bongojava.com.*

THE BELCOURT THEATRE: A MUST-SEE

The Belcourt Theatre has been a Nashville institution for nearly a century, hosting, in turns, the Nashville Children's Theatre and the Grand Ole Opry, and serving as the first "twin cinema" theater in middle Tennessee. Since its opening in 1925 as a silent movie house complete with a Kimball organ, The Belcourt has become Nashville's premier nonprofit film center, where movie lovers can view the latest avant-garde indies, groundbreaking documentaries, and hot new releases. After a $5-million renovation project in 2016, the Belcourt boasts state-of-the-art upgrades, including a newly designed lobby, upstairs classroom space for film education and community outreach, and an additional viewing room for private film screenings. However (and luckily), some things never change: moviegoers can still enjoy a glass of wine or beer with their popcorn, and can still expect riveting post-film discussions with filmmakers and other experts. The Belcourt has also kept some of its other movie traditions, including Music Mondays, where music buffs can watch iconic biopics or films with epic sound tracks; Weekend Classics; and seasonal features, like Twelve Hours of Terror (an all-night horror marathon) and The Ornaments in Convert, where musicians play the entire score of *A Charlie Brown Christmas.*

★ Fido

$ | American. Local favorite Fido is part of the Bongo Java family and has one of the coffee shop group's more extensive food menus. In addition to Fido's own take on the creatively made, ethically sourced espresso drinks found at other Bongo locations, the restaurant serves locally sourced breakfast, lunch, and dinner. Pro tip: try the burger. **Known for:** fresh, local food; creative espresso drinks; funky environment. *Average main: $10* ✉ *1812 21st Ave. S, Hillsboro Village* ☎ *615/777–3436* 🌐 *www.bongojava.com.*

Revelator Coffee

$ | American. If you're looking for a cup of coffee to take on the go while you explore Hillsboro Village, Revelator Coffee is a great place to stop. A small shop, Revelator is geared more toward in-and-out visitors than it is to those looking to sit down and sip drinks with friends. The bright, airy space also makes a nice spot to post a photo of your perfectly made latte. **Known for:** thoughtfully crafted espresso drinks; bright, trendy space. *Average main: $5* ✉ *1817 21st Ave. S, Hillsboro Village* ☎ *615/457–3175* 🌐 *www.revelatorcoffee.com.*

Dining

Biscuit Love

$ | American. Biscuit Love opened its first outpost in the Gulch, with the hip new breakfast spot so popular that lines poured out the door each morning. Now the popular eatery is open in Hillsboro

Village, serving up homemade biscuits and breakfast plates until 3 pm each day. Be warned: unless you get there early, be prepared to wait in line. **Known for:** sweet and savory biscuits; extensive breakfast menu; biscuit donuts ("bonuts"). *Average main: $10 ✉ 2001 Belcourt Ave., Hillsboro Village ☎ 615/610–3336 🌐 www.biscuitlove.com.*

★ **Brown's Diner**

$ | American. One of Nashville's oldest restaurants still in operation, the famed Brown's Diner first opened its doors in 1927. This spot, housed in a large trailer, is popular with celebrities and regular ol' locals alike, and the burger is one of the best in town. **Known for:** classic, no-frills burgers; friendly service; historic restaurant. *Average main: $7 ✉ 2102 Blair Blvd., Hillsboro Village ☎ 615/269–5509.*

Cabana

$$ | American. While new restaurants and bars continue to pop up all over Nashville, Hillsboro Village mainstay Cabana continues to hold strong. It's a great spot for large groups or parties of two alike, with a host of different seating options catered to different crowds. Visit for a reasonably priced classic cocktail and a house-made pizza. **Known for:** inexpensive cocktails; private seating; outdoor patio. *Average main: $20 ✉ 1910 Belcourt Ave., Hillsboro Village ☎ 615/577–2262 🌐 www.cabananashville.com.*

★ **Copper Kettle Café**

$$ | Southern. If you're looking for good old-fashioned Southern comfort food, look no further than the Copper Kettle Café. A Nashville institution since 2002, this "meat and three" (a restaurant serving up one meat alongside three sides) offers Southern staples like fried chicken, country-style meat loaf, and crispy pork chops. Pro tip: don't miss the Sunday brunch buffet. **Known for:** can't-miss Sunday brunch buffet; comfort food; vegetarian options. *Average main: $20 ✉ 4004 Granny White Pike, Hillsboro Village ☎ 615/383–7242 🌐 copperkettlenashville.com ⏲ Closed Sat.*

Etc. Restaurant

$$$ | American. Etc. Restaurant is tucked away behind the Mall at Green Hills, making it the kind of place an out-of-towner could easily miss. The menu, though, makes getting out the GPS worth it, as new American favorites are reimagined using international ingredients. Etc. also has an extensive dessert menu and a generous happy hour. **Known for:** extensive dessert menu; generous happy hour; hard to find, but worth looking for. *Average main: $30 ✉ 3790 Bedford Ave., Hillsboro Village ☎ 615/988–0332 🌐 www.etc.restaurant.*

The Grilled Cheeserie

$ | American. Long before the Grilled Cheeserie opened a brick-and-mortar shop, it was one of Nashville's most loved food trucks, slinging grilled cheese and tater tots to long lines of eaters who often tracked the truck down. Now, though, it's easier to indulge in some melty goodness at the restaurant's first permanent location. You can't go wrong with a grilled cheese, but don't sleep on the homemade soups and desserts, either. **Known for:** inventive twists on grilled cheese; seasoned tater tots; homemade soup. *Average main: $8* ✉ *2003 Belcourt Ave., Hillsboro Village* ☎ *615/203–0351* 🌐 *www.grilledcheeserie.com.*

Hopdoddy Burger Bar

$ | American. Hopdoddy Burger Bar has been popular in Texas for some time now, but the new Hillsboro Village location marks its first outpost in Nashville. The restaurant serves up a variety of freshly made burgers, as well as thick, creamy milk shakes and perfectly crisp fries. Long line? No worries! The Hopdoddy team regularly hands out free samples of beer, fries, and shakes to folks waiting for a table. **Known for:** craft burgers and local beer; free beer samples, fries, and shakes while you wait; house-made margaritas. *Average main: $7* ✉ *1805 21st Ave. S, Hillsboro Village* ☎ *615/823–2337* 🌐 *www.hopdoddy.com.*

★ Martin's Bar-B-Que Joint

$ | Barbecue. Martin's proudly proclaims they don't own a microwave or a freezer. They are committed to the west-Tennessee style of whole-hog barbecue, smoking their hogs for a full day and serving it until it runs out—period. This is the type of place where you may find yourself stupefied by just how much you've managed to eat. **Known for:** large portions; delicious beef brisket; veggie sides. *Average main: $11* ✉ *3108 Belmont Blvd., Belmont* ☎ *615/200–1181* 🌐 *www.martinsbbqjoint.com.*

VIEWFINDER

One of Nashville's oldest murals sits across the street from the entrance to the Belcourt Theatre. It depicts a large dragon beneath the words "Hillsboro Village" in homage to neighboring Fannie Mae Dees Park, known colloquially as "Dragon Park" for its large, climbable dragon statue. Both landmarks make for great photos for kid and adult dragon-lovers alike.

Share your photo with us! @FodorsTravel #FodorsOnTheGo

McDougal's Chicken Fingers and Wings

$ | American. Whether you're traveling with a finicky eater or just enjoy a well-done chicken wing, McDougal's is a great spot for a quick, casual meal. Their perfectly cooked chicken comes with a variety of sauce options, with heat levels that should satisfy even the most daring of eaters. And the best part? Free soft-serve! **Known for:** fried chicken fingers and wings in tasty sauces; local beer; free soft-serve. *Average main: $12* ✉ *2115 Belcourt Ave., Hillsboro Village* ☎ *615/383–3005* 🌐 *www.mcdougalschicken.com*.

Pancake Pantry
$ | **Southern.** A Nashville institution, Pancake Pantry is the place to go for breakfast. It's a favorite with locals, students, and celebrities. Breakfast is the specialty, with 20 kinds of pancakes (sweet to savory) and homemade syrups. There are good soups and sandwiches for lunch—or you can stick with the pancakes, which are served till closing in late afternoon. Get there by 8:15 weekdays to avoid lines, but be prepared to wait on weekends. **Known for:** 20 kinds of pancakes; sweet and savory homemade syrups; long wait times. *Average main: $12* ✉ *1796 21st Ave. S, Hillsboro Village* ☎ *615/383–9333* 🌐 *www.thepancakepantry.com*.

Proper Bagel
$ | **American.** Some say you can't get a proper bagel outside New York City, but Belmont Boulevard's Proper Bagel makes a good argument otherwise. Each day, the small eatery prepares a variety of freshly made bagels alongside numerous flavored cream cheese options. Pair your bagel with one of their many side items, like pasta salad, and a dessert (try a black-and-white cookie!) and you're all set. **Known for:** house-made bagels and cream cheese; variety of salads and sides; minimalist, modern atmosphere. *Average main: $12* ✉ *2011 Belmont Blvd., Hillsboro Village* ☎ *615/928–7276* 🌐 *www.properbagel.com*.

Table 3 Restaurant and Market
$$$ | **Brasserie.** If you're looking for an upscale dinner spot before a movie or trip to the Mall at Green Hills, check out nearby Table 3 Restaurant and Market. The French-style brasserie offers dishes like escargot, foie gras, and coq au vin, as well as one of the city's better curated lists of wines. It's also a great spot to stop for a snack, like one of Table 3's thoughtfully paired cheeses. **Known for:** extensive wine list; French classics; cheese pairings. *Average main: $25* ✉ *3821 Green Hills Village Dr., Hillsboro Village* ☎ *615/739–6900* 🌐 *www.table-3nashville.com*.

Bars and Nightlife

Double Dogs
If you're looking to watch the big game in Hillsboro Village, look no further than Double Dogs. The brewpub has TV screens on TV screens, so they're sure to be broadcasting whichever sporting event you're after, which you can enjoy with a long list of craft beers. It's also a full restaurant, making it a nice spot for a casual meal. ✉ *1807 21st Ave. S, Hillsboro Village* ☎ *615/292–8110* 🌐 *www.doubledogs.biz*.

Joe's Place

Green Hills isn't a neighborhood known for its dives or holes-in-the-wall, but Joe's Place is a lively antidote to the surrounding area's polished sheen. Stop in for a cold beer or mixed drink, and stay for arcade games, karaoke, TVs, and well-prepared bar fare like pizzas and sandwiches. ✉ *2227 Bandywood Dr., Hillsboro Village* ☎ *615/383–9115.*

The Villager Tavern

Much of Hillsboro Village is hip and manicured, but not the Villager Tavern, which remains one of the neighborhood's longest-running establishments. A true dive, the Villager, which is wildly popular among locals, serves up a limited menu of cheap beer and occasionally has potato chips for when you need something to munch on. The real draws are the front-room jukebox and the back-room dartboards, the latter of which draw serious competitors on any night of the week. ✉ *1719 21st Ave. S, Hillsboro Village* ☎ *615/298–3020* 🌐 *www.thevillagertavern.com.*

Performing Arts

★ Belcourt Theatre

The Belcourt Theatre is Nashville's only independent movie theater, first established in 1925 as the Hillsboro Theater. Reopened after extensive renovations in 2016, the newly updated and expanded Belcourt plays host to new films, old classics, special events, speakers, concerts, and more. The Belcourt has all kinds of snacks and drinks (including alcoholic beverages) available, so come hungry. ✉ *2102 Belcourt Ave., Hillsboro Village* ☎ *615/846–3150* 🌐 *www.belcourt.org.*

★ The Bluebird Café

You can't get the full Nashville experience without a visit to the Bluebird Café, one of the city's most famous music venues. Catch a show on any given night and you're bound to see some of the world's best songwriters performing new and old material in a truly intimate setting. Be mindful of the Bluebird's admission policy, and do your research before you visit. ✉ *4104 Hillsboro Pike, Hillsboro Village* ☎ *615/383–1461* 🌐 *www.bluebirdcafe.com.*

5 | # East Nashville

GO FOR

Great bars and restaurants

Hip, artsy atmosphere

Walkable

Sightseeing ★★☆☆☆ | Shopping ★★★★☆ | Dining ★★★★★ | Nightlife ★★★★★

East Nashville is one of the city's hippest enclaves. Made up of several smaller neighborhoods, it is home to some of the city's best local dining and nightlife, as well as unique local shopping, scenic views, and beloved small and midsize music venues. East Nashville epicenter Five Points boasts local favorite watering holes like 3 Crow Bar, the 5 Spot, Red Door East, and Rosemary & Beauty Queen. Adjacent neighborhoods like Lockeland Springs and McFerrin Park are home to many excellent restaurants, including Lockeland Table and Mas Tacos Por Favor, respectively. Running along the eastern edge of East Nashville is Shelby Park, a 1,000-acre urban greenspace with playgrounds, a dog park, a golf course, and hiking and biking trails. East Nashville doesn't have many hotel options, but there are plenty of homes and apartments available for rent, which let visitors live like locals. Give yourself plenty of time to explore East Nashville—there are charming pockets of businesses and attractions tucked away across the area, and you never know what delicious bites or must-have buys you'll stumble across next.—*by Brittney McKenna*

Sights

Shelby Park

Shelby Park (as well as the connecting Shelby Bottoms and Cornelia Fort Airpark) is an east Nashville gem. With more than 336 acres of park land, hiking trails, public recreational facilities, and bike/pedestrian paths, Shelby offers a wide variety of free outdoor activities to locals and visitors alike. There's a public 18-hole golf course, too, so bring your clubs. ✉ *Shelby Ave. at S. 20th St., East Nashville* 🌐 *www.nashville.gov.*

Shopping

Apple and Oak

Located close to the restaurants and coffee shops on Eastland Avenue, Apple and Oak is a haven for lovers of good design. You'll find furniture, rugs, and home decor galore in this locally owned boutique, as well as clothing, accessories, and small gifts. The store has a sister location in Hillsboro Village. ✉ *717 Porter Rd., East Nashville* ☎ *615/568-8633* 🌐 *www.appleandoaknash.com.*

Fanny's House of Music

If your trip to Nashville has you itching to make music of your own, stop by Fanny's House of Music to pick out the guitar of your dreams.

Situated in East Nashville's Five Points neighborhood, the mom-and-pop shop boasts a wide variety of new and vintage instruments, many of which are unusual or hard to find. The store also sells music accessories, so you'll find everything you need to plug in and rock out. ✉ *1101 Holly St., East Nashville* ☎ *615/750-5746* 🌐 *www.fannyshouseofmusic.com*.

Fond Object Records
Nestled in East Nashville's charming Riverside Village neighborhood is Fond Object Records. The locally owned store sells new and used music, vintage clothing, and housewares, and original artwork from a rotating roster of visual artists. Most weekends, the shop hosts concerts and events in its spacious backyard. If you're downtown, check out the store's newer location just south of Broadway. ✉ *1313 McGavock Pike, East Nashville* ☎ *615/499-4498* 🌐 *www.fondobjectrecords.com*.

★ **Grimey's New and Preloved Music**
Grimey's is a Nashville institution. A purveyor of new and used music as well as music-geek accessories, Grimey's, which recently relocated to a larger building in East Nashville, is a must-visit for music fans touring Nashville. Before you visit, check the store's in-store events calendar—there's a good chance you'll catch some great music while browsing the vinyl crates. ✉ *1060 E. Trinity La., East Nashville* ☎ *615/254-4801* 🌐 *www.grimeys.com*.

GETTING HERE

East Nashville hub Five Points is easily accessible via bus, particularly for visitors traveling from the downtown area. Once in Five Points, visitors will find adjacent neighborhoods easily accessible by a short walk, rideshare, or additional bus trip. The majority of East Nashville's neighborhoods have sidewalks and bike lanes and are very friendly to pedestrians and cyclists.

★ **Old Made Good**
Old Made Good is your one-stop shop for all things vintage and fun. From old-school band T-shirts to the perfect mid-century modern side table, everything at Old Made Good, located in East Nashville's Inglewood neighborhood, is carefully curated and stocked by the store's staff. In addition to vintage items, Old Made Good also stocks locally made candles, crafts, jewelry, and gifts. ✉ *3701b Gallatin Pike, East Nashville* ☎ *615/432-2882* 🌐 *www.oldmadegoodnashville.com*.

Opry Mills
The more than 200 stores at Opry Mills include a mix of high-end and casual stores like Coach, Cole Haan, Fossil, and other mall perennials. There's also a carousel and kiddie train, IMAX theater, movie screens, restaurants, and sporting goods stores. To avoid crowds, shop this mall mornings, Monday through Wednesday. ✉ *433 Opry Mills Dr., Franklin* ☎ *615/514-1000* 🌐 *www.simon.com*.

East Trinity Lane
McGavock Pike
East Trinity Lane
East Hill
Burchwood Avenue
Spain Avenue
Delmas Avenue
Fairwin Avenue
Carolyn Avenue
Cahal Avenue
Gallatin Pike
Litton Avenue
Ellington Parkway
Jones Avenue
Cherokee Avenue
Chickasaw Avenue
Highland Heights
Rosedale Avenue
Montgomery Avenue
Renraw
Cahal Avenue
East Nashville
Strouse Avenue
Douglas Avenue
Douglas Avenue
Straightway Avenue
Douglas Avenue
North 7th Street
8th Street
Greenwood Avenue
Sharpe Avenue
Granada Avenue
Greenwood
Greenwood Avenue
Roberts Ave
Sharpe Ave
Eastwood
Chapel Avenue
Scott Avenue
North 14th Street
Gallatin Avenue
Cleveland Park
Ellington Parkway
Petway Ave
Seymour Ave
Chicamauga Ave
Sumner Ave
Franklin Ave
Cleveland St
West Eastland Ave
Eastland Avenue
Porter Rd
Stratton Avenue
North 9th St
Myrtle Avenue
Hart Avenue
Mc Ferrin Avenue
McEwen Avenue
N 12th St
Ordway Place
Gartland Avenue
Forrest Avenue
Maxwell Heights
Lockeland Springs
Woodland St
Main Street
Woodland St
Russell St
Fatherland St
Holly Street
Russell Street
Fatherland St
Lillian St
East End
South 10th St
South 11th St
South 14th St
South 16th St
South 17th St
South 18th St
South 19th St
Shelby Avenue
Shelby Park
1 2 3 9 10 11 12 13 14 15 16 17 18 19 20 21 22 23 24 25 26 27 28 29 30 31 32 33 34 35 36 37 38

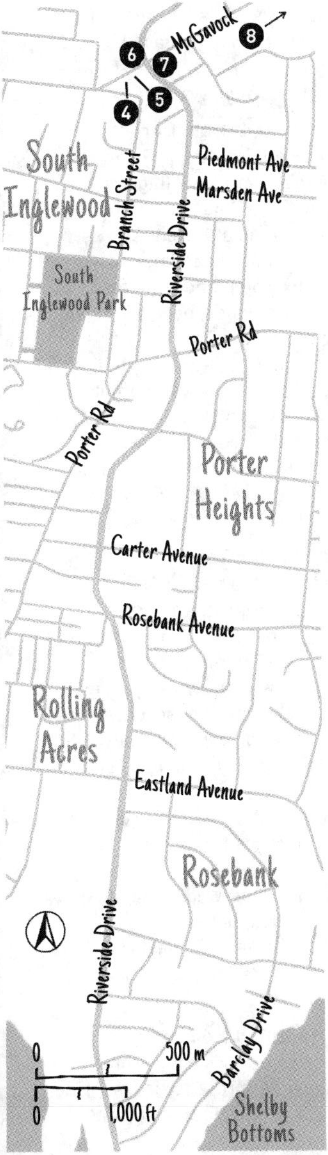

SIGHTS

Shelby Park 38

SHOPPING

Apple and Oak 16

Fanny's House of Music 26

Fond Object Records 6

Grimey's New and Preloved Music 2

Old Made Good 1

Opry Mills 8

Two Son 28

COFFEE & QUICK BITES

Barista Parlor 17

Bongo Java East 25

Dose Café and Dram Bar 7

High Garden Tea 27

Jeni's Splendid Ice Creams 14

The Post East 37

Ugly Mugs 15

DINING

Butcher and Bee 30

Edley's Bar-B-Que... 32

Five Points Pizza 23

Folk 11

Lockeland Table 35

Marché Artisan Foods 21

Margot Café and Bar 22

Mitchell Delicatessen............... 4

The Pharmacy 12

Rosepepper Mexican Grill 13

BARS & NIGHTLIFE

The Crying Wolf........ 31

Dino's 18

Lipstick Lounge 34

Mickey's Tavern 3

No 308 19

Pearl Diver 10

Smith and Lentz Brewing 29

3 Crow Bar 24

Urban Cowboy Public House 36

Village Pub and Beer Garden 5

PERFORMING ARTS

The Basement East 33

The Cobra 9

The 5 Spot................. 20

Two Son
East Nashville is known for its quirky sense of style. Convenient to Five Points, clothing boutique Two Son offers a bright, airy spot to take a little of that style back home. The store carries men's and women's clothes in a number of brands, including its own in-house clothing line. They also carry a curated selection of accessories, beauty supplies, and home decor. *918 Main St., East Nashville 615/678–4953 www.twoson.co Closed Mon.*

Coffee and Quick Bites

Barista Parlor
$ | American. The East Nashville location of Barista Parlor is the spot that started it all for the growing local coffee chain. Barista Parlor is known for paying almost an excruciating level of detail to all of its coffee beverages, so you know you're getting a quality cup of coffee every time you visit. **Known for:** carefully made coffee drinks; hip, trendy setting; knowledgeable staff. *Average main: $5 519B Gallatin Ave., East Nashville 615/712–9766 www.baristaparlor.com.*

Bongo Java East
$ | American. The eastern outpost of the local Bongo Java empire, this location is in East Nashville's bustling Five Points neighborhood. Stop in for coffee, tea, pastries, sandwiches, and more, served up in a refreshingly unpretentious environment by a friendly, knowledgeable staff. **Known for:** ethically sourced coffee; locally sourced food; friendly staff. *Average main: $5 107 S. 11th St., East Nashville 615/777–3278 www.bongojava.com.*

Dose Café and Dram Bar
$ | American. Located in East Nashville's Riverside Village neighborhood, Dose Café and Dram Bar serves up some of the city's finest espresso drinks. In addition to a caffeine fix, you'll find a full food menu, baked goods, beer, wine, and cocktails, making Dose the perfect one-stop shop for exploring the neighborhood. **Known for:** breakfast and lunch options; beer, wine, and cocktails; specialty coffee. *Average main: $10 1400 McGavock Pike, East Nashville 615/730–8625 www.dosecoffeeandtea.com.*

★ **High Garden Tea**
$ | Café. Nestled away in an otherwise nondescript strip of businesses, High Garden is an oasis for tea lovers, kombucha drinkers, and anyone who enjoys a chance to disconnect. Grab a house-brewed tea or a flight of fermented beverages with a locally baked pastry, and chill out in the relaxing atmosphere; High Garden does not allow laptops and discourages cell phone use. **Known for:** curated teas and herbal drinks; locally brewed kombucha; magical atmosphere. *Average main: $4 935 Woodland St., East Nashville 615/919–4195 www.highgardentea.com Closed Sun.*

Jeni's Splendid Ice Creams
$ | American. Jeni's has become such a popular presence in Nashville that many people, locals included,

forget the string of ice cream shops is actually based in Ohio. No matter, though, as the colorful shop and its artful flavors of ice cream and sorbet fit right in here in Music City, particularly in East Nashville. **Known for:** fresh ingredients; creative flavors; modern, minimal atmosphere. *Average main: $5* ✉ *1892 Eastland Ave., East Nashville* ☎ *615/262–8611* 🌐 *www.jenis.com.*

The Post East

$ | American. The Post East is a quaint, friendly spot to grab coffee, juice, breakfast, and lunch while you catch up on a little work or reconnect with a friend. For the gluten-free eaters out there, the Post East has one of the city's more extensive gluten-free menus, as well as a number of vegan options. **Known for:** cozy atmosphere; gluten-free options; juices and smoothies. *Average main: $10* ✉ *1701 Fatherland St., Suite A, East Nashville* ☎ *615/457–2920* 🌐 *www.theposteast.com.*

Ugly Mugs

$ | American. Ugly Mugs is a neighborhood coffee shop on the edge of East Nashville's Lockeland Springs neighborhood. For those staying in the area, it's a great spot to grab coffee, breakfast, or a simple lunch or dinner, and it's also a popular hangout for local musicians, so you never know who you might run into. **Known for:** well-crafted espresso drinks; fresh, locally sourced food; friendly, comfortable atmosphere. *Average main: $5* ✉ *1886 Eastland Ave., East Nashville* ☎ *615/915–0675* 🌐 *www.uglymugsnashville.com.*

VIEWFINDER

New tiki bar Pearl Diver has all kinds of colorful nooks and crannies, perfect for eye-popping photos (the drinks are pretty 'grammable, too). Shelby Park is the perfect spot for those who prefer to take their photos in nature. There are also plenty of eye-catching murals along Gallatin Pike, so grab your camera (or your phone) and explore.

Share your photo with us!
@FodorsTravel #FodorsOnTheGo

Dining

Butcher and Bee

$$ | Eclectic. Though it only opened in 2015, Butcher and Bee is already a Nashville culinary mainstay. The restaurant is convenient both to downtown and to East Nashville's Five Points, and offers guests a variety of dining options, from a casual weekend brunch to an elegant dinner of small, shared plates, all of which find the middle ground between Middle Eastern and Southern American influences.

Known for: shareable small plates; large, lively space; Middle Eastern influences. *Average main: $14 ✉ 902 Main St., East Nashville ☎ 615/226-3322 🌐 www.butcherandbee.com.*

Edley's Bar-B-Que

$ | Barbecue. At Edley's it's first come, first served for their mouth-watering brisket. If you miss the brisket, there are plenty of other delectable Southern barbecue favorites, quickly made to order and enjoy on polished-wood picnic tables inside or on the large patio; you can wash it down with a local craft beer or their signature Bushwacker, a chocolate rum milk shake. **Known for:** house-smoked barbecue; delectable sides; extensive beer list. *Average main: $12 ✉ 908 Main St., East Nashville ☎ 615/873-4085 🌐 www.edleysbbq.com.*

★ **Five Points Pizza**

$ | Pizza. A lively strip of bars wouldn't be complete without a pizza joint, and Five Points Pizza fills that void in the Five Points neighborhood, slinging slices, pies, and brews to the crowds heading to nearby 3 Crow Bar or the Five Spot. For the late-night set, Five Points offers a walk-up window for ordering slices to go. **Known for:** fresh, fast pizza; lively, neighborhood feel; local craft beer. *Average main: $9 ✉ 1012 Woodland St., East Nashville ☎ 615/915-4174 🌐 www.fivepointspizza.com.*

★ **Folk**

$$ | Eclectic. Chef Philip Krajeck's first Nashville restaurant Rolf and Daughters has been a runaway success since opening in 2012, and he has another success on his hands with new spot Folk, situated in East Nashville's Cleveland Park neighborhood. Seasonal salads and small plates round out a well-balanced menu. **Known for:** wood-fired pizza; fresh, seasonal ingredients; hip, artsy interior. *Average main: $20 ✉ 823 Meridian St., East Nashville ☎ 615/610-2595 🌐 www.goodasfolk.com.*

Lockeland Table

$$ | Eclectic. Equipped with a wood-burning stove, a smoker, and a garden of fresh vegetables, Chef Hal Holden-Bache gets down to business preparing some serious down-home cooking at his popular neighborhood restaurant, which serves comfort-gourmet food in a relaxed setting. Don't miss their cocktail menu, which features seasonal-inspired mixed drinks. **Known for:** creative comfort food; thoughtful beverage program; neighborhood atmosphere. *Average main: $22 ✉ 1520 Woodland St., East Nashville ☎ 615/228-4864 🌐 www.lockelandtable.com ⊗ Closed Sun.*

★ **Marché Artisan Foods**

$ | American. The glassed-in dining area of this bustling European-style café and bakery is charming on snowy Saturday mornings, sunny afternoons, or at night. Desserts and breads from the bakery are delicious, as are the soups, omelets, and dinner entrées featuring lamb, pork, fish, and seasonal items. **Known for:** bustling weekend brunch; seasonal ingredients; charming atmosphere. *Average main: $10 ✉ 1000 Main St., East Nashville ☎ 615/262–1111 ⊕ www.marcheartisanfoods.com.*

Margot Café and Bar

$$ | Eclectic. In 2001, when Nashville native Margot McCormack brought her Culinary Institute of America/New York City café-pedigree back home to establish Margot Café, she sparked a food revolution that has since swept through East Nashville. Her local dining institution consistently offers a delightfully inconsistent menu, with Southern-influenced rustic Italian and French dishes served daily. **Known for:** locally sourced ingredients; creatively prepared comfort food; intimate atmosphere. *Average main: $22 ✉ 1017 Woodland St., East Nashville ☎ 615/227–4668 ⊕ www.margotcafe.com ⏲ Closed Mon.*

★ Mitchell Delicatessen

$ | Deli. Mitchell Delicatessen is one of the pillars of East Nashville's Riverside Village neighborhood, and having relocated from across the street to a larger space in 2014, it's one of the more spacious delis in town (with a large covered patio, to boot). Come for classics like the Turkey Avocado; come back for Mitchell creations like the Turkey Apple Brie and Asian Flank Steak. **Known for:** creative and traditional sandwiches; generous portions; gluten-free and vegetarian options. *Average main: $7 ✉ 1306 McGavock Pike, East Nashville ☎ 615/262–9862 ⊕ www.mitchelldeli.com ⏲ No dinner Sun.*

★ The Pharmacy

$ | Burger. If you have a hankering for good burgers and good beer, look no further than the Pharmacy to cure what ails you. The outdoor beer garden is hard to beat for both its size and ambience, and the food itself is fresh, locally sourced, and thoughtfully served. **Known for:** house-made phosphates (sodas) and milkshakes; hard-to-find beers; large outdoor dining space. *Average main: $10 ✉ 731 McFerrin Ave., East Nashville ☎ 615/712–9517 ⊕ www.thepharmacynashville.com.*

Rosepepper Mexican Grill

$$ | Mexican. Even if you haven't been to Rosepepper, it's possible you've seen a photo of the restaurant's front sign, which features humorous comments like, "We love margaritas as much as Kanye loves Kanye." Luckily for guests, the food and drinks, which span classic Mexican fare like tacos as well as Americanized hybrids like the Mexican Caesar salad, are as good as the restaurant's sense of humor. They have a great outdoor space, too, so visit when the weather's nice. **Known for:** strong, flavorful margaritas; vegetarian options; Instagram-worthy sign and great outdoor seating space. *Average main: $13 ✉ 1907 Eastland Ave., East Nashville ☎ 615/227–4777 ⊕ www.rosepepper.com.*

EAST NASHVILLE BREWERY CRAWL

Nashville has become a major craft beer destination in recent years, with breweries like Yazoo and Jackalope achieving national recognition. And while there are worthwhile craft brewers scattered throughout the city, East Nashville has some of the best. Here are the breweries worth checking off your list during an East Nashville beer crawl.

Smith and Lentz Brewing: Having opened in late 2015, Smith and Lentz Brewing has since established itself as one of Nashville's more acclaimed craft brewers. Favorites include the Mosaic IPA and German Pils, but you can't go wrong with rotating seasonal offerings, either. The taproom sells light snacks and has two Ping-Pong tables, so come with your game face on.

Southern Grist Brewing: For lovers of adventurous varieties of beer, Southern Grist Brewing is a must-visit. Located at a quaint four-way stop and situated by some good local eats, the brewery is equally suited to starting or ending a night on the town. Check out inventive brews like the Money Moves milk stout and the Broconut coconut IPA (note that all offerings are seasonal and vary depending on availability).

East Nashville Beer Works: Located on main thoroughfare Trinity Lane, East Nashville Beer Works is a neighborhood gem. The brewery and taproom serve up beers like blonde ale Miro Miel as well as an eclectic menu of pizza, salads, and appetizers. The back patio is dog-friendly.

Bars and Nightlife

The Crying Wolf

The Crying Wolf is a bar first and foremost, though a taste of one of their handcrafted burgers may have you wondering otherwise. The bar, which is decked out in taxidermy, serves an eclectic selection of local and craft beer, as well as inventive original cocktails. The Crying Wolf also hosts live music and events periodically, so check their calendar before you visit if that your kind of thing. There's a nice size patio, too, for a quick smoke or a bit of fresh air. ✉ *823 Woodland St., East Nashville* ☎ *615/953–6715* 🌐 *www.thecrying-wolf.com.*

★ Dino's

Billed as Nashville's oldest dive bar, Dino's has maintained its charm by changing little over the years. The bar stocks a handful of cheap beer selections and can make simple cocktails, while the kitchen serves up hot chicken, Frito pie, and sneakily delicious burgers. On the weekends, Dino's serves one of the best brunches in town, with offerings like hot chicken French toast. ✉ *411 Gallatin Ave., East Nashville* ☎ *615/226–3566* 🌐 *www.dinosnash-ville.com.*

Lipstick Lounge

Tucked away in East Nashville's Lockeland Springs neighborhood is the Lipstick Lounge, a long-standing queer bar with a friendly, community feel. The bar has all of your standard options, plus excellent brunch offerings like Bloody Marys on the weekend. Don't sleep on the food, which is better than your typical bar fare and has a Tex-Mex influence. Karaoke lovers, rejoice: Lipstick Lounge offers up some of the best in town. ✉ *1400 Woodland St., East Nashville* ☎ *615/226-6343* 🌐 *www.thelipsticklounge.com.*

Mickey's Tavern

Located in East Hill in a small strip with like-minded bars and restaurants, Mickey's Tavern is a no-frills dive with a neighborhood vibe. Serving local beer and simple mixed drinks to a diverse mix of patrons, Mickey's offers darts, foosball, and outdoor seating options. Big bonus points to Mickey's for allowing patrons to bring over a meal from next-door local Italian establishment Nicoletto's Italian Kitchen. ✉ *2907 Gallatin Pike, East Nashville* ☎ *615/852-5228* 🌐 *www.mickeystavernnashville.com.*

No. 308

No. 308 is a versatile bar near East Nashville's Five Points that serves creative cocktails, tasty small bites, and a host of local and craft beer. The intimate spot has a variety of nooks and crannies for seating, as well as a large back booth for big parties. Happy hour crowds will find the bar cozy and quiet, while those who come later in the evening can take advantage of 308's many dance and theme nights. ✉ *407 Gallatin Ave., East Nashville* ☎ *615/650-7344* 🌐 *www.bar308.com.*

Pearl Diver

New East Nashville bar Pearl Diver is an island vacation in bar form. From the tropical decor to the extensive list of tiki drinks, no detail at Pearl Diver was left unconsidered. The drink menu features island classics like daiquiris and mai tais, as well as new signature drinks whipped up by Pearl Diver's bartenders. They also serve small bites like dumplings and skewers. Charge your phone before hitting Pearl Diver—it's one big photo op. ✉ *1008 Gallatin Ave., East Nashville* ☎ *615/988-2265* 🌐 *www.pearldivernashville.com* ☞ *Closed Sun.*

★ **Smith and Lentz Brewing**

A host of craft breweries have opened in Nashville over the last few years, and Smith and Lentz Brewing ranks among the best of them. Located convenient to Five Points, Smith and Lentz offers a number of house and rotating brews in various glass sizes, also making each available to take home in a crowler or growler. They don't serve much food but do allow guests to bring in takeout. Ping-Pong tables and a solid selection of board games round out the experience. ✉ *903 Main St., East Nashville* ☎ *615/436-2195* 🌐 *www.smithandlentz.com.*

3 Crow Bar

A pillar of East Nashville's Five Points, 3 Crow Bar is a relaxed dive with a great beer selection, lively atmosphere, and a solid menu of bar food favorites. The bar does allow smoking inside, but on nice days they keep their large windows open. Don't leave without ordering a Bushwacker, which is basically just a delicious chocolate milk shake loaded down with booze. ✉ *1020 Woodland St., East Nashville* ☎ *615/262-3345* 🌐 *www.3crowbar.com.*

Urban Cowboy Public House
Adjacent to the Urban Cowboy Bed and Breakfast, Urban Cowboy Public House is one of east Nashville's trendiest cocktail bars. Serving up high-end libations and a thoughtfully designed food menu in a cozy backyard setting, Urban Cowboy caters to hip, younger crowds. Most seating is outdoors, so plan accordingly. ✉ *103 N. 16th St., East Nashville* ☎ *347/840-0525* 🌐 *www.urbancowboybnb.com.*

Village Pub and Beer Garden
East Nashville neighborhood Riverside Village is one of the few remaining stretches in town that has managed to retain a true community feel. Part of the reason is Village Pub, a friendly neighborhood bar serving up craft beer and specialty mule cocktails alongside a menu heavy on soft pretzels and pretzel sandwiches. Outdoor seating goes quickly on nice days, so get there early if you prefer to drink alfresco. ✉ *1308 McGavock Pike, East Nashville* ☎ *615/942-5880* 🌐 *www.riversidevillagepub.com.*

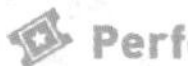

Performing Arts

The Basement East
Affectionately known as "the Beast," the Basement East is an East Nashville offshoot of the long-popular Basement venue located across the river. The midsize venue draws an eclectic array of local bands and nationally touring acts and hosts shows in an intimate environment convenient to Five Points. If you're hungry before or after a show, head around back to the Pub, which serves a full menu of entrées and snacks and a wide variety of booze. ✉ *917 Woodland St., East Nashville* ☎ *615/645-9174* 🌐 *www.thebasementnashville.com.*

The Cobra
While the Cobra is open on non-show nights, too, the East Nashville bar/venue is especially known for its live music. If your tastes venture outside country and Americana, you'll be pleased with the variety of music represented in the Cobra's nightly lineups, which often include local and national rock acts. The Cobra is also lively spot for a drink or a quick bite, so stop in early to enjoy the divey atmosphere. ✉ *2511 Gallatin Ave., East Nashville* ☎ *629/800-2515* 🌐 *www.thecobranashville.com.*

★ **The 5 Spot**
Five Points favorite the 5 Spot is a great place to grab a quick drink and an even better spot to catch a show or cut a rug. The venue/bar hosts a bevy of local musical talent as well as a number of weekly dance nights, including the wildly popular Motown Mondays, which features, you guessed it, a danceable selection of soul and R&B classics. Keep an eye out for Two Dollar Tuesdays, too, a regular concert series hosted by local musician Derek Hoke. ✉ *1006 Forrest Ave., East Nashville* ☎ *615/650-9333* 🌐 *www.the5spotlive.com.*

6 | **12 South**

GO FOR

People-watching

Good restaurants

Quirky shops

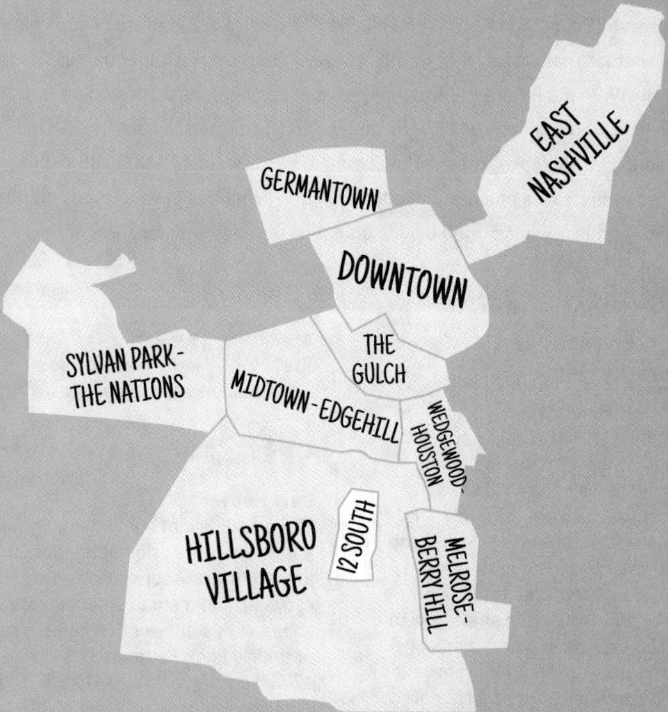

EAST NASHVILLE
GERMANTOWN
DOWNTOWN
SYLVAN PARK-THE NATIONS
THE GULCH
MIDTOWN-EDGEHILL
WEDGEWOOD-HOUSTON
12 SOUTH
HILLSBORO VILLAGE
MELROSE-BERRY HILL

Sightseeing ★☆☆☆☆ | Shopping ★★★☆☆ | Dining ★★★★☆ | Nightlife ★★★☆☆

On any given weekend, 12 South's eponymous road might be filled with crowds for a street fair, cyclists, scooter-riders, and traffic. The strip of shops, restaurants, and coffee establishments is smack in the middle of a residential neighborhood that has quickly morphed from one of long-established retirees to young families in newly constructed dwellings. It's a great place to people-watch and stroll. Locals come here for dining, college kids for hanging out or taking photos in front of murals. The road is also one of several parallel streets forming a major commuter corridor. Shopping at some of the celebrity-owned and -curated shops here is another main draw to 12 South. Reese Witherspoon (Draper James) and Holly Williams (White's Mercantile) have shops here, as do designers and stylists who regularly work with singers and other performers (HERO and Judith Bright, for example). The compact, easily walkable 12 South neighborhood is also a popular place for weekend brunches at which you could easily find yourself seated beside an entertainment luminary.—*by MiChelle Jones*

Sights

★ Sevier Park

A much-loved 20-acre site at one end of the 12 South neighborhood, Sevier Park is the site of festivals and a weekly farmers' market Tuesday from May through late October. The park opened in 1948 and features trails, a creek, two playgrounds, a shelter, picnic tables, and a historic mansion (currently undergoing renovation). The updated community center was opened in 2014 and offers $3 drop-in fitness classes, including yoga. There are also tennis and basketball courts, as well as bike rentals. Open 6 am until dark. ✉ *3021 Lealand La., Nashville* ☎ *615/862–8466* 🌐 *nashville.gov/parks-and-recreation/parks.aspx.*

Shopping

Ceri Hoover

The small, bright showroom/atelier features original handbags and other accessories, including eyewear and a small selection of shoes with solid wooden heels (one of their design hallmarks). ✉ *2905 12th Ave. S, Nashville* ☎ *615/200–0991* 🌐 *cerihoover.com* 🕓 *Closed Mon.*

Craft South

This small shop stocks fabric, yarn, patterns, books, and other items for sewing and needle crafts. The shop also holds workshops and classes and sells sewing machines. ✉ *2516 12th Ave. S, Nashville* ☎ *615/928-8766* 🌐 *craft-south.com* ⏲ *Closed Mon.*

Draper James
Follow the bright blue bags swinging from the arms of seemingly every other woman on 12th Street to find Nashville native Reese Witherspoon's charming flagship store for her line of stylish, feminine clothing, pretty home accents, and gifts. Once you step under the blue-and-white-striped awning and into the Southern fantasy, you'll be greeted by friendly sales associates who, at least in warm months, will offer you (very) sweet iced tea in a pretty blue paper cup. ✉ *2608 12th Ave. S, Nashville* ☎ *615/997-3601* 🌐 *draperjames.com.*

★ **Emerson Grace**
This beautifully curated collection of women's clothing features the work of numerous designers and is showcased in a rustic-industrial space matching the casual-chic aesthetic of the apparel. Local lines include Jamie + the Jones and Ceri Hoover handbags. ✉ *2304 12th Ave. S, Nashville* ☎ *615/454-6407* 🌐 *emersongracenashville.com.*

Halcyon Bike Shop
This shop not only sells and repairs bikes, it also rents City Bikes and tandem bikes. Cycling accessories are sold here, as are locally made music, art, and home goods. ✉ *2802 12th Ave. S, Nashville* ☎ *615/730-9344* 🌐 *halcyonbike.com* ⏲ *Closed Mon.*

GETTING HERE

Bus route 17 runs along 12th Avenue South to and from Nashville. Route 2 runs along Belmont Boulevard. From downtown, take any stop between Paris and Kirkwood, cross Belmont, and walk east to 12th Avenue South.

HERO
This is one of three Nashville-area boutiques (each has a different name) owned by Claudia Robertson Fowler, stylist to country music stars such as Faith Hill, Trisha Yearwood, Martina McBride, and Miranda Lambert. The items here have a certain rock-star flair: flowing frocks, fuzzy fur jackets in bright hues, and sparkly tops. The store also stocks hats by Nashville hat makers such as Claire West. ✉ *2306 12th Ave. S, Nashville* ☎ *615/457-1206* 🌐 *hero12s.com.*

Imogen + Willie
If you really love denim or indigo, this is your store. Known for handmade jeans, overalls, and other denim wear, as well as small-batch T-shirts and other items, the store is as comfortable as your favorite pair and is worth a look even if you can't splurge. The building is a

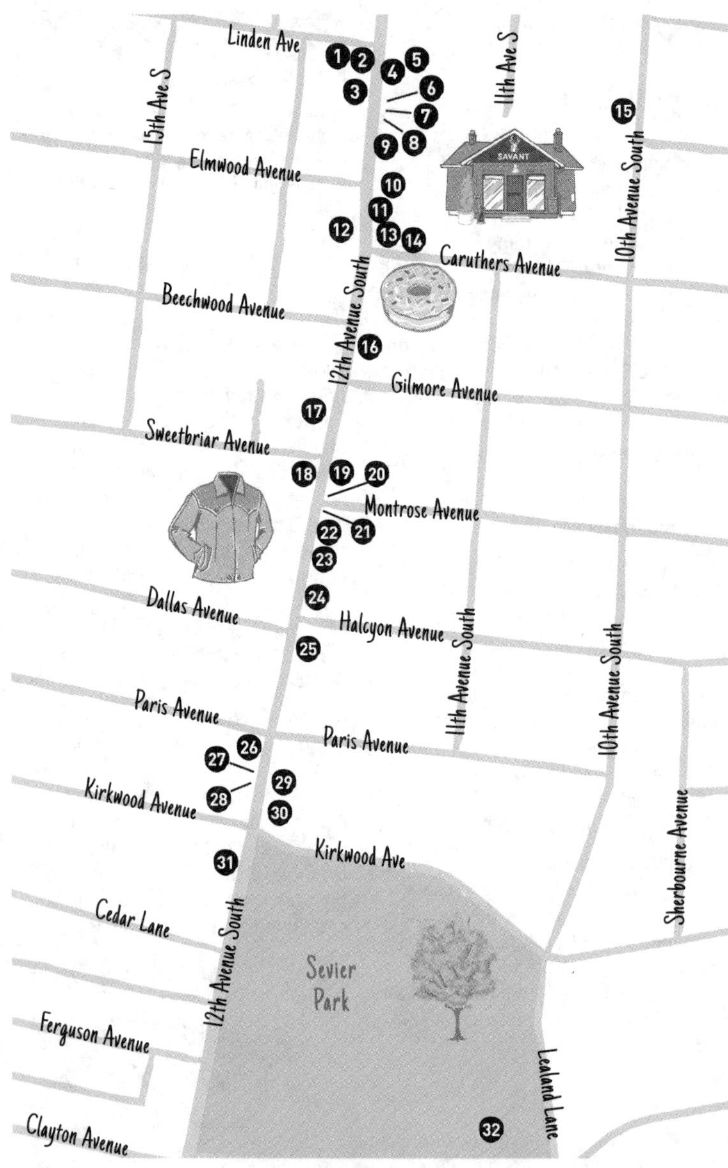
Linden Ave
15th Ave S
11th Ave S
SAVANT
Elmwood Avenue
10th Avenue South
Caruthers Avenue
Beechwood Avenue
12th Avenue South
Gilmore Avenue
Sweetbriar Avenue
Montrose Avenue
Dallas Avenue
Halcyon Avenue
11th Avenue South
Paris Avenue
Paris Avenue
10th Avenue South
Kirkwood Avenue
Kirkwood Ave
Sherbourne Avenue
Cedar Lane
12th Avenue South
Sevier Park
Ferguson Avenue
Lealand Lane
Clayton Avenue
1
2
3
4
5
6
7
8
9
10
11
12
13
14
15
16
17
18
19
20
21
22
23
24
25
26
27
28
29
30
31
32

Bradford Ave
Bradford Ave
9th Avenue South
Waldkirch Ave
Vaulx Lane
Caruthers Ave
12 South
Gilmore Ave
Montrose Avenue
Montrose Ave
9th Avenue South
Halcyon Avenue
Sunnyside
Knox Avenue

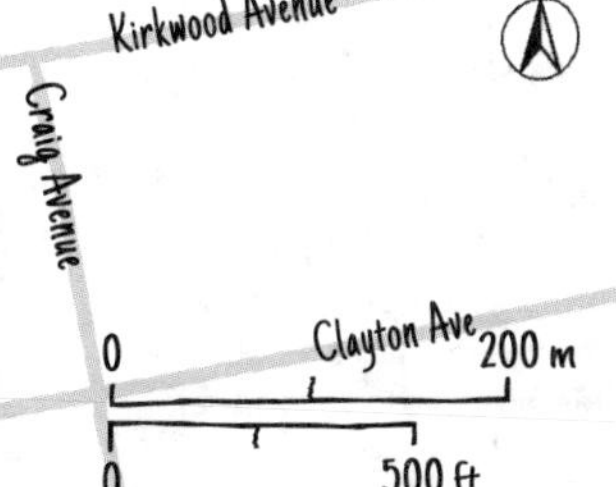

SIGHTS

- Sevier Park.............32

SHOPPING

- Ceri Hoover.............27
- Craft South.............19
- Draper James..........23
- Emerson Grace..........6
- Halcyon Bike Shop.............25
- HERO.........................7
- Imogene + Willie......18
- Judith Bright.............3
- MODA Boutique........17
- Savant Vintage...........4
- Serendipity................1
- Summer Classics Nashville..................21
- Vinnie Louise.............8
- Wags & Whiskers.......5
- White's Mercantile...30

COFFEE & QUICK BITES

- BOX..........................15
- Christie Cookie........22
- Five Daughters Bakery.....................14
- Franklin Juice Bar.....2
- Las Paletas..............31

DINING

- 12 South Taproom & Grill.......10
- bartaco......................20
- Burger Up.................26
- Edley's Bar-B-Que...24
- Epice.........................29
- Firepot Nomadic Teas..........28
- The Flipside.............12
- Josephine's................9
- MAFIAoZA's..............11
- Urban Grub...............16

BARS & NIGHTLIFE

- Embers Ski Lodge ...13

former gas station dating from the 1950s, which gives you an idea of how this neighborhood looked in a former incarnation. ✉ *2601 12th Ave. S, Nashville* ☎ *615/292–5005* 🌐 *imogeneandwillie.com*.

Judith Bright

Selling stylish and delicate handmade pieces combining metal with beads, gemstones, or birthstones, a crew of artisans work on-site in this light aqua cottage, so stones or other elements can be changed on the spot. Some of Judith Bright's creations have been featured in movies and TV shows. ✉ *2307 12th Ave. S, Nashville* ☎ *615/269–5600* 🌐 *judithbright.com*.

MODA Boutique

One of several 12 South shops. MODA is housed in a converted cottage. This small shop offers designer clothes ranging from casual to edgy. Jeans and denim jackets, novelty T-shirts, small gift items, and a jewelry selection that includes pieces made by local designers can all be found here. ✉ *2511 12th Ave. S, Nashville* ☎ *615/298–2271* 🌐 *modanashville.com*.

Savant Vintage

A visit here is like combing through an older relative's overstuffed closet or attic where you'll find vintage gems like leather handbags and satchels, jeans, wool blankets, games, and tchotchkes. ✉ *2302 12th Ave. S, Nashville* ☎ *615/385–0856*.

Serendipity

Behind the red front door of this corner shop you'll find lots and lots of gifts for everyone. Travel games, novelty items, little books, and locally made candles with scents such as "Nashville" (whiskey and leather) abound. The store stocks women's clothing and accessories and has quite a collection of children's books, games, and more. ✉ *2301 12th Ave. S, Nashville* ☎ *615/279–5570* 🌐 *www.serendipity12th.com*.

Summer Classics Nashville

Though it's a chain store with locations in nine other states, the brick-and-mortar Summer Classics Nashville, which occupies the former Becker's Bakery (a century-old landmark), is a reflection of local style and culture. It's soothing to browse here, if only for inspiration. They specialize in design-forward outdoor furniture built to withstand all weather. ✉ *2600 12th Ave. S, Nashville* ☎ *615/264–8061* 🌐 *summerclassics.com*.

★ **Vinnie Louise**

Named after the owner's grandmother, this boutique stocks casual trendy women's clothing at accessible prices along with a small selection of footwear and jewelry. Greeting cards, candles, and a few other gift items are available. The store's earthy vibe is enhanced by its brick floor laid in a herringbone pattern. There's a second location northeast of Nashville. ✉ *2301 12th Ave. S, Nashville* ☎ *615/730–8253* 🌐 *vinnielouise.com* ⏲ *Closed Mon.*

Wags & Whiskers

This charming store sells pet supplies and holistic treats for dogs and cats, along with pet toys and clothing. ✉ *2222 12th Ave. S, Nashville* ✥ *Entrance at the back of the building* ☎ *615/292–9662* 🌐 *wagsandwhiskersnashville.com.*

★ **White's Mercantile**

The flagship location of singer-songwriter Holly Williams's shop stocks shirts and tees for men and women; gifts and greeting cards; and a quirky collection of housewares. This is a great stop for Nashville- or Southern-themed gifts. Beautiful leather totes, shoulder bags, and more from Nashville-based ABLE can be found, and they do an impressive job of gift-wrapping your purchase. To immerse yourself further into the lifestyle, you can stay at a White's Mercantile Room and Board property. ✉ *2908 12th Ave. S, Nashville* ☎ *615/750–5379* 🌐 *whitesmercantile.com.*

Coffee and Quick Bites

BOX

$ | Bakery. This jewel box of a place has quickly become a popular hangout for people coming from the adjacent yoga studio or dropping kids off at the nearby elementary school. Part of Nashville's Bongo Java coffee universe (the name stands for Bongo + Bakery on 10th), BOX serves hot and cold beverages, fresh-baked goods, and breakfast items and sandwiches. **Known for:** Pink Radio Cake; vegan Beet-It muffin; pumpkin-chocolate muffin. *Average main: $10* ✉ *2229 10th Ave. S, Nashville* ☎ *615/777–5282* 🌐 *www.bongojava.com/box.*

Christie Cookie

$ | Bakery. You can't miss the bright red facade or the window where you can order the signature chocolate chip or oatmeal raisin cookies; sometimes there's a tray of samples at the window. This location opened in the summer of 2018, but the bakery has been around since 1985 and tins of the cookies are familiar and beloved holiday and celebratory gifts. **Known for:** snickerdoodle; white chocolate macadamia nut; cookie of the month (limited editions). *Average main: $3* ✉ *2606 12th Ave. S, Nashville* ☎ *615/279–3767* 🌐 *christiecookies.com.*

★ **Five Daughters Bakery**

$ | Bakery. You know the offerings are good when the hours include a "or till sold out" proviso, and that's the case with this bakery located just off 12th Avenue South. They serve pastries and cookies, but the large, beautifully decorated gourmet doughnuts are what people talk about most. It is locally owned and named for the family's five daughters. **Known for:** cronuts; "paleo" varieties; choices like King Kong (with bacon and maple glaze). *Average main: $4 ✉ 1110 Caruthers Ave., Nashville ☎ 615/490–6554 🌐 fivedaughtersbakery.com.*

Franklin Juice Bar
$ | American. This is the second location of a juice company that was founded in 2014 in neighboring Franklin, Tennessee. They serve juices, smoothies, and other healthful menu items in addition to lattes. A large selection of logo merchandise is also available. **Known for:** trail mix bowl; green lemonade; cold-pressed juices. *Average main: $10 ✉ 2301 12th Ave. S, Nashville ☎ 615/750–2992 🌐 franklinjuice.com/pages/12th-south.*

Las Paletas
$ | Mexican. Located across from Sevier Park, this busy shop run by two sisters serves creamy, fruity, and even sugar-free Mexican-style popsicles. The menu changes daily and features traditional flavors as well as new ones born of customer requests. **Known for:** Mexican chocolate; strawberry kiwi; melon flavors. *Average main: $4 ✉ 2911 12th Ave. S, Nashville ☎ 615/386–2101 🌐 laspaletasnashville.com ⏲ Closed Mon.*

Dining

bartaco
$$ | South American. This open yet cozy space, with woven baskets as light fixtures, serves upscale bites influenced by the street food and beach cultures of Southern California, Uruguay, and Brazil. Tacos and rice bowls dominate the menu, as well as fresh-squeezed juice and cocktails. **Known for:** fresh cocktails; outdoor dining; delicious fresh fish tacos. *Average main: $8 ✉ 2526 12th Ave S Nashville, TN, Nashville ☎ 615/269-8226 🌐 bartaco.com/location/nashville-tn.*

Burger Up
$$ | Burger. A comfortable neighborhood hangout (there's a second location in east Nashville) serving—you guessed it—burgers, as well as soups and salads, Burger Up is popular with all ages, including young families. Beef and other meats are sourced from a local farm and butcher shop; some desserts feature Nashville-made Pied Piper ice cream. **Known for:** truffle fries; pimento cheeseburger; well-stocked bar. *Average main: $16 ✉ 2901 12th Ave. S, Nashville ☎ 615/279–3767 🌐 www.burger-up.com.*

Edley's Bar-B-Que
$ | Barbecue. One of three locations in Nashville, weekend brunch here includes the "Nashville Nasty"—fried chicken served on top of homemade biscuits and covered with sausage gravy. This location has a large patio, and a small cocktail menu that includes the signature Bushwacker. **Known for:** brisket tacos; barbecue nachos; whipped banana pudding. *Average main: $10 ✉ 2706 12th Ave. S, Nashville ☎ 615/953–2951 🌐 edleysbbq.com.*

Epice
$$$ | Lebanese. A family-owned restaurant serving traditional Lebanese and Greek dishes with foodie flair, Epice has a large patio, serves lunch and dinner, and has a popular weekend brunch. **Known for:** lamb; shawarma; egg dishes. *Average main: $28 ✉ 2902 12th Ave. S, Nashville ☎ 615/720–6765 🌐 epicenashville.com ⏲ Closed Mon.*

Firepot Nomadic Teas
$ | Café. Owner Sarah Scarborough traveled the world discovering the kinds of teas now available in this tiny tea bar and shop. The aroma is intoxicating and the atmosphere is lively; the space is also available for private parties and tastings. **Known for:** chocolate chai; free tastings and classes; locally created blends. *Average main: $3.50 ✉ 2905 12th Ave. S, Nashville ☎ 615/988–4269 🌐 firepot.com ⏲ Closed Mon.*

The Flipside
$ | Diner. The Instagram-ready decor is inspired by 1950s diner culture, and while the menu may have its roots in roadside eateries, the chicken dishes and burgers have updated twists like sriracha thrown into the mix. They serve a simple brunch on the weekends, host a trivia night on Thursday, and have a small outdoor dining area. **Known for:** tater tot nachos; Bloody Caesar cocktail; shakes and malts. *Average main: $12 ✉ 2403 12th Ave. S, Nashville ☎ 615/292–9299 🌐 theflipside12south.com.*

ART IN THE WILD

Popular photo ops in 12 South include the "I Believe in Nashville" mural at 2700 12th Avenue South (there's another one in east Nashville); another mural on Paris Avenue features wildlife and the Nashville skyline dotted with its latest accessory: construction cranes. A window display on the side of Reese Witherspoon's Draper James store is another favorite.

Josephine's
$$$ | American. Expect upscale American "farmhouse cuisine" in an elegant setting with menus that change monthly at Josephine's. Their weekend brunch is good for lingering over delicious food, and for a unique foodie experience, RSVP for one of the Friday and Saturday "XIX" tasting dinners which can accommodate 10 guests. **Known for:** chicken and waffles; duck fat hash browns; deconstructed lemon layer cake. *Average main: $28 ✉ 2316 12th Ave. S, Nashville ☎ 615/292–7766 🌐 josephineon12th.com.*

MAFIAoZA's

$$ | Pizza. This fun pizza place is where all ages gather for deep-dish pizzas made in an open kitchen. Beyond pizza they serve meatballs, sautéed spinach, and salads, and for dessert, cannoli of course. **Known for:** theme pizzas; lasagna; caprese. *Average main: $16 ✉ 2400 12th Ave. S, Nashville ☎ 615/269–4646 🌐 mafiaozas.com ⏲ Closed Mon.*

12 South Taproom & Grill

$$ | American. Part of the 12 South scene before there was one—and still a favorite with a large, covered street-facing patio and small performance space inside—12 South Taproom has a menu that's surprisingly large with seemingly endless variations of quesadillas (rib-eye!), tacos, salads with vegetarian options, and a kids' menu. Your fellow diners will include families, couples, friends, local college kids, and visitors. Enjoy the walls papered in Hatch Show and other concert posters. **Known for:** extensive beer selection; grass-fed beef; chocolate banana bread. *Average main: $17 ✉ 2318 12th Ave. S, Nashville ☎ 615/463–7552 🌐 12southtaproom.com.*

Urban Grub

$$$ | Contemporary. A former car wash, Urban Grub is now a sophisticated dining space serving seafood and locally sourced meat that's cured on-site. Outdoor seating offers a view of the oversized fireplace for cooking. **Known for:** charcuterie boards; handmade pasta; donut holes with dulce de leche and chocolate. *Average main: $28 ✉ 2506 12th Ave. S, Nashville ☎ 615/679–9342 🌐 urbangrub.net.*

Bars and Nightlife

Embers Ski Lodge

A kitschy hangout with a 1960s après-ski vibe, Embers Ski Lodge serves gastropub fare—burgers, hand-cut Belgian fries—with a hint of the Pacific Northwest and East Asia, and a selection of cocktails, beer, and wine. Their large patio is located on a great corner for people-watching. *✉ 2410 12th Ave. S, Nashville ☎ 615/866–5652 🌐 embersskilodge.com.*

7 | # Wedgewood-Houston

GO FOR

Art scene

New shops

One of the newest hot spots

Sightseeing ★☆☆☆☆ | Shopping ★★☆☆☆ | Dining ★★★☆☆ | Nightlife ★★★☆☆

Longtime Nashvillians may cringe at the WeHo moniker increasingly applied to the Wedgewood-Houston neighborhood, but the shortened name is just one of the many transformations coming to the area. Higher-end residential offerings, a variety of restaurants, and a couple of craft distilleries may have arrived, but the remaining warehouses, train tracks, and commercial buildings help the expanding art scene maintain an appropriate edge. Most of the converted spaces have kept a bit of their rough origins, like the garage doors at the back of galleries on Hagan Street that hint at the building's former life as a truck repair shop. The pace of change in Wedgewood-Houston is astounding, with new businesses opening (and others closing) almost on a monthly basis. This trend should continue to develop as the former minor league baseball stadium and a 1930s hosiery mill are repurposed.—*by MiChelle Jones*

Sights

★ Adventure Science Center

Yes, this is a space designed with kids in mind, but there are also several elements that adults can enjoy, such as virtual reality stations, planetarium and laser shows, and the Blue Max flight simulator. Popular "Way Late Play Dates" are after-hours events exclusively for adults 21 and older and features themes like Harry Potter and Star Wars versus Star Trek. The Adventure Science Center sits on a bluff making it a great spot to watch Nashville's Fourth of July fireworks during the center's annual "Red, White & BOOM!" event. ✉ *800 Fort Negley Blvd., Wedgewood-Houston* ☎ *615/862–5160* 🌐 *www.adventuresci.org* 🎟 *$15.95; planetarium shows $9; Blue Max $6.*

Corsair Distillery

This second Corsair location opened in 2016 and serves as the headquarters for this creator of small-batch whiskeys and other spirits. Three types of tours are offered, ranging from 30-minute general ones that end with a five-spirit tasting to cocktail classes and "master tours." Tastings are also offered without tours, and Corsair has an outdoor area where dogs are welcome. ✉ *601 Merritt Ave., Wedgewood-Houston* ☎ *615/200–0320* 🌐 *corsairdistillery.com* ⏲ *Closed Mon.*

David Lusk Gallery

David Lusk's Memphis gallery has been around since 1995; the Nashville location opened in 2014 and features paintings, photography, and sculpture by regional and national artists. The gallery takes part in the Wedgwood-Houston art crawls and also hosts receptions and other events. ✉ *516 Hagan St., Wedgewood-Houston* ☎ *615/780–9990* 🌐 *davidluskgallery.com* ⏲ *Closed Sun. and Mon.*

Fort Houston
A makers' space offering classes, workshops, and studio and workspaces, the on-site gallery at Fort Houston has changing exhibits and is a key part of the monthly Wedgewood-Houston art crawls. Tours of the 17,000-square-foot facility are available by appointment. There is also an on-site eatery called The Loading Dock Cafe. ✉ *2020 Lindell Ave., Wedgewood-Houston* ☎ *615/730–8865* 🌐 *forthouston.com.*

Fort Negley Park
The history of the Civil War–era fort is told through videos in the visitor center and panels along outdoor pathways. This is also the site of veterans events throughout the year. There's a gift shop and views of the Nashville skyline. ✉ *1100 Fort Negley Blvd., Wedgewood-Houston* ☎ *615/862–8470* 🌐 *nashville.gov/parks-and-recreation/historic-sites/fort-negley.aspx.*

GETTING HERE

The best way to get to Wedgewood-Houston is via auto or bike. If you're coming via interstate, take I–65 (south from downtown, north from Brentwood and Franklin). Take exit 81 and turn onto Wedgewood Avenue (left if coming from I–65 South, right if from I–65 North). Turn left from Wedgewood onto Martin Street, which you can take into the heart of the neighborhood.

Julia Martin Gallery
Founded in 2013, artist Julia Martin's eponymous gallery plays a leading role in the monthly Wedgwood-Houston art crawl. The gallery shows contemporary work by local and national artists working in painting, sculpture, and other media. ✉ *444 Humphreys St., Suite A, Wedgewood-Houston* ☎ *615/336–7773* 🌐 *juliamartingallery.com* ☞ *Closed Sun.–Wed.*

Nashville Craft Distillery
Part of the official Tennessee Whiskey Trail, this facility offers tours for those 21 and older. They are known for small-batch spirits with clever names inspired by Nashville, such as Naked Biscuit Sorghum Spirit and Crane City Gin. ✉ *514 Hagan St., Wedgewood-Houston* ☎ *615/457–3036* 🌐 *nashvillecraft.com* ⏲ *Closed Mon.*

Nashville Fairgrounds
Site of auto races and other sporting events, craft fairs and monthly flea markets, the annual Christmas Village holiday market, concerts, and other special events throughout

the year, the Tennessee State Fair has been held here for more than 100 years, but may need a new home if the fairgrounds are redeveloped to include a soccer stadium for Nashville's new pro soccer team. ✉ *625 Smith Ave., Wedgewood-Houston* ✥ *Entrance location varies with event* ☎ *615/862–8989* 🌐 *thefairgrounds.com.*

The Packing Plant
This building with the asymmetrical slanted roof and the changing sculpture installation on the front lawn is home to tiny contemporary galleries—including those from the COOP Curatorial Collective and Watkins College of Art—and artist studios. This is a popular stop during the neighborhood's monthly art crawls. ✉ *507 Hagan St., Wedgewood-Houston* 🌐 *thepackingplant.com* ☞ *Closed Sun. and Mon.*

Zeitgeist Gallery
The anchor of the Wedgewood-Houston art scene, this gallery shares space with an architectural studio responsible for designing several of Nashville's most popular—dare one say, hip—places. Zeitgeist shows artists who explore daring concepts through intelligent, sophisticated work. Zeitgeist's receptions draw a large, knowledgeable crowd of local art insiders and often include cross-genre performances of dance, live music, and/or spoken word. ✉ *516 Hagan St., Suite 100, Wedgewood-Houston* ☎ *615/256-4805* 🌐 *zeitgeist-art.com* ⏲ *Closed Sun.–Mon.*

Shopping

★ **Cotten Music Center**
The interior of this Houston Station shop is as beautiful as the many acoustic guitars (plus banjos, mandolins, pedal steel, and electric guitars) on display here. The floor is a basketball court from a Memphis high school that was built in 1905, the same year this building was constructed. ✉ *434 Houston St., Suite 131, Wedgewood-Houston* ☎ *615/383-8947* 🌐 *cottenmusic.com* ⏲ *Closed weekends.*

★ **Flip Nashville**
A very particular consignment shop opened in 2014, a companion to the men's store that opened nine years earlier. Come here for high-end brands like Louis Vuitton, Tom Ford, Jimmy Choo, Burberry, etc. The men's shop is located nearby at 1100 8th Avenue South and includes sneakers. ✉ *1016 8th Ave. S, Wedgewood-Houston* ☎ *615/732–3547* 🌐 *hip2flip.com.*

Fork's Drum Closet
Fork's has been around since 1982, and opened in their newest location near Wedgewood-Houston as of fall 2018. They carry a full stock of items to keep percussionists happy, everything from sticks and mallets to drumheads to cases. ✉ *308 Chestnut St., Wedgewood-Houston* ☎ *615/383–8343* 🌐 *forksdrumcloset.com/forks-drum-closet.html* ⏲ *Closed Sun.*

Royal Circus

Wandering through the selection of mid-century (and older) desks, bookcases, and benches at this Houston Station store that opened in the spring of 2018 is not the worst way to spend an afternoon. A purple leather Chesterfield is the comfortable centerpiece. Look for the vintage-inspired silk-screened posters and postcards. ✉ *428 Houston St., Wedgewood-Houston* ☎ *615/727–7267* 🌐 *www.royalcircus.com* 🕓 *Closed Mon.*

Coffee and Quick Bites

Crest Cafe

$ | Café. Opened in the summer of 2018, Crest is billed as Nashville's first donation-based coffeehouse—in other words, it's pay what you wish for the coffee and teas. It hosts trivia nights, open-mics (welcome to Nashville!), and also takes part in the Wedgewood-Houston art crawls. **Known for:** London Fog tea; salted caramel; cider. *Average main: $3* ✉ *1601 Martin St., Wedgewood-Houston* 🌐 *crest.cafe* ☞ *Check for early closing times.*

Dozen Bakery

$ | Bakery. This small space is airy and bright, and maintains a bit of its pop-up-shop origins. Serving breakfast and lunch items—including soups and sandwiches—the best options are the cookies and pastries made on-site and also sold at a number of Nashville eateries. **Known for:** artisanal breads; cupcakes; pumpkin pie. *Average main: $5* ✉ *516 Hagan St., Suite 103, Wedgewood-Houston* ☎ *615/712–8150* 🌐 *www.dozen-nashville.com.*

Falcon Coffee Bar

$ | Café. Falcon opened in spring 2018 in a small former church. A light menu includes sandwiches after 11 am. **Known for:** empanadas; toast; Cubano coffees. *Average main: $5* ✉ *509 Houston St., Wedgewood-Houston* ☎ *786/942–8279* 🌐 *flamingo-cocktailclub.com.*

★ **Humphreys Street Coffee Shop**

$ | Café. The bright, pleasant shop opened in 2018; the nonprofit enterprise behind it was established in 2008 to train and mentor students. In addition to prepared coffees, the shop sells the beans, soaps, and scrubs made by the students, as well as mugs and T-shirts bearing the coffeehouse logo. **Known for:** 100% of profits support students; delicious French toast latte; great atmosphere. *Average main: $4* ✉ *424 Humphreys St., Wedgewood-Houston* ✥ *Look for the entrance on Pillow St.* ☎ *615/647–7554* 🌐 *humphreysstreet.com.*

Dining

Americano Coffee Lounge

$ | Bakery. Opened in fall 2018, this Houston Station coffee shop, or rather, lounge, has baked goods made fresh in its tiny kitchen, a large selection of syrups that are used in its house-made Italian sodas, and, of course, hot and iced coffee. The atmosphere is old-school cozy, even more so on Saturday afternoons when there

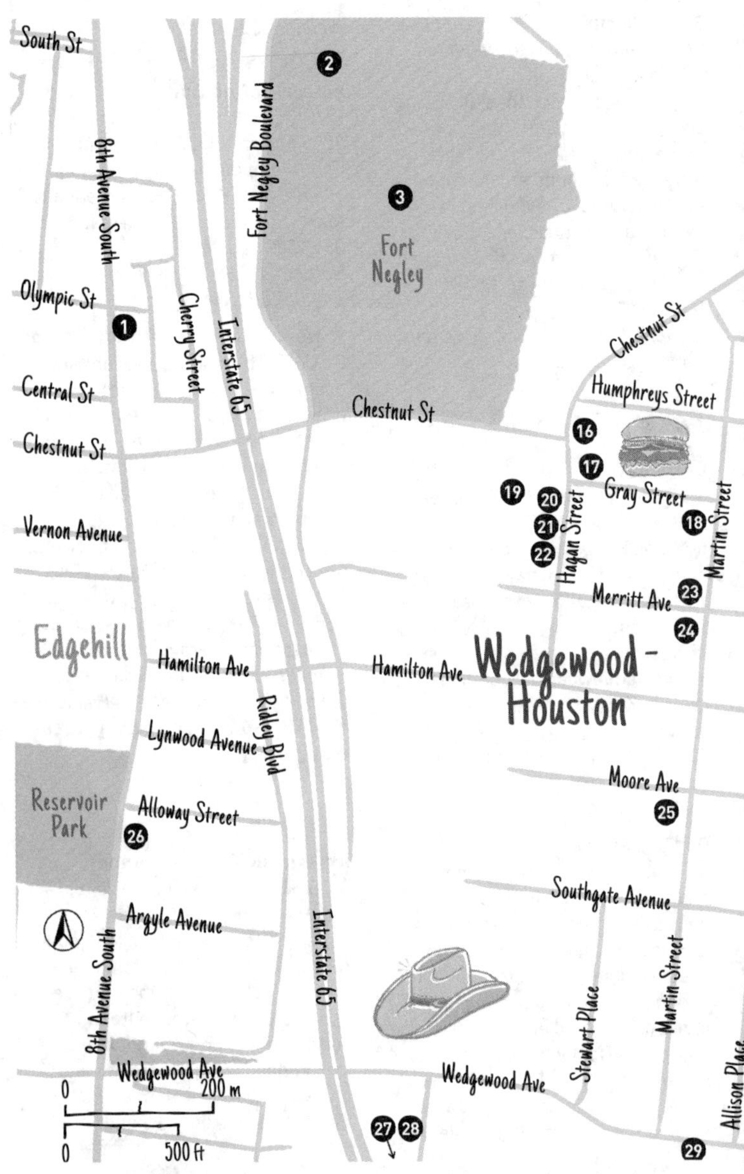

South St
8th Avenue South
Fort Negley Boulevard
Fort Negley
Olympic St
Cherry Street
Interstate 65
Central St
Chestnut St
Chestnut St
Chestnut St
Humphreys Street
Gray Street
Hagan Street
Martin Street
Vernon Avenue
Merritt Ave
Edgehill
Hamilton Ave
Hamilton Ave
Wedgewood-Houston
Ridley Blvd
Lynwood Avenue
Moore Ave
Reservoir Park
Alloway Street
Southgate Avenue
Argyle Avenue
Interstate 65
8th Avenue South
Stewart Place
Martin Street
Allison Place
Wedgewood Ave
Wedgewood Ave
0
200 m
0
500 ft
1
2
3
16
17
18
19
20
21
22
23
24
25
26
27
28
29

SIGHTS

Adventure Science Center........... 2
Corsair Distillery 24
David Lusk Gallery... 21
Fort Houston 27
Fort Negley Park 3
Julia Martin Gallery 13
Nashville Craft Distillery 19
Nashville Fairgrounds.............. 31
The Packing Plant.... 17
Zeitgeist Gallery....... 20

SHOPPING

Cotten Music Center 8
Flip Nashville 1
Fork's Drum Closet........................... 4
Royal Circus 6

COFFEE & QUICK BITES

Crest Cafe 25
Dozen Bakery........... 22
Falcon Coffee Bar.... 15
Humphreys Street Coffee Shop 12

DINING

Americano Coffee Lounge 9
Bastion........................ 7
Clawson's Pub & Deli 5
Gabby's Burgers & Fries....... 16
Hemingway's Bar and Hideaway.... 10
The Loading Dock Café........................... 28
Sassafras Market & Deli........... 23
Smokin Thighs 29

BARS & NIGHTLIFE

The Basement.......... 26
Diskin Cider.............. 18
Flamingo Cocktail Club........................... 14
Jackalope Brewing Company–The Ranch Taproom + Brewery 11
Santa's Pub 30

BACK IN THE DAY

A look around Wedgewood-Houston shows you Nashville's past, present, and future as old buildings, many of them industrial spaces like warehouses and textile mills, are being repurposed, renovated, and in some cases torn down and replaced. Early in the area's rebirth, a former truck garage on Hagan Street became the sleek home of art galleries and a bakery—and now there's a craft distillery at the back of the gravel parking lot. Across the street from this cluster, the one remaining building in a sausage-making factory is now the Packing Plant, home to a number of tiny art galleries.

The oldest of the two Houston Station buildings dates from around 1885; the younger from circa 1905. Both retain much of their rustic charm as you'll notice in the eateries and shops now found in this former textile mill and syrup and preserves factory (parts of the buildings were also used as tobacco warehouses). Meanwhile, the sprawling former May Hosiery complex (where the operation moved when it outgrew Houston Station) was an outlier in the neighborhood's turnaround, full of artist studios and makeshift galleries; now it's undergoing demolition and redevelopment and will eventually be the site of the area's first hotel.

is live jazz. **Known for:** jazz; cozy atmosphere; lemon berry torte with mascarpone. *Average main: $6 ✉ 434 Houston St., Wedgewood-Houston ☎ 629/203–6991 🌐 americanocoffeelounge.com.*

Bastion

$$ | American. Opened in February 2016, this small restaurant (and bar) seats only 24 diners (RSVPs are encouraged; walk-ins are welcomed when space is available). Parties of four to six are offered a five-course, prix fixe meal; smaller groups may order à la carte from a selection of American fare. **Known for:** seafood; punch of the day; desserts. *Average main: $19 ✉ 434 Houston St., Wedgewood-Houston ☎ 615/490–8430 🌐 bastionnashville.com ⏲ Closed Sun.–Tues.*

Clawson's Pub and Deli

$ | Deli. Look for the large gravel parking lot at the Track One development and you'll find this delightful spot serving large, fresh sandwiches with foodie-worthy options—and any sandwich can be made into a salad. The interior is cozy, there are several picnic tables on the front porch; fill out one of the postcards next to the checkout and Clawson's will mail it. **Known for:** the #2 (ham, Brie, strawberry preserves on toasted sourdough); extensive beer selection; house-made sauces. *Average main: $10 ✉ 1205 4th Ave. S, Wedgewood-Houston ☎ 615/484–6069 🌐 clawsonspub.com ⏲ Closed weekends.*

★ Gabby's Burgers & Fries
$ | Burger. Gabby's is where real people of all sorts go for really good burgers (grass-fed beef or vegan) and addictive sweet potato fries. The ever-present line moves quickly; eat at the tables or small counter overlooking the grill, or grab and go. **Known for:** huge portions; shakes made with house-made syrups; quirky wall decor. *Average main: $10 ✉ 493 Humphreys St., Wedgewood-Houston ☎ 615/733–3119 🌐 gabbysburgersandfries.com 🕙 Closed Sun.*

Hemingway's Bar & Hideaway
$$$ | American. The spacious interior shares the rustic elegance—rough brick walls, rich hardwood floors—found throughout Houston Station. The hearty menu's large portions are balanced by sampler-sized chocolate mousse and other desserts. **Known for:** heirloom tomato salad; double-cut pork rib chop; Nicoletto's kale gnocchi. *Average main: $35 ✉ 439 Houston St., Suite 160, Wedgewood-Houston ☎ 615/915–1715 🌐 hemingwaysbarandhideaway.com.*

The Loading Dock Cafe
$ | Café. Located within the Fort Houston arts complex, this small café resembles the open-plan dwelling of your trendy friend's apartment. Breakfast—bagels, scrambles, sandwiches—is available all day; sandwiches are served at lunch (gluten-free bread is available). **Known for:** avocado toast; Caitypies (sweet and savory hand pies); Bob's Grilled Fluffernutter. *Average main: $7 ✉ 2028a Lindell Ave., Wedgewood-Houston ☎ 615/640–0733 🌐 loadingdocknashville.com 🕙 Closed Sun.*

Sassafras Market & Deli
$ | Deli. A small specialty grocery, Sassafras also has a window-filled deli space with great views of the fast-changing neighborhood from its corner location; picnic tables out front are a warm-weather seating option. The menu features sandwiches and breakfast items, including a number of vegetarian and vegan options. **Known for:** specialty sodas; kids menu; Kennebec fries. *Average main: $10 ✉ 610 Merritt Ave., Wedgewood-Houston ☎ 615/835–2920 🌐 sassafrasmarket.com.*

Smokin Thighs
$ | American. Lots of chicken—wings, quarters and, of course, thighs—all smoked or grilled using a signature applewood blend, is served here; they also offer salads and chicken burgers and tacos. The restaurant gets especially crowded at lunch. **Known for:** pimento mac-and-cheese; "moonshine" selection; menu of rubs, sauces, and seasoning. *Average main: $10 ✉ 611 Wedgewood Ave., Wedgewood-Houston ☎ 615/601–2582 🌐 smokinthighs.com.*

Bars and Nightlife

The Basement

This small venue seating 100 people is one of two venues under the "Basement" umbrella (their other venue is the Basement East in East Nashville close to Little Five Points). Indie acts like Lucy Dacus and Dilly Dally are some of the artists you'll see perform at this intimate spot, in addition to storytelling and holiday events. Tickets are generally affordable, ranging from free to $15. ✉ *1604 8th Ave., Suite 330, Wedgewood-Houston* ☎ *615/645–9174* 🌐 *thebasementnashville.com.*

Diskin Cider

The 8,000-square-foot facility includes a tasting room and patio. The menu includes cider cocktails and food, such as wings, crab cakes, grilled cheese, and more. Live music, art crawl after-parties, and other special events are held here. ✉ *1235 Martin St., Wedgewood-Houston* ☎ *615/248–8000* 🌐 *diskincider.com* ☞ *Closed Mon.–Wed.*

Flamingo Cocktail Club

Drawing inspiration from Miami clubs of the 1950s and '60s, this new space has a large open area and minimalist seating. They host theme parties, live music, workshops for makers and creatives, and other special events. ✉ *509 Houston St., Wedgewood-Houston* ☎ *786/942–8279* 🌐 *flamingococktailclub.com.*

Jackalope Brewing Company–The Ranch Taproom + Brewery

This second location, referred to as "The Ranch," opened in fall 2018. There are 16 beers on tap; the menu is limited, but you can bring your own food and food trucks are on-site on Saturday. Tours of the brewing facility are available (and are open to children); there's shuffleboard on the patio. ✉ *429B Houston St., Wedgewood-Houston* ☎ *615/873–4313* 🌐 *jackalopebrew.com* ☞ *Closed Mon. and Tues.*

Santa's Pub

It's five o'clock somewhere, and it's certainly always Christmas at Santa's Pub, a double-wide trailer festooned with holiday decorations inside and out. Open until the wee hours with cheap beer (no liquor is served), nightly karaoke, and a house band performing on Sunday night, this kitschy pub is located between Wedgewood-Houston and the Melrose neighborhoods. ✉ *2225 Bransford Ave., Wedgewood-Houston* ☎ *615/593–1872* 🌐 *santaspub.com* ☞ *Cash only—ATM located outside of bar.*

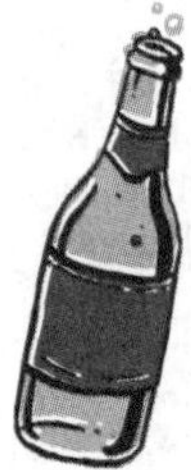

8 | **Melrose and Berry Hill**

GO FOR

Low-key atmosphere

Casual dining

Antiques shopping

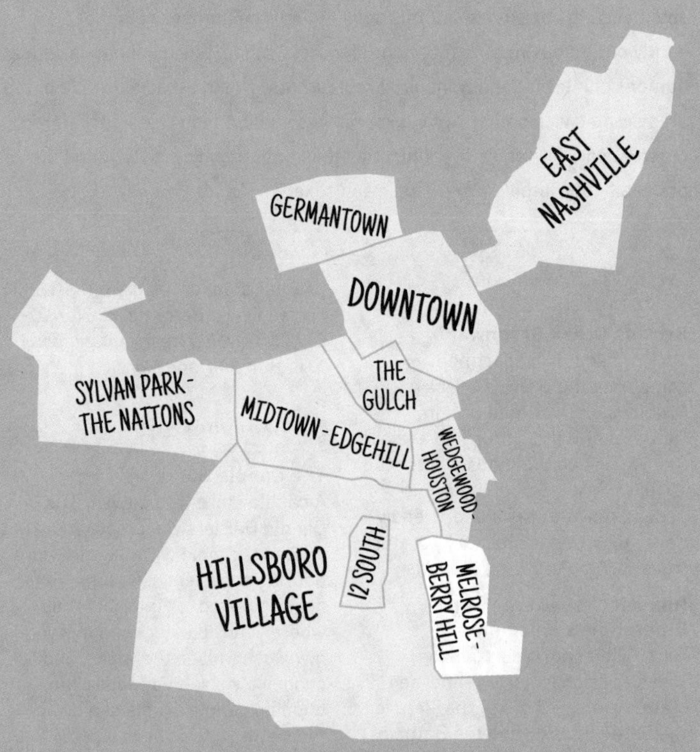

Sightseeing ★☆☆☆☆ | Shopping ★★★☆☆ | Dining ★★★★★ | Nightlife ★★☆☆☆

Berry Hill, with just 500-some residents, has one of the highest number of recording studios per capita for a neighborhood: in its 1-square-mile area, around 30 recording studios call Berry Hill home. Northwest of Berry Hill, Melrose is a growing neighborhood, with shops and housing blossoming on 8th Avenue. Melrose also features one of the city's richest pockets of antiques and vintage resale stores, all centered around 8th Avenue and Wedgewood. Both areas feel a bit suburban with chain and big box stores, but this doesn't limit the number of independently owned businesses that flourish here. Diverse cuisine abounds with a number of internationally inspired restaurants. The laid-back attitude of the area creates welcoming dining experiences without long waits or required reservations. The eclectic yet functional neighborhood attracts young professionals, families, and musicians alike.—*by Laura Pochodylo*

Sights

Browns Creek Greenway

Tucked behind an apartment complex is the Browns Creek Greenway, a 0.65-mile trail in Battlemont Park. Occupying a space that was cleared of houses after the 2010 Nashville Flood, the repurposed area features a dog-friendly paved loop that is shaded by mature trees. ✉ *816 Park Terr., Nashville.*

Historic Travellers Rest Plantation & Museum

Berry Hill and the surrounding areas are rich in early Tennessee state history, full of key markers for the battle lines during the Battle of Nashville and housing homesteads like Judge John Overton's, which has been preserved as Travellers Rest Plantation. With archaeological finds and Civil War significance, the plantation is a museum and is a popular stop for history buffs. ✉ *636 Farrell Pkwy., Berry Hill* ☎ *615/832-8197* 🌐 *travellersrestplantation.org* ⏲ *Closed Sun. and Mon.*

Shopping

The Candle Bar

A candle store with a twist, The Candle Bar lets you create your own artisanal candle with their in-store pouring experience. Reservations are suggested for the workshop, where you will select and mix your own scent, place the wicks, and choose a vessel. For added fun, budding candle artists can bring their own wine or beer. ✉ *2934 Sidco Dr., Suite 140, Berry Hill* ☎ *615/630-7135* 🌐 *thecandlebar.co* ⏲ *Closed Mon.*

Cat Shoppe & Dog Store

Located in a classic Berry Hill bungalow, this independent pet shop sells pet supplies and gifts, and has cats for adoption. Pet lovers will feel at home in the store and can even offer to spend time helping socialize the store cats who are waiting for their forever homes. ✉ *2824 Bransford Ave., Berry Hill* ☎ *615/297-7877* 🌐 *www.thecatshoppedogstore.com* ⏲ *Closed Sun.*

Classic Modern

Classic Modern is a spotless, well-organized antiques and vintage furniture store with quality items, whether the style is Victorian or Space Age. Not to be missed is the wall of '50s and '60s costume and fine jewelry, curated by a local collector. ✉ *2116 8th Ave. S, Waverly* ☎ *615/297-5514* 🌐 *classicmodernonline.com* ⏲ *Closed Sun.*

Designer Renaissance

Designer Renaissance is a women's fashion resale shop that features upscale consignment items at reasonable prices. Find both one-of-a-kind treasures and popular labels among the selection, including some vintage frocks. ✉ *2822 Bransford Ave., Berry Hill* ☎ *615/297-8822* 🌐 *www.designerrenaissance.com* ⏲ *Closed Sun.*

8th Avenue Antique Mall

Part of 8th Avenue's antiquing alley, 8th Avenue Antique Mall is a standout choice with a variety of vendors selling furniture, audio equipment, vintage clothing, and various collectibles. The welcoming staff is known to offer free donuts and helpful advice about their antiques and the neighborhood. ✉ *2015 8th Ave. S, Waverly* ☎ *615/279-9922.*

GETTING HERE

Berry Hill and Melrose are south of downtown, clustered around the bottom of the downtown loop at the junction of the 440 and I-65. A car is required to get to the area, and recommended to travel between most points of interest. City bus service is sparse and found on the main thoroughfares of Thompson Lane in Berry Hill and 8th Avenue in Melrose.

Gas Lamp Antiques

Gas Lamp Antiques features vendor booths that stock furniture, vintage jewelry, and pop culture memorabilia. More items are available at the nearby Gas Lamp, Too (128 Powell Place). ✉ *100 Powell Pl., Berry Hill* ☎ *615/297-2224* 🌐 *www.gaslampantiques.com.*

Gruhn Guitars

This long-standing mecca sells rare and vintage guitars, banjos, mandolins, and more. Music fans will be in awe of their extensive inventory and knowledgeable staff. ✉ *2120 8th Ave. S, Waverly* ☎ *615/256-2033* 🌐 *guitars.com* ⏲ *Closed Sun.*

8th Ave S
Wedgewood Ave
Stewart Pl
Martin St
Allison Pl
Neal Ter
Carvell Ave
Wingrove St
Wedgewood Ave
4th Avenue South
Benton
Benton Ave
Douglas Ave
Lindell Ave
White Ave
Interstate 65
Vine Hill Rd
Bransford Avenue
Craighead Street
Berry Hill
Bradford Ave
Napoleon
Seminole Ave
Gladstone Ave
Utopia Ave
Hillview Heights
Westwood Dr
Vaulx Lane
Inverness Ave
SINEMA
Rosedale Avenue
Fessy Park Rd
Horner Ave
Four-Forty Parkway
Kirkwood Avenue
8th Avenue South
Berry Road
Melrose Ave
Clayton Ave
Bransford Ave
Gale Lane
Melrose
Interstate 440
Battlefield Dr
Sutton Hill Rd
Browns Creek Park
McNairy Lane
Thompson Lane
Woodmont Boulevard
Rainbow Pl
Crestridge Dr
Franklin Pike
Interstate 65
Powell Avenue
Kraft Drive
0
500 m
Caldwell Lane
0
1,000 ft
1 2 3 4 5 6 7 8 9 10 11 12 13 14 15 16 17 18 19 20 21 22 23 24 25 26 27 28 29 30 31 32 33

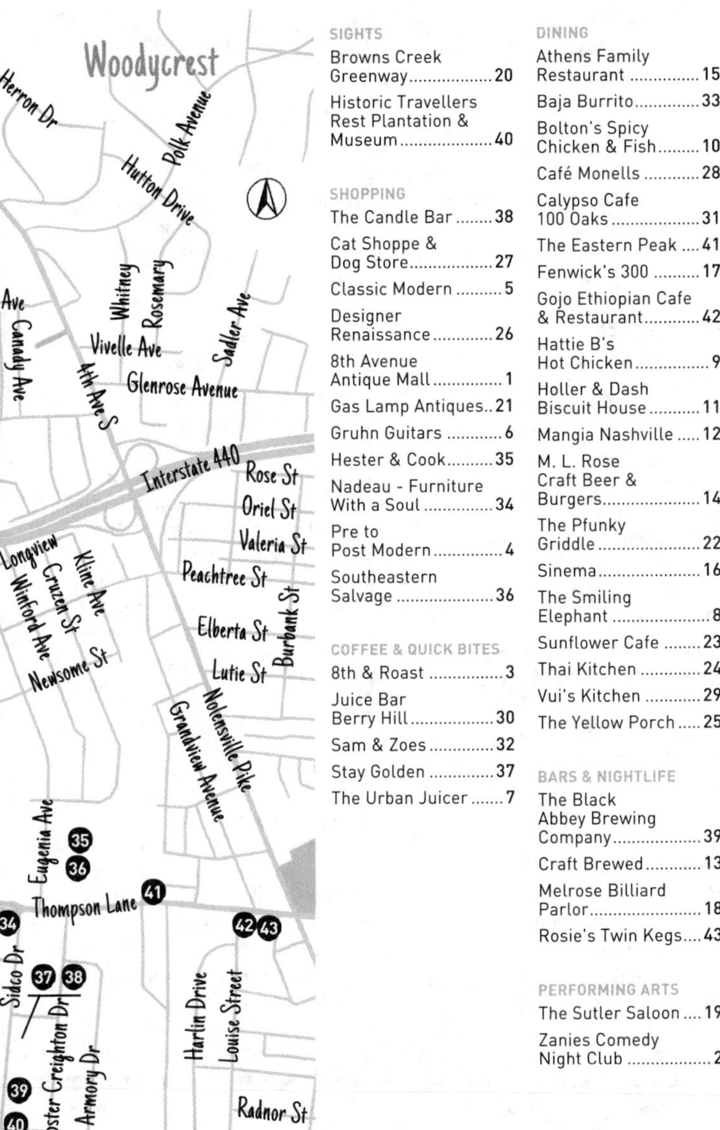

SIGHTS

Browns Creek Greenway 20

Historic Travellers Rest Plantation & Museum 40

SHOPPING

The Candle Bar 38

Cat Shoppe & Dog Store 27

Classic Modern 5

Designer Renaissance 26

8th Avenue Antique Mall 1

Gas Lamp Antiques.. 21

Gruhn Guitars 6

Hester & Cook.......... 35

Nadeau - Furniture With a Soul 34

Pre to Post Modern 4

Southeastern Salvage 36

COFFEE & QUICK BITES

8th & Roast 3

Juice Bar Berry Hill 30

Sam & Zoes 32

Stay Golden 37

The Urban Juicer 7

DINING

Athens Family Restaurant 15

Baja Burrito.............. 33

Bolton's Spicy Chicken & Fish......... 10

Café Monells 28

Calypso Cafe 100 Oaks 31

The Eastern Peak 41

Fenwick's 300 17

Gojo Ethiopian Cafe & Restaurant............ 42

Hattie B's Hot Chicken................ 9

Holler & Dash Biscuit House 11

Mangia Nashville 12

M. L. Rose Craft Beer & Burgers..................... 14

The Pfunky Griddle 22

Sinema...................... 16

The Smiling Elephant 8

Sunflower Cafe 23

Thai Kitchen 24

Vui's Kitchen 29

The Yellow Porch 25

BARS & NIGHTLIFE

The Black Abbey Brewing Company................... 39

Craft Brewed............ 13

Melrose Billiard Parlor........................ 18

Rosie's Twin Kegs.... 43

PERFORMING ARTS

The Sutler Saloon 19

Zanies Comedy Night Club 2

LOCAL Q&A

Berry Hill's House of Blues Studios is surrounded by a fence featuring musician portraits, the work of painter Scott Guion.

Q: **How long does each portrait take?**

A: About two days.

Q: **What inspires your distinctive style?**

A: I love decorative art, folk art, and traditional painting of all regions, cultures, and styles.

Q: **Best part of the project?**

The most inspirational thing is watching people's reactions! I love seeing people enjoying it and want to make their eyeballs pop out a little.

Hester & Cook
The original Berry Hill location of this local chain features elevated homewares, lighting fixtures, and thoughtfully curated stationary and gifts, plus playful party supplies and gift wrap. Started by a husband-and-wife duo, Hester & Cook feels like an inspiring trip to a well-designed home. ✉ *2728 Eugenia Ave., Berry Hill* ☎ *615/736–2692* 🌐 *hesterandcook.com.*

Nadeau - Furniture With A Soul
Not your average furniture store, Nadeau features quirky furnishings, often with bright colors and an international twist. Their bold selections are fairly priced and always rotating, making it a fun stop in Nashville's Design District. ✉ *647 Thompson La., Berry Hill* ☎ *615/298–2474* 🌐 *www.furniturewithasoul.com.*

★ **Pre to Post Modern**
A rotating stock of mid-century furniture, vintage clothing, jewelry, entertainment memorabilia, and more from the 1950s to the 1990s can be found at Pre to Post Modern. Explore their multiple rooms and you're likely to find something unique at a reasonable price. ✉ *2110 8th Ave. S, Waverly* ☎ *615/292–1958.*

Southeastern Salvage
Eclectic furniture and unbeatable closeout deals are the hallmarks of Southeastern Salvage, a large warehouse store for both home renovators and decorators. The ever-rotating stock of home furnishings, housewares, lawn and garden accessories, and more, make for a treasure hunt at discount prices. ✉ *2172 Eugenia Ave., Suite 109, Berry Hill* ☎ *615/244–1001* 🌐 *southeastern-salvage.com.*

Coffee and Quick Bites

★ **8th & Roast**
$ | Café. The original location of this growing local coffee roaster serves ethically sourced coffee roasted in-house, plus seasonal treats, breakfast sandwiches, and lunch items. Lined with exposed brick, the bright space is industrial yet cozy, featuring seating for both individuals and larger groups. **Known for:** in-house coffee bean roasting; slow-style pour-over coffee; quick service. *Average main: $10* ✉ *2108*

8th Ave. S, Waverly ☎ 615/730–8074 🌐 www.eighthandroast.com.

Juice Bar Berry Hill

$ | Modern American. Using only raw fruits and vegetables, Juice Bar serves up healthy juices, energy shots, and smoothies in a welcoming converted bungalow. Partnering with local farms and vendors, they also offer a lunch menu and açai bowls, which you can enjoy at their outdoor seating. **Known for:** gluten-free menu; healthy ingredients; juice cleanse programs. *Average main: $7 ✉ 522 Heather Pl., Berry Hill 🌐 ilovejuicebar.com.*

Sam & Zoe's

$ | Café. This pleasantly low-key coffee shop is decorated with quirky local art and is typically quiet, making it a relaxing place to work or chat. In addition to coffee, Sam & Zoe's offers tea, breakfast food, salads, sandwiches, smoothies, and desserts. **Known for:** large porch; all-day breakfast; creative latte art. *Average main: $8 ✉ 525 Heather Pl., Berry Hill ☎ 615/385–2676 🌐 www.samandzoes.com.*

Stay Golden

$ | Café. Founded by veterans of the Nashville coffee scene, Stay Golden is a stylish and sophisticated spot to sip on single-origin coffee and teas, try a craft cocktail, or check out local brews on draft. In addition to their beverages, seasonally inspired breakfast and lunch options are available. **Known for:** high-quality coffee beverages; knowledgeable staff; well-styled interior. *Average main: $10 ✉ 2934 Sidco Dr., Suite 130, Berry Hill ☎ 615/241–5105 🌐 stay-golden.com.*

The Urban Juicer

$ | Café. Fresh, locally sourced ingredients are front and center at The Urban Juicer, which focuses on fresh juices, smoothies, and superfood-laden bowls. Whether grabbing a breakfast sandwich or made-to-order juice, or signing on for a cleanse, the helpful staff will guide you through their health food options. **Known for:** made-to-order juices; vegan options; meal-replacement smoothies. *Average main: $10 ✉ 2206 8th Ave. S, Melrose ☎ 855/905–8423 🌐 theurbanjuicer.com.*

Dining

Athens Family Restaurant

$ | Greek Fusion. Once featured on the Food Network, the Athens Family Restaurant is a diner that has all the appearances of a classic greasy spoon but instead serves delicious Greek food for all three meals. Enjoy gyro, pitas, and Greek sides as well as American diner favorites like burgers and breakfast sandwiches. **Known for:** Greek cuisine; filling breakfasts; family-friendly diner environment. *Average main: $10 ✉ 2526 8th Ave. S, Berry Hill ☎ 615/383–2848 🌐 www.athens-familyrestaurant.com.*

★ **Baja Burrito**

$ | Mexican Fusion. This colorful neighborhood staple is a locally owned Baja Californian–style

Mexican food restaurant, with build-your-own counter service featuring local meats, handmade salsas, and delicious fruit teas. In addition to their namesake burritos, they offer plentiful taco and salad options, all in generous portions, making this funky and fun spot a local favorite. **Known for:** colorful atmosphere; quick counter service; pineapple salsa made in-house. *Average main: $7 ✉ 722 Thompson La., Berry Hill ☎ 615/383–2252 🌐 www.bajaburrito.com ⏲ Closed Sun.*

Bolton's Spicy Chicken & Fish

$ | Southern. Bolton's Spicy Chicken and Fish keeps a no-frills focus on their food, and it pays off—their chicken is solidly in the running for Nashville's best hot chicken. Classic Southern sides ordered at the window pair well with the boldly spiced chicken, fish, pork, and ribs. **Known for:** hot chicken; hole-in-the-wall atmosphere; fast service. *Average main: $10 ✉ 2309a Franklin Pike, Melrose ☎ 615/383–1421 🌐 www.boltonsspicy.com ⏲ Closed Sun.*

Café Monell's

$ | Southern. Look no further than Monell's for Southern staples, including their famous fried chicken, hearty sides, and rich desserts. Serving breakfast, lunch, and dinner in a relaxed café setting, Café Monell's differs from the other Monell's locations which serve their food family-style. **Known for:** rich Southern dishes; panfried chicken; country breakfast. *Average main: $10 ✉ 2826 Bransford Ave., Berry Hill ☎ 615/298–2254 🌐 monellstn.com.*

INTERNATIONAL CUISINE

Bordering Berry Hill to the east is South Nashville and Woodbine, which have a growing immigrant and refugee population. Nashville is home to the nation's largest Kurdish population and has one of the fastest growing immigrant populations in the country. This diversity has made its main thoroughfare, Nolensville Pike, the city's epicenter of delicious international food: in addition to its famed taco trucks, there is also delicious Turkish food, multiple Thai options, and a food court with Mexican and Latin American options called Plaza Mariachi.

Calypso Cafe 100 Oaks

$ | American. Casual healthy dining that is easy on the wallet is Calypso Cafe's focus, making it a popular, laid-back lunch spot. Calypso Cafe's menu features Caribbean influences, with an emphasis on chicken and fresh produce, creating tropical flavor combinations like their Lucayan salad and famed corn muffins that easily satisfy nutrition-focused eaters and those with dietary restrictions. **Known for:** budget-friendly; light lunch fare; vegetarian and vegan options. *Average main: $10 ✉ 700 Thompson La., Berry Hill ☎ 615/297–3888 🌐 calypsocafe.com.*

The Eastern Peak

$ | Thai. Asian fusion entrées, Thai curries, and sushi come together in a stylish setting at The Eastern Peak. Enjoy well-priced lunch specials on the covered porch, or pair a cocktail with a sushi combo for happy hour. **Known for:** chic finishes; Thai favorites made fresh; porch seating. *Average main: $12 ✉ 536 Thompson La., Berry Hill ☎ 615/610–4888 🌐 www.theeasternpeak.com.*

Fenwick's 300

$ | Diner. Bright and airy, this diner-style restaurant features a standalone coffee bar within the dining room, where Bongo Java's coffee and signature drinks are paired with thoughtful, hearty brunch selections and breakfast cocktails. The large center bar is topped with a bowling lane, a nod to the building's past life. **Known for:** upscale coffee bar; open design concept; breakfast tacos. *Average main: $10 ✉ 2600 8th Ave. S, Suite 103, Berry Hill ☎ 615/840–6462 🌐 fenwicks300.com.*

Gojo Ethiopian Cafe & Restaurant

$ | Ethiopian. A standout in the pocket of international eateries clustered around Nolensville Pike, Gojo Ethiopian Cafe serves authentic dishes in a cozy, brightly colored building. The lunch buffet is a favorite of both vegetarians and meat eaters. **Known for:** traditional Ethiopian coffee service; abundant injera (sourdough flatbread); good for Ethiopian food rookies. *Average main: $11 ✉ 415 W. Thompson La., Berry Hill ☎ 615/332–0710 🌐 www.gojoethiopiancafenashville.com.*

Hattie B's Hot Chicken

$ | Southern. One of three Nashville Hattie B's locations, the Melrose Hattie B's provides the hot chicken hookup often with less of a line. Enjoy hot chicken of varying heat levels, wash it down with a sweet tea or craft brew, and finish off your meal with a delicious Southern-inspired side or two. **Known for:** hot chicken; expansive covered patio; yard games. *Average main: $10 ✉ 2222 8th Ave. S, Melrose ☎ 615/970–3010 🌐 hattieb.com.*

Holler & Dash Biscuit House

$ | Southern. Fresh takes on Southern tastes for breakfast, brunch, and lunch can be found at Holler & Dash, located in the base of the Eighth South condominium complex. Specializing in imaginative biscuit sandwiches, everything at Holler & Dash is handmade, right down to the stools you sit on. **Known for:** biscuit sandwiches; breakfast bowls; Southern-inspired ingredients. *Average main: $8 ✉ 2407 8th Ave. S, Suite 105, Berry Hill ☎ 615/970–7181 🌐 holleranddash.com.*

Mangia Nashville

$ | Italian. Authentic New York–style Italian food is the name of the game at Mangia Nashville, and they bring it to a new level with their reservation-only weekend Italian Feasts. Their dinner-only menu during the week features pizza, sandwiches, shareables, and sweets, while their prix fixe feast menu features multiple courses served family-style. **Known for:** family-style feasts; Italian favorites with a New York twist; bocce ball. *Average main: $12 ✉ 701 Craighead St., Berry Hill ☎ 615/750–5233 🌐 mangianashville.com ⏲ Fri. and Sat. by reservation only.*

M.L. Rose Craft Beer & Burgers
$ | American. This bustling brewpub serves more than 90 varieties of craft beer, focusing on local taps and seasonal flavors in a warm setting featuring an ivy-covered back patio with picnic tables. Their food is simple pub food done well, with a focus on juicy burgers and waffle fries. **Known for:** broad beer selection; creative burgers; trivia night. *Average main: $12* ✉ *2535 8th Ave. S, Melrose* ☎ *615/712-8160.*

The Pfunky Griddle
$ | American. One of the city's most inventive brunch experiences puts you in control of your pancakes and more with an in-table griddle set up for a DIY menu. In addition to creative toppings for the all-you-can-eat pancakes, you can also griddle-cook your own eggs and potatoes and order from the kitchen if you aren't up for the task of making your own. **Known for:** cook-your-own brunch experience; pancakes with many toppings; family-friendly. *Average main: $10* ✉ *2800 Bransford Ave., Berry Hill* ☎ *615/298–2088* 🌐 *www.thepfunkygriddle.com* ⏲ *Closed Mon.*

Sinema
$$ | Modern American. With upscale American dining featuring elevated entrées, inventive cocktails, and a bottomless brunch, Sinema is housed in the stylish setting of a former movie theater, with screens inside that still play classic movies. The design of the dining room, lounge, and even the restrooms is eclectic yet elegant, much like the menu. **Known for:** bottomless brunch; Southern-inspired entrées; Instagrammable ambience. *Average main: $21* ✉ *2600 8th Ave. S, Suite 102, Melrose* ☎ *615/942–7746* 🌐 *www.sinemanashville.com.*

The Smiling Elephant
$$ | Thai. Arguably Nashville's most popular Thai restaurant, The Smiling Elephant serves classic Thai dishes featuring a daily rotating curry menu in a quirky, cottage-like environment. Given its popularity and no-reservations policy, expect a moderate wait, especially at peak mealtimes. **Known for:** authentic Thai dishes; ample portions; health-conscious preparation. *Average main: $15* ✉ *2213 8th Ave. S, Melrose* ☎ *615/891–4488* 🌐 *www.thesmilingelephant.com* ⏲ *Closed Sun. and Mon.*

Sunflower Cafe
$ | Vegetarian. Welcoming and straightforward, Sunflower Cafe feeds the vegans, vegetarians, and gluten-free eaters of Nashville with mouthwatering veggie burger options, vegan barbecue, ample salads, and enticing happy hour specials. The menu features both Southern staples and international-inspired flavors, providing many options for diners who are used to feeling restricted by other menus. **Known for:** daily specials; ample seating; helpful staff. *Average main: $7* ✉ *2834 Azalea Pl., Berry Hill*

615/457-2568 www.sunflowercafenashville.com Closed Sun.

Thai Kitchen

$ | Thai. Don't let the spartan appearance of this hole-in-the-wall Thai restaurant trick you: their authentic dishes are anything but plain. With an extensive curry menu, multiple dishes featuring duck, and a range of sushi choices, your taste buds and wallet will be pleased with the well-priced entrées. **Known for:** cheap eats; abundant portions; no-frills atmosphere. *Average main: $9 738 Thompson La., Berry Hill 615/385-9854 www.thaikitchentn.com.*

★ **Vui's Kitchen**

$ | Vietnamese. Chic yet inviting, the fresh Vietnamese fare at Vui's Kitchen includes favorite dishes like pho and bun garnished with local greens, as well as a seasonal selection of local beer and wine. Their counter is one of the few places in Nashville where you can find a fresh coconut, which is best enjoyed in their ample outdoor seating area. **Known for:** fresh noodle bowls; ample outdoor seating; vegan options. *Average main: $10 2832 Bransford Ave., Berry Hill 615/241-8847 www.vuiskitchen.com Closed Sun.*

The Yellow Porch

$ | American. The Yellow Porch is a popular neighborhood restaurant with a cozy interior and expansive patio. Favorite selections include soups, crab cakes, and the pork chops cured in sweet tea. **Known for:** vegetable garden; attentive service; covered patio. *Average main: $10 734 Thompson La., Berry Hill 615/386-0260 www.theyellowporch.com Closed Sun.*

Bars and Nightlife

The Black Abbey Brewing Company

While Black Abbey beers can be found on taps throughout Nashville, a visit to their monastery-themed brewery in Berry Hill is an experience all its own. Enjoy a brewery tour, then sample their flavorful beers in the Fellowship Hall located in the middle of the working brew house. *2952 Sidco Dr., Berry Hill 615/755-0070 blackabbeybrewing.com.*

Craft Brewed

Both a bottle shop and tasting room, Craft Brewed features more than 30 craft beer taps, a menu of sandwiches and shareables, plus a dog-friendly patio. Pick up a six-pack of craft beer, fill your growler, or shop their selection of spirits and wine—you can even drink a pint while you browse. *2502 8th Ave. S, Melrose 615/873-1992 www.craftbrewednashville.com.*

Melrose Billiard Parlor

Originally opened in 1944 but recently reimagined under new ownership, Melrose Billiard Parlor is a classic dive where you can play pool, Ping-Pong, darts, and shuffleboard on a basement level that stays smoke free until 10 pm every day. Enjoy classic bar food like burgers, or more inventive options like fried

Spam or a Frito pie, with a cold beer. ✉ *2600 8th Ave. S, Suite 108, Melrose* ☎ *615/678–5489* 🌐 *dirtymelrose.com*.

Rosie's Twin Kegs
The sign touts popular local hang Twin Kegs as internationally famous, and once you try one of their juicy burgers you'll understand why. This classic dive features cheap beer, karaoke, a pinball machine, shuffleboard, and inventive Burgers of the Month. ✉ *413 W. Thompson La., Berry Hill* ☎ *615/832–3167* 🌐 *rosiestwinkegs.com*.

 Performing Arts

The Sutler Saloon
A restaurant and bar with a creative, Southern-inspired menu, the Sutler has an extensive whiskey list that pairs nicely with their live entertainment. Catch the live Bluegrass Brunch on the weekends, or see a variety of local bands of all genres and even DJs grace the dining room stage in the evening. ✉ *2600 8th Ave. S, Suite 109, Melrose* ☎ *615/840–6124* 🌐 *thesutlersaloon.com*.

Zanie's Comedy Night Club
As Nashville's only major comedy club, the intimate setting of Zanie's is shared between big-name touring acts and local talent. Shows typically have a two-drink or food-item minimum from the bar's menu, and the venue's up-close seating is a plus for many comedy fans. ✉ *2025 8th Ave. S, Waverly* ☎ *615/269–0221* 🌐 *nashville.zanies.com*.

9 | # Sylvan Park and The Nations

GO FOR

Laid-back locals

Diverse dining and shopping

Green spaces

Sightseeing ★☆☆☆☆ | Shopping ★★★★☆ | Dining ★★★★★ | Nightlife ★★☆☆☆

Sylvan Park and The Nations are constantly growing, with new shops and restaurants frequently opening along Charlotte and 51st avenues. Sylvan Park's quiet residential areas feature a variety of architectural styles, from bungalows to Victorian homes, whereas The Nations, west Nashville's last major urban enclave before the rolling hills, hiking trails, and green spaces of neighboring Bellevue, is notorious for new development. The economic transition in the neighborhood has caused tension among developers and residents of the area. Despite the changing landscape, though, down-to-earth local establishments remain strongholds here. Those seeking diverse dining, boutiques, green spaces, and a low-key atmosphere will find much to explore.—*by Laura Pochodylo*

Sights

England Park

This long strip of park bordering Richland Creek is The Nations' greenway. Featuring a paved loop trail that is part of the Richland Creek Greenway, picnic tables, and large trees, England Park offers serenity in the city. ✉ *811 Delray Dr., Sylvan Park.*

Shopping

ABLE

Chic, elevated basics are ABLE's hallmark, which they sell in their stylish flagship boutique. Popular around Nashville for their simple yet sophisticated leather bags, clothing, and jewelry, ABLE is also known for their commitment to employing women in need both locally and worldwide to create their goods. ✉ *5022 Centennial Blvd., The Nations* 🌐 *www.livefashionable.com.*

Cool Stuff Weird Things

This flea-market-style space selling salvaged items, vintage finds, and oddities lives up to its name. The friendly and unassuming environment is great for shoppers who live to dig for treasure. Take home one of their rustic, metal, lighted Nashville signs as a souvenir. ✉ *4900 Charlotte Pike, Sylvan Park* ☎ *615/460–1112* 🌐 *coolstuffweirdthings.com.*

Elle Gray Boutique

Elle Gray is a locally owned boutique selling chic, on-trend women's apparel and accessories at reasonable prices. They also carry gifts and baby items. ✉ *4429 Murphy Rd., Sylvan Park* ☎ *615/679–9854* 🌐 *www.ellegrayboutique.com.*

The Great Escape

A collector's heaven, The Great Escape features a wide-ranging collection of vinyl records, video games, comic books, CDs, and more. The vinyl record selection is one of the best in Music City, and their thrifty prices are often further discounted with frequent specials and sidewalk sales. ✉ *5400 Charlotte Ave., Sylvan Park* ☎ *615/385–2116* 🌐 *www.thegreatescapeonline.com*.

Haus of Yarn
For the broadest selection of yarns in Nashville, look no further than Haus of Yarn. The store focuses on natural fibers and often hosts classes, knitting groups, and pop-up shops for fans of the fiber arts. ✉ *265 White Bridge Rd., Whitebridge* ☎ *615/354–1007* 🌐 *www.hausofyarn.com*.

The Mill Boutique
Opened by a pair of sisters living in The Nations, The Mill Boutique features a broad range of women's clothing at attractive prices. In addition to apparel, The Mill also has a selection of gifts and accessories. ✉ *812 51st Ave. N, The Nations* ☎ *615/873–4432*.

★ **OAK Nashville**
Bringing together both vintage and handmade items, OAK Nashville is a beautifully curated home-goods store that you might want to live in after visiting. They specialize in vintage furniture, rugs, textiles, and decor, as well as an assortment of gifts and candles. ✉ *4200 Charlotte Ave., Sylvan Park* ☎ *615/499–1817* 🌐 *www.oaknashville.com* 🕒 *Closed Mon.*

Project 615 West Nashville
A favorite for fun Nashville-themed apparel, Project 615 has a broad selection of trendy tees, tanks, sweatshirts, and more that celebrate Music City and the company's values. Project 615 employs people recovering from homelessness, addiction, and mental illness, and donates to charities locally and worldwide. ✉ *1404 51st Ave. N, The Nations* ☎ *615/864–8175* 🌐 *www.project615.org*.

GETTING HERE

Located west of downtown Nashville, Sylvan Park is situated south of 1–40 between the 440 and Briley Parkway junctions. The Nations is directly north of Sylvan Park over I–40, and east of Briley Parkway. While parts of each neighborhood are walkable, a car is essential for traveling between most points of interest. The area's primary bus route runs along Charlotte Avenue in northern Sylvan Park.

Coffee and Quick Bites

★ **Bobbie's Dairy Dip**
$ | American. This classic ice cream and burger stand feels like a blast from the past with retro decor, classic diner fare, ice cream, and milk shakes that can be enjoyed on their covered patio. This family-friendly staple embraces their throwback energy, even naming their delicious signature shake flavors after 1950s rockers. **Known for:** dipped soft-serve ice cream; creatively flavored milk shakes; hand-dipped corn dogs. *Average main: $5* ✉ *5301 Charlotte Ave., Sylvan Park* ☎ *615/463–8088*.

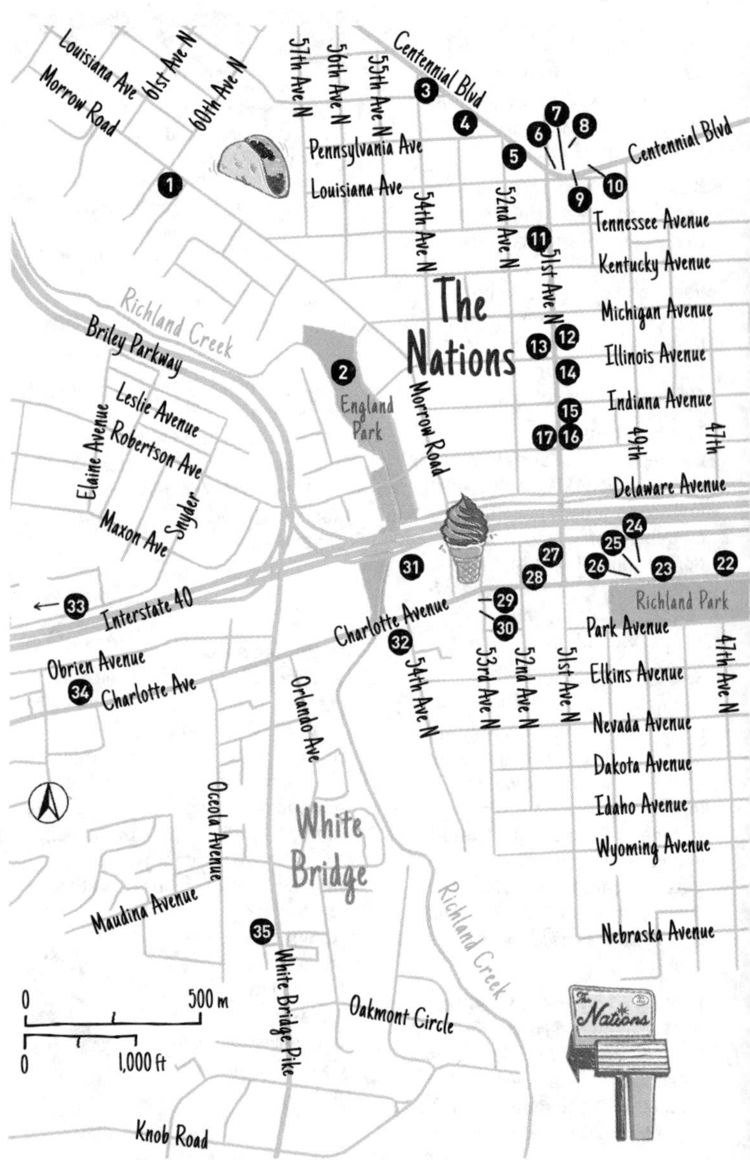
Louisiana Ave
Morrow Road
61st Ave N
60th Ave N
57th Ave N
56th Ave N
55th Ave N
Centennial Blvd
Pennsylvania Ave
Louisiana Ave
54th Ave N
52nd Ave N
51st Ave N
Centennial Blvd
Tennessee Avenue
Kentucky Avenue
Michigan Avenue
Illinois Avenue
Indiana Avenue
49th
47th
Delaware Avenue
The Nations
Richland Creek
Briley Parkway
England Park
Morrow Road
Leslie Avenue
Robertson Ave
Elaine Avenue
Maxon Ave
Snyder
Interstate 40
Charlotte Avenue
Richland Park
Park Avenue
Elkins Avenue
Obrien Avenue
Charlotte Ave
54th Ave N
53rd Ave N
52nd Ave N
51st Ave N
47th Ave N
Orlando Ave
Nevada Avenue
Dakota Avenue
Idaho Avenue
Wyoming Avenue
Oceola Avenue
White Bridge
Maudina Avenue
Richland Creek
Nebraska Avenue
White Bridge Pike
Oakmont Circle
0
500 m
0
1,000 ft
Knob Road
The Nations
1
2
3
4
5
6
7
8
9
10
11
12
13
14
15
16
17
22
23
24
25
26
27
28
29
30
31
32
33
34
35

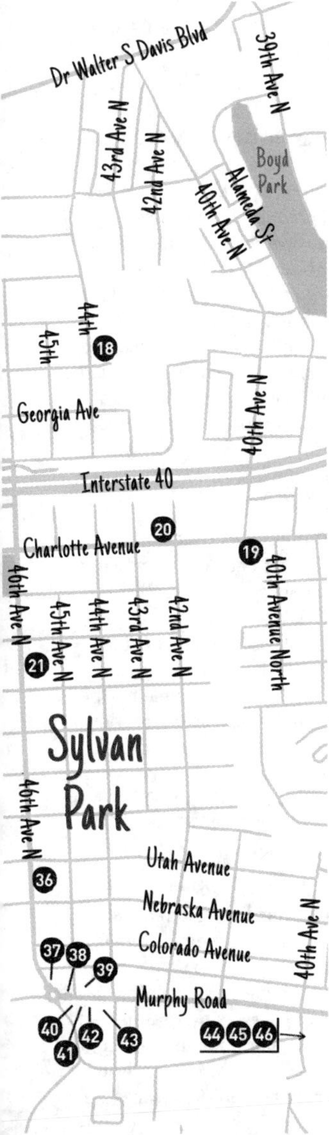

SIGHTS

England Park 2

SHOPPING

ABLE 9
Cool Stuff Weird Things 25
Elle Gray Boutique ... 41
The Great Escape 31
Haus of Yarn 35
The Mill Boutique 14
OAK Nashville 20
Project 615 West Nashville 8

COFFEE & QUICK BITES

Bobbie's Dairy Dip ... 29
The Fountain of Juice 12
Frothy Monkey 7
Headquarters 26
Red Bicycle Coffee & Crepes 15
Star Bagel Cafe 37
Three Corners Coffee 3
Vegan Vee Gluten-Free Bakery 21

DINING

Answer 36
Blue Moon Waterfront Grille 33
The Café at Thistle Farms 28
Caffe Nonna 40
Chateau West 44
Coco's Italian Market 27
Daddy's Dogs 4
Edley's Bar-B-Que ... 38
Farm Burger 19
51 North Taproom ... 16
51st Kitchen & Bar .. 13
Hugh-Baby's 23
McCabe Pub 39
Miel 30
Nations Bar & Grill. 17
Nicky's Coal Fired...... 6
Park Cafe 43
The Ridge 32
Taquería La Juquilita 1
VN Pho & Deli 34

BARS & NIGHTLIFE

Betty's Grill 24
The Centennial 5
Fat Bottom Brewing. 18
Neighbors of Sylvan Park 42
Southern Grist Brewing Company - Nations Taproom 10
The Original Corner Pub 11

PERFORMING ARTS

Darkhorse Theatre .. 22
Nashville Ballet 45
Nashville Opera 46

The Fountain of Juice

$ | Vegetarian. Locally minded small-batch juicery The Fountain of Juice brings raw, unpasteurized cold-pressed juices, plant-based shots, and nut "mylks" to The Nations. Predominantly organic ingredients are blended to create a rainbow selection of healthful juices, and an assortment of baked snacks are available at the pickup counter. **Known for:** plant-based juices; juice cleanse packages; healthy snacks. *Average main: $9 ✉ 908 51st Ave. N, The Nations ☎ 615/873-4289 🌐 www.tfojuice.com.*

★ Frothy Monkey

$ | Café. Giant warehouse windows hearken back to The Nations' industrial roots and shed bright light on the stylish wood-laden interior of this coffee shop and all-day café. The variety of seating options make Frothy Monkey a favorite for remote workers with laptops, and their health-focused menu features locally roasted coffee, fresh pastries, and farm-sourced ingredients for all meals. **Known for:** imaginative coffee beverages; elevated café food; cocktail offerings. *Average main: $10 ✉ 1400 51st Ave. N, The Nations ☎ 615/600-4756.*

Headquarters

$ | American. Blink and you could miss the narrow, 9-foot-wide storefront of Headquarters, which serves locally roasted coffee, seasonal lattes, and locally sourced snacks. Small in size but not personality, relax in the cozy interior or head outside to the inviting back patio and deck area. **Known for:** cozy surroundings; locally crafted flavored syrups; friendly baristas. *Average main: $5 ✉ 4902 Charlotte Ave., Sylvan Park ☎ 615/386-6757 🌐 www.hqsnashville.com.*

Red Bicycle Coffee & Crepes

$ | Café. More than just a coffee shop, Red Bicycle offers a wide selection of sweet and savory crepes, beer, wine, sandwiches, and tacos. A variety of seating options in the large space, including outdoor tables in the Astroturf yard, make this a popular meeting place and work space. **Known for:** large patio and outdoor space; creative crepe flavors; specialty lattes. *Average main: $7 ✉ 712 51st Ave. N, The Nations ☎ 615/457-1117 🌐 redbicyclecoffee.com.*

Star Bagel Cafe

$ | Deli. This deli specializing in bagel sandwiches serves breakfast all day. In addition to bagels, the café offers granola, baked goods, coffee, and fresh-pressed juices from their in-house partner, Nashville Roots. **Known for:** flavored bagels; fresh juices; welcoming neighborhood atmosphere. *Average main: $7 ✉ 4502 Murphy Rd., Sylvan Park ☎ 615/292-7993 🌐 www.starbagelcafe.com.*

Three Corners Coffee

$ | Café. Quirky, welcoming, and homey, Three Corners Coffee feels like you stepped into someone's living room for a cup of coffee and a chat. They serve simple coffee and tea drinks, homemade pastries, and breakfast sandwiches. **Known for:** quaint and quirky environment;

delicious brioche; unpretentious coffee selection. *Average main: $5 ✉ 5307 Centennial Blvd., The Nations ☎ 615/818–0717.*

Vegan Vee Gluten-Free Bakery
$ | Bakery. This weekend-only takeout-style bakery can satisfy your sweet tooth with their vegan, gluten-free, peanut-free, and mostly organic treats. Vegan Vee baked goods—donuts, cupcakes, cookies, savory rolls, and even dog treats—can also be found in coffee shops and cafés all around Nashville. **Known for:** no artificial flavors or colorings; inventive donut flavors; German desserts. *Average main: $5 ✉ 306 46th Ave. N, Sylvan Park 🌐 www.veganvee.com ⏲ Closed Mon.–Thurs.*

Dining

Answer
$$ | Eclectic. This chef-driven restaurant, with its relaxed yet upscale feel and menu full of character, fits seamlessly into the Sylvan Park neighborhood that surrounds it. Their laid-back Sunday brunch has familiar favorites with thoughtful touches, and their dinner entrées tout flavors that can satisfy even refined palates. **Known for:** enticing happy hour; Sunday brunch; internationally inspired entrées. *Average main: $20 ✉ 132 46th Ave. N, Sylvan Park ☎ 615/942–0866 🌐 www.answerrestaurant.com.*

Blue Moon Waterfront Grille
$$ | American. This floating restaurant and bar is on a secluded marina, tucked away in a combination neighborhood and industrial area in true Nations fashion. The dockside dining options include many seafood options, large salads, and shareable appetizers. **Known for:** waterfront dining; Sunday brunch; live music. *Average main: $17 ✉ 525 Basswood Dr., Charlotte Park ☎ 615/356–6666 🌐 bluemoongrille.com.*

The Café at Thistle Farms
$ | American. An eatery at nonprofit Thistle Farms, The Café employs women survivors of trafficking, prostitution, and addiction, and partners with local suppliers for fresh produce. The Café also touts Nashville's only full afternoon tea service, available by reservation. **Known for:** tea service; mission-driven purpose; fresh, locally sourced breakfast and lunch entrées. *Average main: $10 ✉ 5122 Charlotte Ave., Sylvan Park ☎ 615/953–6440 🌐 thecafeatthistlefarms.org ⏲ Closed Sun.*

Caffe Nonna
$$ | Italian. A long-standing staple of Sylvan Park, Caffe Nonna serves Italian dinner in an inviting and intimate café setting. Pizzas are baked fresh in a brick oven, pasta is served with house-made sauces, and the wine list rounds out the experience. **Known for:** made-to-order dishes from scratch; Italian favorites; cozy seating area. *Average main: $15 ✉ 4427 Murphy Rd., Sylvan Park ☎ 615/463–0133 🌐 www.caffenonna.com ⏲ Closed Sun.*

Chateau West

$$$ | French Fusion. A Southern answer to French cuisine, Chateau West serves French-inspired lunch, dinner, and weekend brunch. Their upscale yet relaxed setting matches the quality and accessibility of their entrées. **Known for:** French cuisine; weekend brunch; chateau-like setting. *Average main: $25* ✉ *3408 West End Ave., West End* ☎ *615/432–2622* 🌐 *chateauwestrestaurant.com.*

Coco's Italian Market

$$ | Italian. Part grocery market, part travel agency, part restaurant, Coco's Italian Market is dedicated to and passionate about all things Italian. Their house specialities remain proudly authentic to original Italian recipes that won't break the bank. **Known for:** bocce ball courts; authentic Italian dishes; imported Italian wine list. *Average main: $15* ✉ *411 51st Ave. N, Sylvan Park* ☎ *615/783–0114* 🌐 *www.italian-market.biz.*

Daddy's Dogs

$ | Hot Dog. A hot dog stand housed in a converted gas station, Daddy's Dogs offers creative topping combos on your choice of a beef or vegan hot dog. They also have a small selection of filling sides. **Known for:** creative topping combinations; juicy hot dogs; fast service. *Average main: $6* ✉ *5205 Centennial Blvd., The Nations* ☎ *615/802–8481* 🌐 *daddys-dogsnash.com.*

★ **Edley's Bar-B-Que**

$ | Southern. Edley's offers a delicious taste of Southern cooking in the classic meat-and-three tradition, and their sides are just as delicious as their melt-in-your-mouth meats. Make sure to try their brisket before it sells out for the day in either taco, sandwich, or platter form, and enjoy a craft beer or a signature spiked milk shake called a Bushwacker for refreshment. **Known for:** heaping barbecue platters; rich Southern sides; boozy Bushwackers. *Average main: $11* ✉ *4500 Murphy Rd., Sylvan Park* ☎ *615/942–7499* 🌐 *www.edleysbbq.com.*

Farm Burger

$ | Burger. Don't knock roasted bone marrow on your locally raised, grass-fed burger patty until you've tried it. In addition to seasonally inspired burgers, Farm Burger serves fresh salads and hot dogs, plus milk shakes and floats. **Known for:** fresh, locally sourced ingredients; sweet potato hush puppies; hamburger lunch combos. *Average*

main: $10 ✉ 4013 Charlotte Ave., Sylvan Heights ☎ 615/810–9492 🌐 farmburger.com.

51st Kitchen & Bar

$$ | American. A relaxed neighborhood bistro serving upscale American fare with Southern elements for brunch and dinner, 51st Kitchen & Bar frequently hosts wine tastings at their homey location in The Nations. Their community-based approach extends to four-legged neighbors as well: they have a dog-friendly patio and an on-site dog park for canine dining companions. **Known for:** warm, community feel; very dog-friendly; bistro-style American menu. *Average main: $20 ✉ 5104 Illinois Ave., The Nations ☎ 615/712–6111 🌐 www.51nashville.com ⏲ Closed Mon. and Tues.*

51 North Taproom

$$ | American. With a menu nearly as broad as its beer selection, the entrées featuring lamb, seitan, and goat cheese alongside more traditional pub food favorites will surprise anyone who imagines 51 North Taproom to be a run-of-the-mill bar and grill. With ample options for vegans and vegetarians, there is something for everyone, plus beer to go with it. **Known for:** local and regional craft beers on tap; board game lounge; locally sourced beef and bread. *Average main: $20 ✉ 704 51st Ave. N, The Nations ☎ 629/800–2454 🌐 www.51northtaproom.com.*

Hugh-Baby's

$ | Burger. Made-to-order diner classics, some with a Southern twist, are served in a retro-style space at Hugh-Baby's. Burger patties ground fresh every day are joined by topping-laden hot dogs and barbecue sandwiches on the family-friendly menu. **Known for:** fresh hamburgers; children's play area; drive-through service. *Average main: $5 ✉ 4816 Charlotte Ave., Sylvan Park ☎ 615/610–3340 🌐 www.hughbabys.com.*

McCabe Pub

$$ | American. Burgers, beer, and pub food done right are the focus of this classic Sylvan Park establishment. The brick-laden interior feels vaguely European while the plant-filled outdoor patio looks out onto Sylvan Park's main business intersection. **Known for:** all-American entrées; late-night happy hour; full bar featuring beer selection. *Average main: $13 ✉ 4410 Murphy Rd., Sylvan Park ☎ 615/269–9406 🌐 www.mccabepub.com ⏲ Closed Sun.*

Miel

$$$ | French Fusion. While Miel has a French name, don't expect classic French cuisine: this artful restaurant pulls from many global tastes for inspiration while following some French conventions, like a complimentary amuse-bouche. The menu is separated into small plates and large plates, with smaller portions intended for tasting and sharing. **Known for:** well-curated wine list; dog-friendly patio; elegant entrée presentation. *Average main:*

$25 ✉ 343 53rd Ave. N, Sylvan Park ☎ 615/298–3663 🌐 www.mielrestaurant.com ⏲ Closed Mon.

Nations Bar & Grill

$ | American. Serving burgers nearly as big as their iconic neon sign, the Nations Bar & Grill keeps it real with substantial pub-style favorites and a full bar. Formerly an auto repair shop, this no-nonsense neighborhood spot won't leave anyone hungry. **Known for:** large, topping-heavy burgers; hearty chili; neighborhood pub atmosphere. *Average main: $12 ✉ 705 51st Ave. N, The Nations ☎ 615/873–4755 🌐 www.nationsbarandgrill.com.*

★ Nicky's Coal Fired

$$ | Modern Italian. Quality ingredients and uncommon preparation come together at Nicky's Coal Fired for a unique pizza and Italian food experience. While their coal-fired pizza—made in the only coal-burning oven in Tennessee—is their speciality, Nicky's also offers house-made pasta, upscale antipasti with local ingredients, and delectable Italian desserts. **Known for:** eclectic cocktail list; personal-sized coal-fired pizza; house-made Italian standards, like daily-spun gelato. *Average main: $17 ✉ 5026 Centennial Blvd., The Nations ☎ 615/678–4289 🌐 www.nickysnashville.com.*

Park Cafe

$$$ | American. Park Cafe serves rich entrées, a selection of small plates, and a full wine program in Sylvan Park. In addition to their dinner service, they also feature an enticing happy hour. **Known for:** quality meats; happy hour menu; Southern-inspired appetizers. *Average main: $26 ✉ 4403 Murphy Rd., Sylvan Park ☎ 615/383–4409 🌐 parkcafenashville.com ⏲ Closed Sun.*

The Ridge

$ | Barbecue. The Ridge serves a wide variety of barbecue, burgers, Tex-Mex-inspired appetizers, and more in their counter-serve location in a converted Sylvan Park house. The restaurant also has a food truck offshoot that is often seen around Nashville. **Known for:** barbecue platters; homey environment; popular food truck. *Average main: $12 ✉ 333 54th Ave. N, Sylvan Park ☎ 615/385–7800.*

Taquería La Juquilita

$ | Mexican. This classic mom-and-pop taqueria serves Oaxacan-style favorites full of flavor at irresistible prices. Surrounded by traditional Mexican decor, diners can expect a menu in Spanish, and hefty portions of freshly cooked items served on disposable plates. **Known for:** authentic Mexican food; welcoming, colorful dining area; cash-only. *Average main: $5 ✉ 5913 Morrow Rd., The Nations ☎ 615/524–9053 💳 No credit cards.*

VN Pho & Deli

$ | Vietnamese. While Nashville has a range of Vietnamese food options, VN Pho & Deli is a standout for its baked goods selection and emphasis on traditional ingredients and preparation. Yet the pho in this plainly decorated, family-owned, cash-only joint is a must-try. **Known for:** large spring rolls; unassuming atmosphere; traditional Vietnamese favorites at affordable prices. *Average main: $8 ✉ 5906 Charlotte Pike, Charlotte Park ☎ 615/356-5995 ⏲ Closed Tues. and Wed. ☞ Cash only ▭ No credit cards.*

 Bars and Nightlife

Betty's Grill

This no-frills beer-only watering hole is the real deal: cheap beer served in plastic cups, pool tables, cash-only, and a straightforward food menu. Don't let appearances fool you, however: this is also one of the best places to see both touring and local live music up close. *✉ 407 49th Ave. N, Sylvan Park ☎ 615/297-7257.*

The Centennial

This classic dive is a stronghold in The Nations, providing all of the fixings necessary for fun: cheap beer, video games, cornhole on the back patio, TVs, and friendly staff. But the real reason The Centennial has withstood the test of time is their simple yet surprisingly good food. *✉ 5115 Centennial Blvd., The Nations ☎ 615/679-9746.*

★ Fat Bottom Brewing

Visiting the Hop Yard at Fat Bottom Brewing turns enjoying the brewer's locally crafted beers into an experience. The large, warehouse-like space features ample seating, multiple outdoor areas with yard games, and brewery tours on weekends. *✉ 800 44th Ave. N, The Nations ☎ 615/678-5715 🌐 fatbottombrewing.com.*

ART IN THE WILD

Nashville is filled with murals, but none as large as the one on an abandoned silo in The Nations. The 15-story-high portrait of an elderly man is the work of Australian artist Guido Van Helten, who chose his subject Lee Estes, age 91, a longtime resident of the neighborhood, as a tribute to The Nations' past and changing future.

Neighbors of Sylvan Park

An authentic neighborhood hangout as the name suggests, Neighbors is the spot in Sylvan Park to watch a game, hear some live music, and enjoy cheap beer on either their front patio or covered back deck. On the deck is where they smoke meats for sandwiches, quesadillas, loaded nachos, and more. *✉ 4425 Murphy Rd., Sylvan Park ☎ 615/942-5052 🌐 neighborsnashville.com.*

The Original Corner Pub

A sports-lover's TV-laden haven, The Original Corner Pub is a great place to watch a game, grab a drink, and eat some of their freshly prepared food. In addition to traditional bar offerings, they also feature a broad whiskey list. *✉ 1105 51st Ave. N, The Nations ☎ 615/298-9698 🌐 originalcornerpub.com.*

Southern Grist Brewing Company - Nations Taproom

Local brewer Southern Grist serves pints and flights of their brews alongside other craft guest brews in their industrial-style taproom in The Nations. Their often fruity, sometimes sour, but always creative brews partner with a food menu of Nashville favorites like barbecue and hot chicken. ✉ *5012 Centennial Blvd., The Nations* ☎ *615/864-7133* 🌐 *www.southerngristbrewing.com*.

Performing Arts

Darkhorse Theater

Darkhorse Theater is Nashville's answer to independent, alternative theater. Housed in a former church, it's comprised of resident companies who share the performance space, with varied productions ranging from Shakespeare to the work of local playwrights, to politically driven shows. ✉ *4610 Charlotte Ave., Sylvan Park* ☎ *615/297-7113* 🌐 *darkhorsetheater.weebly.com*.

Nashville Ballet

Like their neighbors the Nashville Opera, the Nashville Ballet holds performances downtown and at their Sylvan Park location. They frequently hold classes and community events in the space as well. ✉ *3630 Redmon St., Nashville* ☎ *615/297-2966* 🌐 *www.nashville-ballet.com*.

Nashville Opera

Nashville's Opera company aims to celebrate a lesser-represented genre in Music City, and to make it accessible and interesting to all audience members, including opera newbies. Shows are held at the Noah Liff Opera Center black box theater on multiple weekends each opera season. The company also performs downtown at the Tennessee Performing Arts Center. ✉ *3622 Redmon St., Sylvan Heights* ☎ *615/832-5242* 🌐 *www.nashvilleopera.org*.

10 | The Gulch

GO FOR

Buzzy upscale eateries

Posh hotels

Urban Southern charm

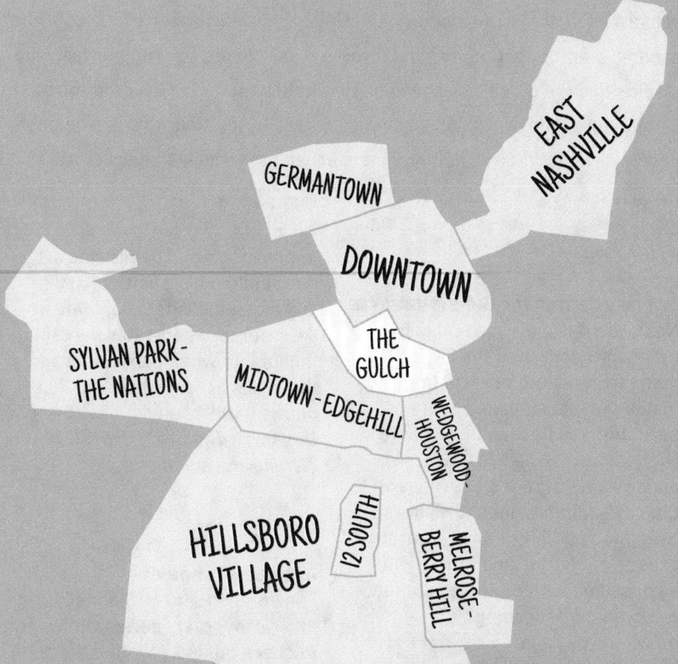

Sightseeing ★★★☆☆ | Shopping ★★★★★ | Dining ★★★★★ | Nightlife ★★☆☆☆

Nashville's Gulch neighborhood has one of the city's most interesting origin stories: Once a busy rail yard anchored by the commuter lines that ran through Union Station, the area fell out of favor after the rail services shut down in 1979. But in the early 2000s, young investors and developers lay the foundation for the hip, walkable mixed-use neighborhood that has blossomed into one of the ritziest and dynamic areas of Nashville. Some might even say the Nashville boom directly followed the Gulch's rise. Now mainly a destination for foodies and savvy, daring restaurateurs from across the country, the Gulch is characterized by its high-end condos, plentiful boutiques, and diverse music venues. From old Nashville staples like the bluegrass haven of The Station Inn to the new rooftop oases serving up skyline views and inventive cocktails, it's clear this is a neighborhood where Southern tradition meets urban progress.—*by Hilli Levin*

Sights

★ Frist Center for the Visual Arts
Nashville has a unique and active arts community, and the city's main art museum reflects that. Instead of focusing on a beefy permanent collection like Atlanta's High Museum, the Frist, which opened in 2001, aims to expose the city's inhabitants and visitors to as many different and disparate artists, mediums, and movements as possible, with multiple rotating exhibitions. Depending on when you're in town, you can catch anything from an extensive focus on a single artist, like Soundsuit sculptor Nick Cave, to an exploration of Impressionism. The historic art deco building is a work of art in and of itself. Visitors can dine in their alfresco café after perusing thought-provoking exhibitions in the 1930s art deco building that once served as a post office. ✉ *919 Broadway, The Gulch* ☎ *615/244–3340* 🌐 *fristartmuseum.org*.

Shopping

Antique Archaeology
Fans of the History Channel's *American Pickers* series will want to check out Mike Wolfe's store in Marathon Village. All of the quirky items—signage, furniture and random finds—were personally selected or approved by Wolfe. ✉ *1300 Clinton St., Ste. 130, Marathon Village* ☎ *615/810–9906* 🌐 *www.antiquearchaeology.com*.

★ **Blush Boutique**
A Nashville staple and frequently voted one of the best women's boutiques in town, Blush specializes in trendy, colorful pieces that won't break the bank. Their focus is on "unique, affordable fashion," and they definitely deliver on that promise. If you fall in love with their carefully curated selection during your trip, you can call to order your favorite pieces that pop up on their Instagram feed even after you head back home. ✉ *606 12th Ave. S, The Gulch* ☎ *615/401–9599* 🌐 *blushboutiques.com*.

Carter Vintage Guitars
Founded in 2012 by friendly and knowledgeable husband-and-wife duo Christine and Walter Carter, this gorgeous showroom is for serious musicians looking for a one-of-a-kind instrument. With price tags that also list the famous musicians who previously owned the piece, this is a shopping experience like no other. Take a vintage guitar, mandolin, or other fretted beauty into one of their private rooms and try it out for yourself. ✉ *625 8th Ave. S, The Gulch* ☎ *615/915–1851* 🌐 *cartervintage.com*.

Colts Chocolates
Founded by a former cast member of the popular country music variety show *Hee Haw*, this charming little chocolate shop serves up seriously sweet treats like whiskey caramel brownies, their signature chocolate peanut butter cups with roasted almonds, and a variety of samplers and gift baskets. This is a great stop to make before you board your flight back home. ✉ *609 Overton St., The Gulch* ☎ *615/251–0100* 🌐 *www.coltschocolates.com*.

GETTING HERE

The city runs a free shuttle called the Music City Circuit that will take you directly to the hot spots in the Gulch—just jump on the Blue Circuit on 4th Avenue North or the Green Circuit on 5th Avenue North. You can also hop on in the Gulch and ride to Nashville's biggest downtown attractions like Bridgestone Arena, the Ryman, the Frist, and more.

Downtown Antique Mall
After you drool over some seriously pricey guitars across the street, head to this rough-around-the-edges antiques paradise to peruse the booths and hopefully grab a fun new piece of decor that you can actually fit in your suitcase, ✉ *612 8th Ave. S, The Gulch* ☎ *615/256–6616*.

The Frye Company
Skip the cowboy boots found at Boot Barn and the rest of the Western-wear shops that litter Broadway and head to Frye for some seriously well-made boots that locals actually wear. They also host small shows and local showcase nights, so you can shop and catch some entertainment at the same time. ✉ *401 11th Ave. S, Space 143, The Gulch* ☎ *615/238-6170* 🌐 *www.thefryecompany.com*.

Lucchese Bootmaker
Skip the two-for-one boot deals on Broadway in favor of the hand-stitched beauties at Lucchese. The luxury Texas brand is renowned for expert craftsmanship and attention to detail, and if you're interested in raising some eyebrows, you can even find boots made of exotic materials like alligator, lizard, ostrich, and more. ✉ *503 12th Ave. S, The Gulch* ☎ *615/242–1161* 🌐 *www.lucchese.com.*

★ **Third Man Records**
Serious Jack White fans won't want to miss his lauded label's Nashville outpost. Drop by to record your own two-minute song on a 1945 Voice-o-Graph machine, dig through the stacks, or grab some exclusive merch. Check their social media and special events pages if you're looking to catch a live performance in the now-legendary Blue Room or attend one of their intermittent film screenings. Tours are available on Fridays and Saturdays at 2 pm, but get there early. ✉ *623 7th Ave. S, The Gulch* ☎ *615/891–4393* 🌐 *thirdmanrecords.com.*

The Turnip Truck Urban Fare
Need quick access to a natural market in the middle of town? Head to Turnip Truck for Nashville's best local produce; hot bars filled with fresh and healthy options for breakfast, lunch, and dinner; locally made bath and beauty products; and more. Most locals skip the trip to Whole Foods altogether since the staff here is always friendly and helpful, the shelves are always stocked, and the local owners are staples of the community. ✉ *321 12th Ave. S, The Gulch* ☎ *615/248–2000* 🌐 *theturniptruck.com.*

Two Old Hippies
Offering up kitschy gifts, clothing, and accessories for men and women and a vault of acoustic guitars, this is an eclectic shop to say the least. You can even see some live music in the evenings, making this one of the city's more unique boutiques. ✉ *401 12th Ave. S, The Gulch* ☎ *615/254–7999* 🌐 *twooldhippies.com.*

Uncommon James
Laguna Beach alum Kristin Cavallari relocated to Nashville in 2017 and opened her posh boutique soon after. You can snag a piece from her understated jewelry collection, a branded tee or hoodie, or a few choice home goods characterized by clean lines and copper accents. Regardless of what you pick up, rest assured it will be chic and Instagram-ready. ✉ *601 9th Ave. S, The Gulch* ☎ *615/915–3180* 🌐 *uncommonjames.com.*

Coffee and Quick Bites

★ **Barista Parlor Golden Sound**
$ | Café. Serious coffee connoisseurs shouldn't leave the city without a visit to one of Barista Parlor's outposts. The Gulch location is housed inside a former transmission shop, and everything inside, from the wood tables and platters to the art and barista aprons, are sourced from local makers and craftspeople, so you better believe

they're serious about keeping it bespoke. **Known for:** bourbon vanilla latte; unique limited-run beans from around the world; homemade Pop-Tarts. *Average main: $7 ✉ 610 Magazine St., The Gulch ☎ 615/227-4782 🌐 baristaparlor.com.*

ZolliKoffee

$ | Café. Nestled next door to Jackalope is this fast and casual coffee spot with plenty of homemade baked goods and tasty sandwiches. If you're cycling through the neighborhood and catch a flat tire, then this bike-friendly shop can help you get patched and back on the road in no time—they actually have repair equipment in-house to fix flats. **Known for:** giant Rice Krispies treats; breakfast-in-a-hurry options; no-frills coffee and espresso. *Average main: $6 ✉ 701 8th Ave. S, The Gulch ☎ 615/873-4315 🌐 zollikoffee.com.*

Dining

★ Adele's

$$$ | Southern. Fresh, open, airy, and never too buttoned-up, Adele's is a favorite for business lunches and date-night dinners alike. This high-end Southern eatery was an early part of the neighborhood's revitalization, and James Beard–winning chef Jonathan Waxman continues to dazzle with his accessible but polished cuisine. **Known for:** surprisingly addictive kale salad; Southern coconut cake; Sunday brunch buffet. *Average main: $25 ✉ 1210 McGavock St., The Gulch ☎ 615/988-9700 🌐 www.adelesnashville.com ⏲ No dinner Fri.–Sun.*

★ Arnold's Country Kitchen

$ | Southern. Newly expanded with more seating room, this old-school cafeteria-style meat and three is the perfect pick for anyone who's serious about some Southern food that will stick to your ribs. The meat and vegetable options vary by day, so check their website to make sure you're not missing your protein of choice, but it's hard to go wrong. **Known for:** fried chicken and savory Southern greens; life-changing bread pudding; long wait during peak hours. *Average main: $10 ✉ 605 8th Ave. S, The Gulch ☎ 615/256-4455 🌐 arnoldscountrykitchen.com ⏲ Closed weekends.*

Biscuit Love

$ | Southern. What started as a beloved Airstream food truck is now a brick-and-mortar staple in the neighborhood that's hailed for its daily scratch-made Southern-style biscuits. There are nine different biscuit sandwiches to choose from, made with a variety of meats, gravies, and toppings, but there are plenty of tempting "Without a Biscuit" options like the surprisingly tasty egg-topped Lindstrom made with shaved brussels sprouts, hazelnuts, and shredded Parmesan. **Known for:** biscuit donuts; long lines at peak hours; a chicken biscuit you'll never forget. *Average main: $8 ✉ 316 11th Ave. S, The Gulch ☎ 615/490-9584 🌐 biscuitlove.com.*

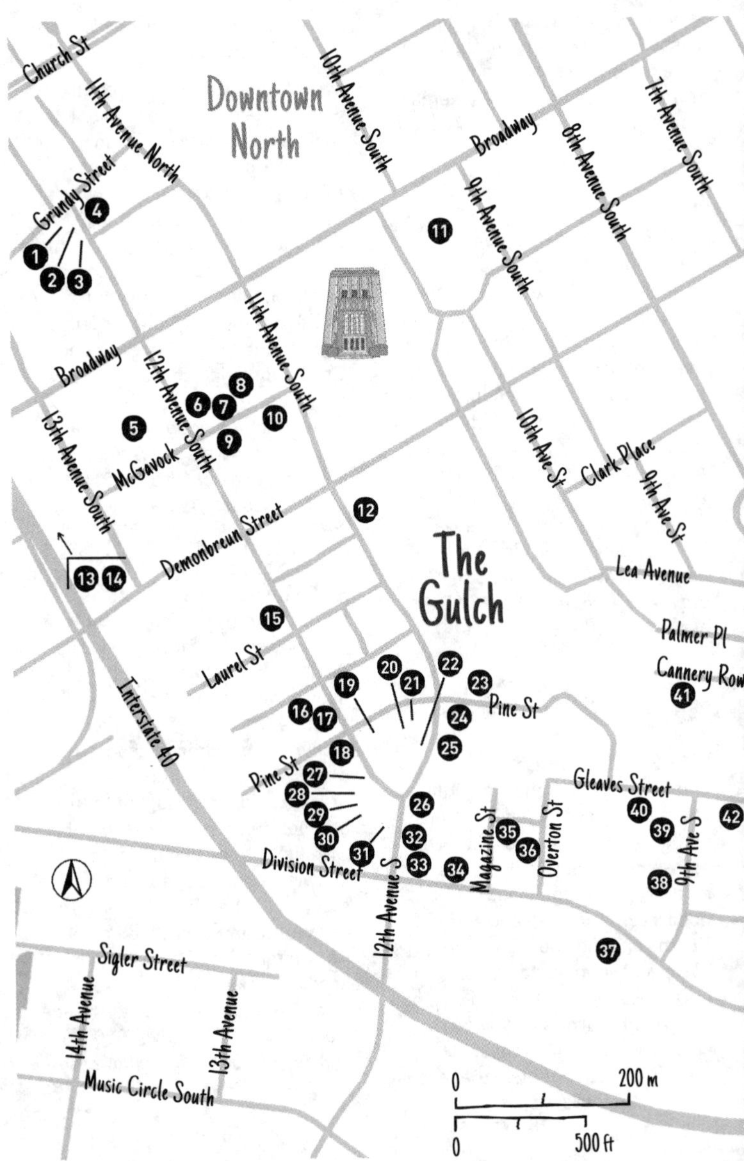

Church St
11th Avenue North
Downtown North
10th Avenue South
Broadway
8th Avenue South
7th Avenue South
Grundy Street
9th Avenue South
Broadway
12th Avenue South
11th Avenue South
13th Avenue South
McGavock
10th Ave St
Clark Place
9th Ave St
Demonbreun Street
The Gulch
Lea Avenue
Laurel St
Palmer Pl
Cannery Row
Interstate 40
Pine St
Pine St
Gleaves Street
Magazine St
Overton St
9th Ave S
Division Street
12th Avenue S
Sigler Street
14th Avenue
13th Avenue
Music Circle South
0
200 m
0
500 ft
1
2
3
4
5
6
7
8
9
10
11
12
13
14
15
16
17
18
19
20
21
22
23
24
25
26
27
28
29
30
31
32
33
34
35
36
37
38
39
40
41
42

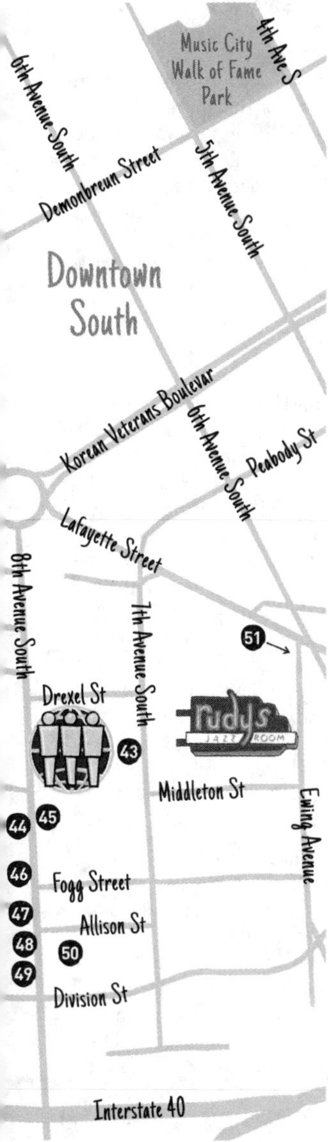

SIGHTS

- Frist Center for the Visual Arts 11

SHOPPING

- Antique Archaeology 13
- Blush Boutique 32
- Carter Vintage Guitars 46
- Colts Chocolates 36
- Downtown Antique Mall 45
- The Frye Company ... 20
- Lucchese Bootmaker 27
- Third Man Records 43
- The Turnip Truck Urban Fare 16
- Two Old Hippies 18
- Uncommon James ... 39

COFFEE & QUICK BITES

- Barista Parlor Golden Sound 35
- ZolliKoffee 48

DINING

- Adele's 5
- Arnold's Country Kitchen 44
- Biscuit Love 23
- Burger Republic 25
- Chauhan Ale & Masala House 1
- The Chef & I on Ninth 38
- City Fire 33
- Fin & Pearl 15
- Flyte World Dining and Wine 50
- The 404 Kitchen 30
- Kayne Prime 10
- Little Octopus 28
- Marsh House 21
- Milk & Honey 12
- The Mockingbird 3
- Moto Cucina + Enoteca 7
- Otaku Ramen 34
- Party Fowl 49
- Peg Leg Porker 40
- The Pub Nashville 24
- Saint Añejo 8
- Sambuca 31
- Sunda New Asian 26
- Tánsuŏ 2
- Virago 6
- Whiskey Kitchen 9

BARS & NIGHTLIFE

- Gertie's Bar 29
- Hops & Crafts 17
- Jackalope Brewing 47
- L.A. Jackson 22
- Marathon Music Works 14
- Primings Cigar Bar and Lounge 51
- The Station Inn 19
- 12th & Porter 4
- UP, a rooftop lounge 37

PERFORMING ARTS

- Mercy Lounge 41
- Rudy's Jazz Room 42

Burger Republic

$ | Burger. For those craving a burger that's a cut above the rest, Burger Republic offers up 15 different variations—like a fancier version of the In-N-Out classic or a Southern-inspired burger with a pimento cheese–stuffed patty—with a focus on locally sourced meats and ingredients. For the full artery-clogging experience, order a hand-made shake spiked with your choice of booze. **Known for:** boozy milk shakes; Tennessee Burger featuring Jack Daniel's honey glaze; tater tot fondue. *Average main: $11 ✉ 420 11th Ave. S, The Gulch ☎ 615/915-1943 🌐 burgerrepublic.com.*

★ Chauhan Ale & Masala House

$$ | Indian. *Chopped* judge and beloved celebrity chef Maneet Chauhan made a splash when she announced that she would be opening her first restaurant not in New York or Chicago, but right here in Nashville. Her playful global Indian fusion is not to be missed, and although you'll find some of the best food in the city here by far, the ambience is never stuffy. **Known for:** hot chicken pakoras; inventive cocktails and unconventional weekend brunch; Tandoori chicken poutine. *Average main: $19 ✉ 123 12th Ave. N, The Gulch ☎ 615/242-8426 🌐 chauhannashville.com ☞ Happy hr weekdays 5–6:30.*

The Chef & I on Ninth

$$$$ | American. If you're looking for a chef's tasting menu that won't necessarily break the bank, check out this stripped-down, rock and roll–inspired intimate restaurant, which is centered around hearty, well-seasoned proteins paired with the freshest possible local produce—this is upscale American that delivers. The space is anchored by a chef's counter, so you'll be able to see each part of your meal as it's prepped and get to know the staff. **Known for:** flexibility with dietary restrictions; generous portions; continually evolving menus. *Average main: $45 ✉ 611 9th Ave. S, The Gulch ☎ 615/730-8496 🌐 www.thechefandi-nashville.com.*

City Fire

$$ | American. One of the more casual and accessible dining options in the neighborhood, City Fire serves up pretty straightforward American cuisine inside a comfortable, unfussy space. The shrimp and grits are a winner during both brunch and dinner, and there are great drink and food deals Monday through Thursday. **Known for:** build-your-own mimosas at brunch; hot chicken mac-and-cheese; breakfast flatbread. *Average main: $20 ✉ 610 12th Ave. S, The Gulch ☎ 615/401-9103 🌐 cityfirenashville.com ⏲ No dinner Sun.*

Fin & Pearl

$$ | Seafood. It might be hard to head to a seafood restaurant in the middle of a landlocked state, but this open and casual space is inviting, and their focus on sustainable, earth-friendly fishing is refreshing. Brunch and lunch are especially lovely times to visit this light-drenched space, but it's also a great idea to grab some oysters during their happy hour. **Known for:**

focus on sustainability; specialty oyster menu; complimentary valet. *Average main: $15 ✉ 211 12th Ave. S., The Gulch ☎ 615/577–6688 🌐 finandpearl.com.*

Flyte World Dining and Wine
$$$ | American. Serving up thoughtful, elevated American cuisine since way back in 2006, Flyte consistently tops the lists of the city's best restaurants. Though there are countless newer, flashier dining options that have popped up in its stead, don't overlook this tried-and-true local favorite with excellent service and a unique wine list. **Known for:** great happy hour; special tasting menus; friendly, attentive service. *Average main: $30 ✉ 718 Division St., The Gulch ☎ 615/255–6200 🌐 flytenashville.com ⏲ Closed Sun. and Mon.*

The 404 Kitchen
$$$ | American. Big on visual presentation and earning high marks in overall aesthetics, The 404 Kitchen is an excellent choice for anyone looking for a sumptuous evening. The menu is small and carefully laid out to ensure that anything ordered lives up to the kitchen's high bar for quality. **Known for:** house-made burrata; dim sum–style brunch; more than 400 whiskies available. *Average main: $27 ✉ 507 12th Ave. S, The Gulch ☎ 615/251–1404 🌐 the404nashville.com.*

Kayne Prime
$$$$ | Steakhouse. If you're craving artfully marbled cuts of meat, then Kayne Prime boasts the best selection in town with top-notch cuts from some of the best ranches in the United States and abroad. The huge interior is filled with raw wood planks, private leather booths, and three different bars, and the starters consistently win top marks from diners. **Known for:** cotton candy bacon; Japanese Wagyu beef; popcorn buttered lobster. *Average main: $60 ✉ 1103 McGavock St., The Gulch ☎ 615/259–0050 🌐 www.mstreetnashville.com/kayne-prime.*

Little Octopus
$$$ | American. What started as a pop-up restaurant in east Nashville is now a full-fledged upscale eatery acclaimed for its unique array of California-inspired small plates. In a chilled-out and modern space characterized by hints of millennial pink, diners can expect inventive flavor combinations like scallops with watermelon and jicama, eggplant cooked with sake, and refreshing cocktails made with cachaça. **Known for:** bottomless brunch; "magic hour"; fresh, bright flavors. *Average main: $25 ✉ 505 5th Ave. S, The Gulch ☎ 615/454–3946 🌐 littleoctopusnashville.com.*

Marsh House
$$$ | Seafood. Southern seafood is no joke: Where the Northeast focuses on lobster and clam, the South emphasizes fried Gulf oysters and gumbo. At Marsh House, they elevate these Southern staples to beautiful heights while also offering up a raw bar to behold and their signature seafood towers, and now with daily brunch, you can choose a more low-key experience until

3 pm. **Known for:** seafood towers; shrimp toast; raw bar. *Average main: $28* ✉ *401 11th Ave. S, The Gulch* ☎ *615/262-6001* 🌐 *marshhouserestaurant.com*.

Milk & Honey
$$ | Café. What started as a tiny coffee-and-gelato shop in nearby Chattanooga, Tennessee, is now a full-service restaurant offering breakfast, lunch, and dinner in this Gulch outpost. Serving up their dreamy gelato—including their signature Milk & Honey flavor—along with wood-fired pizzas, pastas, and seriously good espresso drinks, this is a great choice when the lines at neighboring joints are too long. **Known for:** homemade gelato; shakshuka; wood-fired pizza. *Average main: $15* ✉ *214 11th Ave. S, The Gulch* ☎ *615/712-7466* 🌐 *milkandhoneynashville.com*.

The Mockingbird
$$ | Diner. Maneet Chauhan's playful take on a diner is situated right next to her Ale & Masala House and features the expected milk shakes, burgers, and fries, but the extensive offerings only start there. Get ready for some seriously great eats served in whimsical and fun ways. **Known for:** tiki taco Tuesday; punch in a bag; tatchos with lamb chili. *Average main: $20* ✉ *121 12th Ave. S, The Gulch* ☎ *615/741-9900* 🌐 *mockingbirdnashville.com*.

Moto Cucina + Enoteca
$$ | Italian. The inside of this ritzy Italian restaurant can be a bit of a maze (it's so much bigger on the inside than expected from its small entrance on a side street), but thankfully it just means there's plenty of seating inside for hungry diners to dive into rich, decadent homemade pastas and gnocchi. **Known for:** black spaghetti made with squid ink; extensive wine list; mod Italian interior design. *Average main: $20* ✉ *1120 McGavock St., The Gulch* ☎ *615/736-5305* ⏲ *www.mstreetnashville.com/moto*.

★ **Otaku Ramen**
$$ | Ramen. Although ramen has always been hiding in Nashville's under-the-radar Japanese spots, Sarah Gavigan returned from 20 years in L.A. and made it her mission to get more Nashvillians interested in slurping it up (and although it isn't the city's only high-end ramen shop, it is the only one that lets you take a bowl to go). Don't miss out on the limited-time bowls or the Sunday Okonomiyaki. **Known for:** Tennessee tonkatsu; hot chicken buns; cocktails with Japanese flair. *Average main: $15* ✉ *1104 Division St., The Gulch* ☎ *615/942-8281* 🌐 *otakuramen.com* ⏲ *Closed Mon.*

★ **Party Fowl**
$$ | Southern. Most Nashville hot chicken joints are smaller grab-and-go affairs, but this spacious sports bar provides table service and full bar. Heat levels on these hot chicken dishes—you can find everything from nachos and tacos to salads—range from mild to the scary spicy "Poultrygeist." **Known for:** pork fat-fried piggy chips; live music; brunch-for-two Bloody Mary.

Average main: $15 ✉ 719 8th Ave. S, The Gulch ☎ 615/624-8255 🌐 partyfowl.com.

★ **Peg Leg Porker**

$ | Barbecue. Owner and longtime pit master Carey Bringle says it all in his biography: "Smoke is in my veins." The line for the lunch rush is often out the door, but many agree that the dry ribs, hickory-smoked for more than 18 hours, are well worth the wait. Peg Leg's wings—offered dry, hot, and extra-hot—also keep people coming back again and again. **Known for:** dry rub ribs; pulled pork platter; fried pie. *Average main: $10 ✉ 903 Gleaves St., The Gulch ☎ 615/829-6023 🌐 www.peglegporker.com ⏲ Closed Sun.*

The Pub Nashville

$$ | British. If you need a break from the sleek, buzzy restaurants, then head to The Pub for a calming dark-wood interior that's filled with stained glass and even a pull-your-own-beer wall of tempting taps. The straightforward menu swears by tall pints and British classics that are served alongside some Southern favorites for good measure. **Known for:** fish-and-chips; pleasant patio; layered beer drinks. *Average main: $15 ✉ 400 11th Ave. S, The Gulch ☎ 615/678-4840 🌐 experiencethepub.com.*

Saint Añejo

$ | Mexican Fusion. For those who are serious about tequila and mezcal, head to this modern Mexican cantina with à la carte taco options like Korean barbacoa, hot chicken, and jerk shrimp. Sugar skulls adorn most surfaces, and the giant mural in the main dining room is just begging for a photo op; if the wait seems too long downstairs, head to the lounge upstairs known as the Tequila Library for quick service, strong drinks, and a quieter atmosphere. **Known for:** late-night menu; the tequila library; 120 varieties of tequila and mezcal. *Average main: $12 ✉ 1120 McGavock St., The Gulch ☎ 615/736-5301 🌐 www.mstreetnashville.com/saint-anejo ☞ Walk-ins only. Call for large party reservations of 15 or more.*

Sambuca

$$$ | American. If you're looking for bold elegance with a dash of drama, the deep plush seating and wrought-iron candelabras and chandeliers at this acclaimed, three-story eatery are sure to hit the spot. For those who prefer to take in a show with dinner, you can catch live music each night starting around 6:30, and if you're more of an early riser, you can opt for some tunes with your brunch instead. **Known for:** accommodates large groups; live music; miso sea bass. *Average main: $28 ✉ 601 12th Ave. S, The Gulch ☎ 615/248-2888 🌐 www.nashville.sambucarestaurant.com ⏲ No lunch Mon.*

★ **Sunda New Asian**

$$$ | Asian Fusion. Celebrity chef and actor Billy Dec has brought his Chicago-based Sunda to Nashville with the recent splashy opening of this new sister restaurant, and the neighborhood is all the better for it. Characterized as "Southeast Asian fusion," you can find a menu of shareable plates that includes twists on classic Filipino dishes, a selection of dim sum, a full sushi bar, crispy rice topped with tuna, and quite a few expertly cooked pork dishes. **Known for:** garlic crab noodles; dim sum; separate gluten-free and vegan menus. *Average main: $30 ✉ 592 12th Ave. S, The Gulch ☎ 615/610–7566 🌐 sundanewasian.com/nashville.*

Tànsuǒ

$$ | Chinese Fusion. Although the street view isn't much, jewel-toned hanging lanterns, cozy wraparound booths, and upbeat tunes await inside Nashville's top spot for Chinese fusion. The Peking Duck is can't-miss, but order ahead or prepare to settle in and have a few cocktails while it's being prepped. **Known for:** dim sum specials on Mondays; live DJs on weekends; bottomless brunch cocktails. *Average main: $19 ✉ 121B 12th Ave. N, The Gulch ☎ 615/782–6786 🌐 www.tansuonashville.com.*

Virago

$$ | Sushi. The best place to go for upscale sushi in town, step inside Virago's sprawling modern interior—or check out their legendary patio—and get ready for some of the freshest fish you can find in the entire landlocked state. Make a reservation if you're smart, and be sure to follow the business-casual dress code. **Known for:** half-price maki and 2-for-1 sake on Mondays; solid late-night menu; wasabi martinis. *Average main: $20 ✉ 1126 McGavock St., The Gulch ☎ 615/254–1902 🌐 mstreetnashville.com/virago.*

Whiskey Kitchen

$$ | Southern. Whiskey and bourbon lovers, rejoice: as you can tell from the name of this neighborhood hot spot, the owners are serious about this tipple. Casual Southern fare is found here, but go for the staff's extensive whiskey, rye, bourbon, and Scotch knowledge—it's also a great pick for late-night bites after a bar crawl. **Known for:** seriously extensive whiskey list; late-night eats; whiskey flights. *Average main: $15 ✉ 118 12th Ave. S, The Gulch ☎ 615/254–3029 🌐 mstreetnashville.com/whiskey-kitchen.*

Bars and Nightlife

★ Gertie's Bar

This inviting downstairs addition to the 404 Kitchen offers up 30 pages of hard-to-find whiskies from around the world on its menu. You'll find some bottles here, all hand-selected by chef Matt Bolus, that you'd be hard-pressed to find in even the most exclusive whiskey bars in New York. *✉ 507 12th Ave. S, 404 Kitchen, 1st fl., The Gulch ☎ 615/251–1404 🌐 gertiesnashville.com.*

Hops & Crafts

Curious about the Southeast's craft beer scene as a whole? Or are you a seasoned beer drinker on the hunt for a certain brew? Make a stop at this shop and taproom to try one of their 36 rotating taps, fill a growler, order a bite from their small but solid food menu, or pick up a chilled and ready-to-drink six-pack from their fridge. Hit up their Sunday all-day "Hoppy Hour" to refuel after a day of walking and shopping. ✉ *319 12th Ave. S, The Gulch* ☎ *615/678–8631* 🌐 *hopscrafts.com*.

Jackalope Brewing
Founded in 2011 by Bailey Spaulding and Robyn Virball, before the Nashville craft beer scene truly exploded, Jackalope quickly gained a foothold as one of Nashville's most beloved breweries. The airy and light-filled taproom has Jenga and board games aplenty, making this an excellent late-afternoon hangout spot. With special seasonal brews like summertime favorite Lovebird or the especially limited Spruce Beerstein (complete with an all-day Bruce Springsteen festival in the parking lot), this is a playful brewery that locals treasure. ✉ *701 8th Ave. S, The Gulch* ☎ *615/873–4313* 🌐 *jackalopebrew.com*.

★ **L.A. Jackson**
At the top of the luxe Thompson Hotel is the city's premiere rooftop bar, where the drinks are strong and the views are just as Instagrammable as the hip, modern decor. Filled to the brim with friendly young professionals on the weekends, this is always a lively spot, especially when there's a local DJ spinning records. The Frozé is always a crowd-pleaser, and they offer a variety of small bites and cocktails. ✉ *401 11th Ave. S, The Gulch* ☎ *615/262–6007* 🌐 *lajacksonbar.com*.

ART IN THE WILD

Visitors can find perhaps the most popular Instagram spot in the city on at 302 11th Avenue South. Stand in front of popular street artist Kelsey Montague's 20-foot-tall mural of two massive outstretched white wings, and don't forget to use the #whatliftsyou hashtag. And yes, there's even a tiny set of wings for your pup's equally angelic photo op.

Marathon Music Works
This 14,000-square-foot open venue in the former automobile factory now known as the Marathon Village complex hosts mid-level artists in its standing-room-only, 1,500-person-capacity space. ✉ *1402 Clinton Ave., Marathon Village* ☎ *615/891–1781* 🌐 *www.marathonmusicworks.com*.

Primings Cigar Bar and Lounge
Of course, Primings is geared toward cigar connoisseurs with their extensive humidor, ritzy membership program, and a selection of hand-rolled smokes, but the bar is where this place truly shines. Yes, you'll find top-notch standbys like a Hemingway Daiquiri or an Aviation on their cocktail menu, but you'll also find a unique selection of smoked cocktails that you absolutely cannot miss. Any cocktail you order can be smoked, but their own creations, like the Burgundy, where cherrywood smoke is paired with Scotch, vermouth, and Averna, are surefire winners that you'll want to sip slowly in one of their plush leather armchairs. ✉ *701 4th Ave. S,*

The Gulch ☎ *615/454-2158* 🌐 *www.primingscigar.com*.

★ The Station Inn
One of the last bastions of old Nashville that locals still frequent despite the influx of tourists, The Station Inn is without a doubt the best place to hear bluegrass, roots music, and Americana in the city. Inside the worn stone building you'll find cheap beer, folding tables, mismatched chairs, and a sea of red-and-white-checkered plastic tablecloths that prove this venue is charmingly frozen in time. ✉ *402 12th Ave. S, The Gulch* ☎ *615/255-3307* 🌐 *www.stationinn.com*.

12th & Porter
This venue has seen 32 years of changes in the city—and it's passed through many hands and seen changes of its own—but it's still a staple of the neighborhood for its great sounding room and eclectic mix of acts. Their events calendar has been scaled down to make way for more private events, but you can still find solid label showcases of their newly discovered darlings if you check their social media pages. ✉ *114 12th Ave. N, The Gulch* ☎ *615/369-6474* 🌐 *12andporter.com*.

UP, a rooftop lounge
Another one of Nashville's trendy rooftop hotel bars (you can even check out their view of the city beforehand on their EarthCam), UP specializes in shareable small plates—like jerk pork flatbreads—and fresh, fruit-forward cocktails. With both indoor and outdoor seating, you can rest easy that you can catch these lovely views year-round. Make sure to cash in on the Fairview's free three-hour parking for bar patrons. ✉ *910 Division St., The Gulch* ☎ *615/690-1722* 🌐 *cityfire-nashville.com*.

Performing Arts

Mercy Lounge / Cannery Ballroom / The High Watt
Built in 1883, this historic former cannery was converted into the Mercy Lounge in 2003 and has grown into a four-story complex with three dedicated music venues and a private events space. Catch smaller buzzy acts on the top floor, strong midsize acts and local rock showcases in the middle, and the bigger leagues on the bottom. ✉ *1 Cannery Row, The Gulch* ☎ *615/251-3020* 🌐 *www.mercylounge.com*.

Rudy's Jazz Room
Looking for an intimate listening room experience, but not a country music fan? Head to Rudy's for incredible local and traveling jazz musicians, Prohibition-style cocktails, a full dinner menu filled with New Orleans cuisine, and cozy mood lighting. Catch an all-ages jazz jam every Sunday night. ✉ *809 Gleaves St., The Gulch* ☎ *615/988-2458* 🌐 *www.rudysjazzroom.com*.

11 | # Midtown and Edgehill

GO FOR

Dining variety

Coffee shops

Central to everything

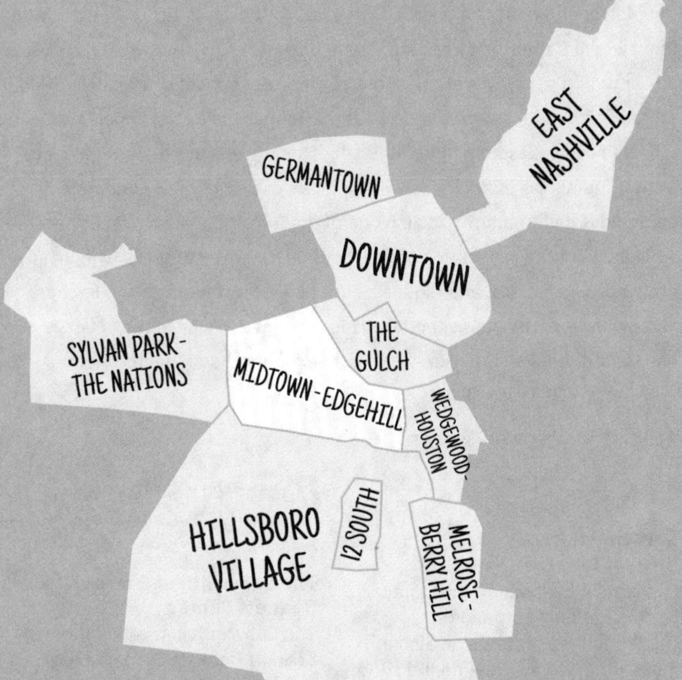

Sightseeing ★★★★☆ | Shopping ★★★☆☆ | Dining ★★★★★ | Nightlife ★★★★★

Tucked between Downtown Nashville and the suburban enclaves of Green Hills and Belle Meade, Midtown is the perfect place for a newcomer to a rapidly growing city. Midtown residents enjoy easy access to the heart of Nashville without the hassle of rush-hour traffic, and the benefit of living near some of the city's most notable attractions, like the Grand Ole Opry and Printer's Alley. With amenities like a direct bus route that travels into and away from downtown, and proximity to I–440, which circumnavigates the city, Midtowners can travel to nearly any part of the Metropolitan Nashville area with ease. In their free time, they can walk the trails of Centennial Park (or play fetch with a furry roommate at the adjacent dog park), or peruse some of the world's most provocative exhibits at the Frist Art Museum. Concerts at the Tennessee Performing Arts Center (TPAC), Nissan Stadium, and the Bridgestone Arena are a quick car ride away. Finding a great place to live is just as easy, with new condominiums being built daily. Midtown is also one of the most pedestrian/cyclist-accessible parts of the city: coffee shops, boutiques, grocery stores with locally grown produce, bars, and taquerias are only a few blocks apart. In short, Midtown offers the best of both worlds: it's close to where the action is, yet has the right kinds of perks to make the neighborhood feel like home.
—by Destiny O. Birdsong

Sights

Centennial Park
Built for the 1897 Tennessee Centennial Exposition, this popular park is not only home to the **Parthenon Museum** but is also a pleasant place for walking, relaxing, and participating in outdoor festivals. Craft fairs, festivals, and performances are often held in the 132-acre park, which includes a small lake, picnic areas, a band shell, an arts center, and a dog park. ✉ *2500 West End Ave., West End* ☎ *615/862–8400* 🌐 *www.centennialpark.com.*

The Labyrinth at Scarritt Bennett Center
The Labyrinth is located at the Scarritt Bennett Center, a former college for Christian workers that now serves as a community-focused meeting space for people of all faiths who are interested in issues of social justice and spiritual enrichment. The Labyrinth is a seven-circuit path based on medieval

models, and is designed to mirror the journey of life: there is only one path, and those who are entering often meet others at various stages who are moving in different directions. Visitors are encouraged to clear their minds and allow their bodies to move at whatever pace feels most comfortable. ✉ *Scarritt Bennett Center, 1027 18th Ave. S, Vanderbilt* ☎ *615/340–7500* 🌐 *www.scarrittbennett.org/programs/soulwork/labyrinth*.

Love Circle

Located in one of Nashville's most picturesque neighborhoods, and offering stunning views of the city (especially at night), Love Circle is a familiar spot for locals, lovers, and anyone else who is looking for a little privacy with a dazzling skyline. Grab a blanket and a few of your favorite snacks, and head to one of the most beautiful spots in Midtown—not to mention the most serene. ✉ *Love Circle Park, 3300 Love Circle, West End*.

Music Row

Music Row is one of Nashville's most famous historical districts; it is a series of streets just southwest of the downtown area that once served as home to the recording studios, record labels, and publishing houses that helped build the genre of country music. While it was once a hub for artists in the mid-20th century, today it is a beloved network of historical sites, such as RCA Studios (where Elvis Presley once recorded music) and Owen Bradley Park, which commemorates the life and legacy of one of the city's most influential musicians and producers. ✉ *Music Row, 1001 17th Ave. S, Nashville*.

GETTING HERE

From I–40, take the Broadway or Church Street exits, heading west. From I–440, take the West End or Murphy Road exits, heading east. Most of Downtown Nashville's main thoroughfares lead to Midtown, including Charlotte Avenue, Church Street/Elliston Place, and Broadway/West End. MTA bus lines can also get you in and out of Midtown in a flash. Route 25 (Midtown) offers the most stops in the area, but Routes 10 and 50 (Charlotte Corridor) and Routes 3 and 5 (The West End Corridor) also offer stops in the area.

Musica

Sitting squarely in the Music Row roundabout (also known as Buddy Killen Circle), *Musica* was originally a point of controversy, but now represents the artistic and cultural diversity of this thriving city. *Musica* is a bronze statue depicting nine dancing nude figures—including African American, Asian American, Native, and Latinx men and women—enthralled by music. At its pinnacle stands a woman holding a tambourine. The 14- and 15-foot-tall figures also stand on limestone boulders, which are native to the area. ✉ *Buddy Killen Circle, 1600 Division St., Midtown* ✣ *At the convergence of 16th and 17th Aves. S and Division St. in downtown Nashville*.

Nashville Pedal Tavern
This BYOB tavern offers guests the option of a bar crawl, where they can hop off to take advantage of exclusive discounts, or they can bring their own alcohol (in plastic containers only), while the tavern provides cups, ice, and, of course, music. There are two routes: one that traverses Lower Broadway, the heart of Nashville's downtown honky-tonk scene, and Midtown, which makes stops on Music Row. Groups of at least six can opt for public tours with other groups, or reserve one (or several) trollies for private tours with family and friends. All guests must be 21 or older to ride. ✉ *1504 Demonbreun St., Unit A, Midtown* ☎ *615/390–5038* 🌐 *www.nashvillepedaltavern.com*.

Parthenon
An exact copy of the Athenian original, Nashville's Parthenon was constructed to commemorate Tennessee's 1897 centennial. Across the street from Vanderbilt University's campus, in **Centennial Park**, it's a magnificent sight, perched on a gentle green slope beside a duck pond. Inside are the 63-piece Cowan Collection of American art, traveling exhibits, and the 42-foot *Athena Parthenos,* the tallest indoor sculpture in the Western world. ✉ *2500 West End Ave., West End* ☎ *615/862–8431* 🌐 *www.nashville.gov* 🎟 *$6* 🕒 *Closed Mon.*

Vanderbilt Arboretum
Vanderbilt's entire 330-acre campus is a designated arboretum, with more than 6,000 identified species of trees and shrubs. Guided tours are available via smartphone, and many famous trees (such as Sir Isaac Newton's Apple Tree, a descendent of the tree whose falling fruit allegedly inspired the physicist's theories on gravity) have plaques that tell visitors the story of their ecological and historical significance. Other trees have QR codes that visitors can scan with their phones to learn more about a specific species. ✉ *Vanderbilt University, 2301 Vanderbilt Pl., Vanderbilt* ☎ *615/322–7311* 🌐 *vanderbilt.edu/trees/about*.

 Shopping

Boutique Bella
Tucked in Midtown's Park Plaza, Boutique Bella caters to women who love classic, sophisticated looks. Splurge on a beautiful silk top, or your favorite pair of designer denim jeans, and don't forget to check out the jewelry. Add a wrap bracelet and a stacked ring set to any ensemble for a little extra bling. ✉ *2817 West End Ave., Suite 111, West End* ☎ *615/467–1471* 🌐 *www.instagram.com/boutiquebellanashville* 🕒 *Closed Sun.*

Cumberland Transit

Nashville may be a bustling metropolis filled with must-see sights and sounds, but its state parks, complete with rolling hills and hiking trails, are also worth the trip. And, if you decide to take an excursion, or if you're just in need of some comfortable gear for bike-riding around town, Cumberland Transit has you covered, from camping equipment to tire repair. Also, look out for the occasional BOGO sale. ✉ *2807 West End Ave., West End* ☎ *615/321–4069* 🌐 *cumberlandtransit.com.*

★ **Dead Ahead Tattoo Co.**

Looking for a longer-lasting souvenir than T-shirts and baseball caps? Then visit one of the seven artists at Dead Ahead Tattoo Co., one of the pioneer studios in Nashville's budding tattoo tourism industry. Clients have traveled from as far as Canada for new ink. ✉ *2916 West End Ave., West End* ☎ *615/490–3857* 🌐 *deadaheadtattoo.com.*

★ **The French Shoppe**

Nestled in Park Plaza is The French Shoppe, a boutique designed to cater to your every fashion whim. Their retail includes everything from designer totes to boho chic dresses to souvenir jewelry (a favorite among patrons is a gold pendant engraved with Nashville's geographic coordinates). In need of evening wear at the last minute? The French Shoppe has a room filled with ballroom gowns in the latest styles. Or, if you'd like a glam look for a night on the town, stop by the cosmetics counter for a dazzling lip color or a fresh new compact. ✉ *2817 West End Ave., Suite 120, West End* ☎ *615/327–8712* 🌐 *www.frenchshoppe.com* ⏲ *Closed Sun.*

LASH

Want a glam look for Nashville's legendary nightlife? LASH is an eyelash extension studio with aestheticians on-site who specialize in lash extension removals, fill-ins, and full-set installations. Sessions are booked by appointment only, which means you can get in and out, with plenty of time left to enjoy the rest of your day in Midtown. ✉ *211 Louise Ave., Elliston Place* ☎ *615/979–6643* 🌐 *www.nashvillelash.com/Lash/Home.html.*

★ **Scarlett Begonia**

Scarlett Begonia is one of the most eclectic shops in Midtown, stocked to the gills with fair trade jewelry and accessories, as well as decorative artwork and handcrafted bags and totes. If you're lucky, you might catch one of their frequent sidewalk sales, where you can snag an adorable peasant blouse or a cozy scarf for Nashville's sometimes unpredictable weather. ✉ *2805 West End Ave., West End* ☎ *615/329–1272* 🌐 *scarlettassociates.shoplightspeed.com.*

Smack Clothing

Smack Clothing is the epitome of "Nashville chic"—think silky kimonos, vintage moto jackets, oversized sunglasses, and glitter-printed T-shirts, all of which you can find here, alongside the occasional punk rocker in search of their latest look. If you want to spend a night

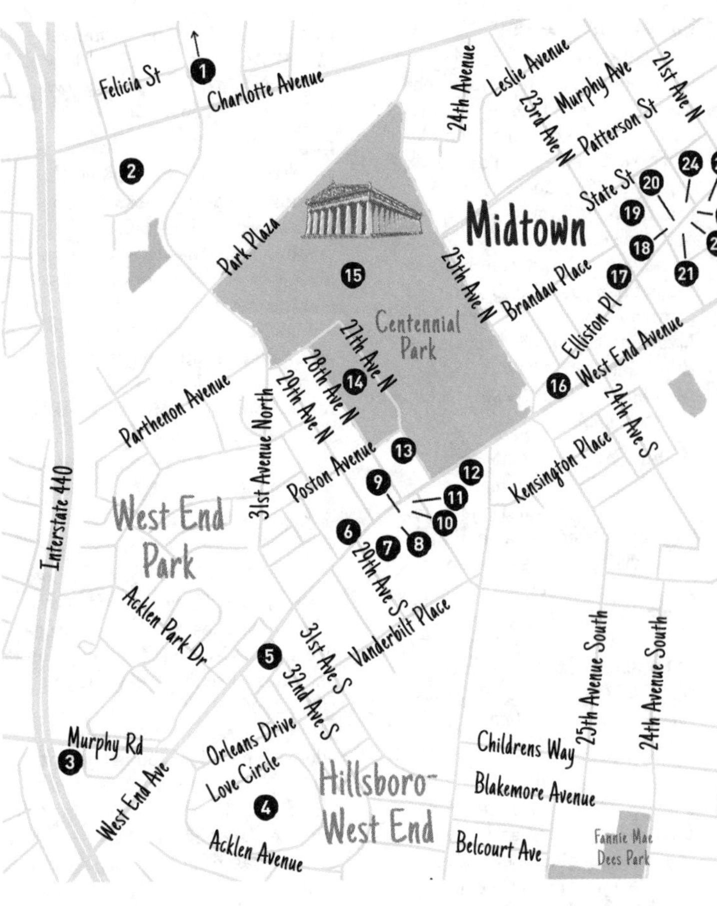

SIGHTS

Centennial Park 14
The Labyrinth at Scarritt Bennett Center 32
Love Circle 4
Music Row 33
Musica 41
Nashville Pedal Tavern 44
Parthenon..................... 15
Vanderbilt Arboretum. 27

SHOPPING

Boutique Bella 8
Cumberland Transit 10
Dead Ahead Tattoo Co... 6
The French Shoppe........ 7
LASH 19
Scarlett Begonia 11
Smack Clothing............ 23

COFFEE & QUICK BITES

Dose (Murphy Road) 3
Edgehill Café................ 28
Le Sel............................ 34
Three Brothers Coffee 9

DINING

AVO................................. 2
Bella Napoli Pizzeria... 29

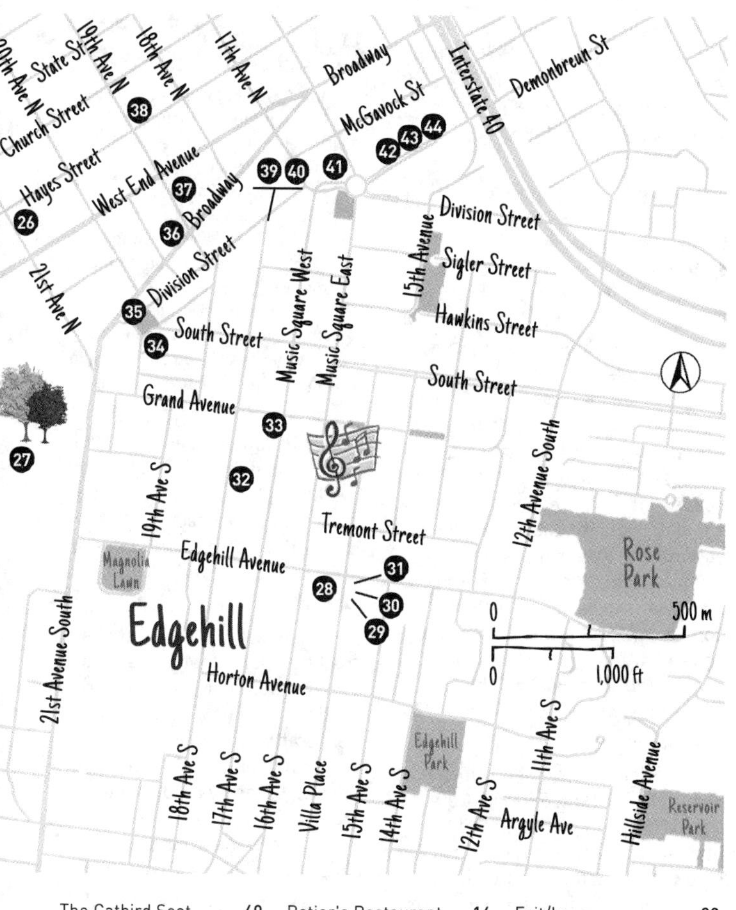

The Catbird Seat 40
Elliston Place Soda Shop.................... 25
Hog Heaven 13
J. Alexander's–Redlands Grill 12
Jamaicaway Restaurant and Catering................. 39
Midtown Cafe 38
Nama Sushi Nashville/Elliston Place 17
Rotier's Restaurant 16
Sitar Indian Cuisine 26
Swett's Restaurant 1
Taco Mamacita 31
Tin Angel 5

BARS & NIGHTLIFE

The Corner Bar 24
The End......................... 21
Exit/In 20
Hurry Back 18
Old Glory........................ 30
The Patterson House... 39
Tavern............................ 37
The Gold Rush 22
Tin Roof 43
Two Bits.......................... 42
Union Common 35

on the town without looking like an out-of-towner, go to Smack for the look that's sure to help you blend in with the locals. ✉ *2201 Elliston Pl., Vanderbilt* ☎ *615/321–9030.*

Coffee and Quick Bites

Dose

$ | American. Dose is one of the neighborhood's better-kept secrets; its location on the border of Midtown and Sylvan Park makes it a less frequented (and, subsequently, quieter) café than the larger chains closer to downtown or Vanderbilt University. This is a good thing, because their daily fresh-baked goods, specially blended coffees, and delicious breakfast and lunch options are ones you're going to want to keep all to yourself. **Known for:** great sandwiches; fresh baked goods; chill (but friendly) atmosphere. *Average main: $8* ✉ *3431 Murphy Rd., West End* ☎ *615/457–1300* 🌐 *dosenashville.com.*

★ Edgehill Café

$ | American. Conveniently located just off Music Row, Edgehill Café is a great place to meet a friend for a midday espresso, but if you're in the mood for something more filling, they've got that, too: the usual fare of salads and quinoa bowls are paired with cheddar grits, hangover hash, and fried green tomatoes to make for a menu that can satisfy appetites of any size. Ample seating, trendy decor, and close proximity to downtown also make this a great place to stop in before a day of sightseeing, or to recover from a late night with a little (Southern) comfort food. **Known for:** hearty breakfast plates; great beer on tap; quick service. *Average main: $10* ✉ *1201 Villa Pl., Suite 101, Edgehill* ☎ *615/942–5717* 🌐 *edgehillcafe.com.*

ART IN THE WILD

Keep an eye out for public artwork throughout the city, including *Thread and Needle*, which appear on the Francis S. Guess Connector, a bridge located between Park Plaza and Charlotte Avenue. Formerly known as the 28th–31st Avenue Bridge, this connector was recently built to unite formerly segregated parts of the city (Midtown and the historically black north Nashville neighborhoods). The needle and thread are meant to symbolize that step towards unity.

Le Sel

$$ | French. While Le Sel styles itself as a place that "doesn't take itself too seriously," with its striped tile floors and neon wall art, the well-crafted cocktails and delectable small plates are nothing to scoff at. Come by for delicious brunch items like beignets and crepes, or for heartier dinner options with rich sauces. Either way, you'll be seriously pleased. **Known for:** whimsical decor; extensive wine list; petit plats. *Average main: $21* ✉ *1922 Adelicia St., Midtown* ☎ *615/490–8550* 🌐 *leselnashville.com.*

Three Brothers Coffee

$ | American. Created by the owners of Cumberland Transit, Three Brothers Coffee caters to the international outdoor enthusiast who knows their way around an Aeropress. In spite of its small size, it has one of the most extensive coffee menus in the area, and often features popular local blends from nearby shops. Visitors can stop in for one of their favorites, then head next door to Cumberland Transit for the latest in quality sporting goods. **Known for:** specialty coffees; featured artwork; convenient location. *Average main: $6* ✉ *2813 West End Ave., West End* ☎ *615/835–2166* 🌐 *threebroscoffee.com.*

Dining

★ AVO

$$ | Vegetarian. AVO is the culinary jewel in the crown of a new, mindful-lifestyle district called OneCity; as such, it offers decadent vegan options, a generous afternoon happy hour, and a thoughtful waitstaff trained to offer helpful information for those with specific nutritional needs. On sunny days, diners can enjoy a locally sourced afternoon meal just minutes from downtown, and top it off with a game of volleyball on a court just off the restaurant's patio. **Known for:** expansive raw food menu (though some cooked dishes are now available); midday happy hour featuring vegan cocktails (such as the avocado margarita); knowledgeable waitstaff. *Average main: $14* ✉ *3 City Ave., Suite 200, West End* ☎ *615/329–2377* 🌐 *www.eatavo.com* 🕓 *Closed Sun.*

★ Bella Napoli Pizzeria

$$ | Italian. Bella Napoli is one of the few authentic Neapolitan pizzerias in the city, and its brick-oven baked pizzas, decadent pasta dishes, and inexpensive happy hour will send you searching for this quaint eatery tucked in an alleyway on the back end of Edgehill Village. On warm nights, you can kick back on the romantically lit patio and enjoy good food, your favorite bottle of wine, and occasional live music. **Known for:** authentic Italian pizza; inexpensive happy hour drinks; beautiful patio seating. *Average main: $16* ✉ *1200 Villa Pl., Suite 206, Edgehill* ☎ *615/891–1387* 🌐 *bellanapolipizzeria.com.*

The Catbird Seat

$$$$ | Fusion. With a 22-seat dining area surrounding an open kitchen, and prepaid reservations, The Catbird Seat might be one of the most exclusive dining experiences in Nashville, but a worthwhile one. Guests watch as the restaurant's world-class chefs prepare signature dishes and experiment with new cuisines, while a beverage director creates cocktails specially designed to pair with every mouthwatering course. **Known for:** interactive dining experience; world-famous visiting chef tastings; intimate

atmosphere. *Average main: $125 ✉ 1711 Division St., Midtown ☎ 615/810–8200 🌐 www.thecatbirdseatrestaurant.com ⏲ Closed Sun.–Tues.*

Elliston Place Soda Shop

$ | American. Elliston Place Soda Shop has been open since 1939, and has retained much of its mid-century decor, including vintage jukeboxes at the tables (though the boxes themselves no longer play), and a lovely soda counter, complete with a fountain. Come for great burgers, frothy ice-cream sodas, and delicious chocolate shakes—or breakfast. **Known for:** shakes; malts; delectable banana splits. *Average main: $8 ✉ 2111 Elliston Pl., Elliston Place ☎ 615/327–1090 🌐 www.ellistonplacesodashop.com ⏲ Closed Sun.*

Hog Heaven

$ | Southern. This casual, outdoor restaurant near Centennial Park is known for its hickory-smoked pork, chicken, and ribs. Its takeout style allows diners to enjoy their meals in the park or take them home. **Known for:** "Kickin' Chicken" white sauce; "Bashin' Bull" hot red sauce; wide selection of vegetable side dishes. *Average main: $10 ✉ 115 27th Ave. N, West End ☎ 615/329–1234 🌐 www.hogheavenbbq.com ⏲ Closed Sun.*

★ J. Alexander's - Redlands Grill

$$ | American. This Midtown location has a decidedly upscale feel, with dark-wood paneling and low lighting. The menu includes hardwood-grilled beef, chicken, and pork; hearty salads; and fresh seafood. **Known for:** superb cocktails; perfectly cooked steaks; friendly and knowledgeable staff. *Average main: $24 ✉ 2609 West End Ave., West End ☎ 615/340–9901 🌐 www.jalexanders.com.*

★ Jamaicaway Restaurant and Catering

$$ | Jamaican. A longtime favorite sit-down spot in Nashville's Farmer's Market, Jamaicaway now has an additional location just off West End Avenue, one of Midtown's main thoroughfares. Its cozy setting, friendly owners, and scrumptious curried dishes make this dining experience feel like you've stepped onto the island itself, where serenity and home-cooked food abound. **Known for:** famous curried dishes; vegetarian and vegan options (including curry tofu); friendly staff (family-owned and -operated). *Average main: $13 ✉ 1812 Hayes St., Midtown ☎ 615/678–4031 🌐 www.jamaicawaycatering.com ⏲ Closed weekends.*

Midtown Cafe

$$$ | American. If you love a decadent late breakfast, or a sumptuous meal before heading out for a night on the town, then Midtown Café is the perfect place for you. Patrons rave about everything from the soups to the desserts. The café also offers diners a complimentary shuttle service to some of Nashville's premier performing arts venues, including the Schermerhorn Symphony Center, the Nashville Opera, and the Ryman Auditorium. **Known for:** late breakfast and brunch options; veal dishes;

downtown shuttle service. *Average main: $25* ✉ *102 19th Ave. S, Midtown* ☎ *615/320–7176* 🌐 *www.midtowncafe.com* 🕙 *Closed Sun.*

Nama Sushi Nashville/Elliston Place

$$ | Asian. Whether you're a sushi novice or connoisseur, Nama is the perfect place to expand your palate, or indulge in some of your favorite rolls. They offer sushi and sashimi, as well as Asian-inspired dishes, such as soups, salads, burgers, and rice or noodle bowls. **Known for:** best sushi in the area; variety of hot and cold dishes; gluten-sensitive menus and kids' menus. *Average main: $15* ✉ *2300 Elliston Pl., Elliston Place* ☎ *615/739–5819* 🌐 *namasushibar.com.*

Rotier's Restaurant

$ | Southern. Rotier's original claim to fame was its French bread cheeseburgers and beers, but it's also a great place for traditional Southern comfort food, like beef tips and rice, pork chops and macaroni-and-cheese, and deep-fried side dishes. If you're in the mood for a little moo (or oink) and brew, this is the place—and be sure to check out their daily dinner specials. **Known for:** ice cold beer; French bread burgers; handmade milk shakes. *Average main: $9* ✉ *2413 Elliston Pl., Elliston Place* ☎ *615/327–9892* 🌐 *www.rotiersrestaurant.com* 🕙 *Closed Sun.*

Sitar Indian Cuisine

$$ | Indian. Locals and visitors pack this popular West End/Vanderbilt area restaurant for the lunch buffet that includes favorites like chicken tikka masala and sag paneer (spinach, cheese, and spices). The lively midday atmosphere becomes more sophisticated for evening meals. **Known for:** reasonably priced lunch buffet; wide variety of meat-based dishes; generous vegetarian options. *Average main: $14* ✉ *116 21st Ave. N, West End* ☎ *615/321–8889* 🌐 *www.sitarnashville.com.*

VIEWFINDER

Take a walk in Centennial Park and get a photo with the geese at Lake Watauga, or in the sunken garden, which offers a brilliant assortment of flowers in the spring and summer, and beautifully colored foliage in the fall.

Share your photo with us!
@FodorsTravel #FodorsOnTheGo

★ **Swett's Restaurant**

$ | Southern. Nashville is known for its meat-and-three-style restaurants, and Swett's is one of its most famous; past patrons run the gamut from presidents to pop stars, and everyone in between. If you're looking for Southern staples like collard greens, baked macaroni-and-cheese, and entrées that range from fried catfish to barbecued ribs, this is the place to be—you might even find the owner out in the dining room with a group of friends, enjoying his meal as much as you will. **Known for:** cafeteria-style dining; down-home Southern cooking; popular pies and cobblers. *Average main: $12* ✉ *2725 Clifton Ave., McKissack Park* ☎ *615/329-4418.*

Taco Mamacita

$ | Mexican. At Taco Mamacita, they believe "a balanced diet is a taco in each hand," and if you feel similarly, head over to Edgehill Village and treat yourself to some fresh-Mex with a little international flair. You can try your hand at tacos, enchiladas, or Peruvian chicken, and top off your meal with something cold, like a margarita or sangria, which come in traditional as well as seasonal flavors. **Known for:** fusion tacos; fresh-made sauces; margarita menu. *Average main: $10* ✉ *1200 Villa Pl., Edgehill* ☎ *615/730-8552* 🌐 *tacomamacita.com.*

Tin Angel

$$ | American. Like the neighborhood it has inhabited for more than a quarter of a century, Tin Angel is the best of both worlds: it draws mature, quiet patrons during the week, but hosts a livelier crowd on weekends. Its building and architecture date back to the 1930s, which is most apparent in its exposed brick walls, walnut bar, and freestanding fireplace, but it serves American food with a modern, international flair—the perfect place to visit any day of the week. Come in for the reasonably priced cocktails during "and be merry hour," and stay for their famous fried green tomatoes, steak and seafood options to die for, and delectable desserts. **Known for:** cozy atmosphere; seasonal menus with locally sourced foods; fried green tomatoes. *Average main: $21* ✉ *3201 West End Ave., West End* ☎ *615/298-3444* 🌐 *sitespace.us/tinangel.*

Bars and Nightlife

The Corner Bar

Like many of its neighbors on the Elliston Place strip, The Corner Bar is heavy on local flavor and flair; its unpretentious clientele, great beer selection, and nightly karaoke make it a favorite among Midtown residents. Stop by for a late-night shot (whiskey or pool), and if you're feeling lucky, try your hand at darts. ✉ *2200 Elliston Pl., Elliston Place* ☎ *615/320-4979.*

The End

The End is a small venue with a big reputation: it's a rock-and-roll dive bar that also doubles as a private event space, and is a known site for breakout performances by some of today's most famous bands. Check out their upcoming events, or visit their website to reserve the space for a listening session with 200 or so close friends. ✉ *2219 Elliston Pl.,*

Elliston Place ☎ *615/321–4457* 🌐 *endnashville.com*.

★ Exit/In

Exit/In showcases the most cutting-edge blues, rock, heavy metal, and hip-hop bands from the United States and beyond. If you want to hear everything *except* country music, come groove in an unpretentious atmosphere. ✉ *2208 Elliston Pl., Elliston Place* ☎ *615/891–1781* 🌐 *www.exitin.com*.

The Gold Rush

Legend has it that The Gold Rush was the first place in Nashville approved to pour and sell liquor by the glass, but it's grown far beyond its days as a dive bar for local musicians. The drinks are still flowing, but the food is equally delectable. Stop by for one of their famous bean rolls, or for $10 burger-and-draft nights on Wednesdays. And, luckily, performers still call The Gold Rush "home": singer-songwriter nights are better than ever, and you can now enjoy your meal as well as listen to some good music in a smoke-free environment. ✉ *2205 Elliston Pl., Elliston Place* ☎ *615/321–1160* 🌐 *www.goldrushnashville.com*.

Hurry Back

Hurry Back's logo boasts ice cold beer, but this Elliston Place pub offers so much more, including board and video games, bingo and trivia nights, and Taco Tuesdays. Even so, the extensive and ever-changing tap and bottle lists are enough to bring any beer-lover calling; stay tuned to their social media pages for new arrivals from craft breweries around the globe. ✉ *2212 Elliston Pl., Elliston Place* ☎ *615/915–0764* 🌐 *www.hurry-back.com*.

Old Glory

One of Nashville's newest speakeasy-style lounges, Old Glory is housed in an old steam-cleaning facility, and retains most of the building's original 1920s fixtures—all except the sign: you'll find it by looking for the large golden triangle at its entrance. Drinks and company take center stage here; while there isn't an expansive food menu, there are craft drinks that highlight fresh and seasonally available ingredients, like the Chiang Mai Fire, a mango-based cocktail that is all the rage among the summer crowd. ✉ *1200 Villa Pl., Suite 103, Elliston Place* ☎ *615/679–0509* 🌐 *oldglorynashville.com*.

★ The Patterson House

The Patterson House is one of Nashville's long-standing speakeasy-style bars, offering a Prohibition-era feel with its obscured entrance, cordoned-off dining area, and house rules, such as one must be seated in order to be served a drink, and men cannot introduce themselves to women without invitation. However, this cultivated vibe makes it one of the most popular nightspots in the city—that, and the amazing drinks, which are crafted by mixologists at a bar in the middle of the chandelier-laden dining room. ✉ *1711 Division St., Midtown* ☎ *615/636–7724* 🌐 *www.thepattersonnashville.com*.

★ Tavern

Don't be fooled by its name—Tavern is a gastropub in every sense of the word, offering hearty dinner entrées like pork chops and short rib tacos, along with a wide selection of whiskeys, wines, and craft beers. Late-night offerings include turkey BLTs and nachos, and the brunch menu—which features red velvet waffles, huevos rancheros, and two-for-one cocktails—is not to be missed. ✉ *1904 Broadway, Midtown* ☎ *615/320-8580* 🌐 *www.mstreetnashville.com/tavern*.

Tin Roof

Strategically located near Music Row, and originally created as a hangout spot for musicians, Tin Roof is the place to go for good music, good drinks, and good food. With a five-hour happy hour, a Tuesday showcase for songwriters, and featured bands throughout the week, there's no way not to have a good time. ✉ *1516 Demonbreun, Midtown* ☎ *615/313-7103* 🌐 *www.theoriginaltinroof.com/food-drink*.

Two Bits

Want to beat your bestie at a board game over beer? Or maybe play some Pac-Man and then nosh on burgers and fries? If so, Two Bits is the perfect place to feed the kid in you, and satisfy the craft beer connoisseur to boot. With its late-night hours and brunch specials, it's the spot for parties, playdates, and impromptu game nights around the clock. ✉ *1520 Demonbreun St., Midtown* ☎ *615/750-3536* 🌐 *twobitsnashville.com*.

Union Common

Union Common touts itself as a wine bar and steak house, but don't sleep on its craft cocktails, delectable seafood dishes (the fried oyster Caesar salad is a must-have), and music. Jazz Champagne Sundays offer half-price bottles and free listening sessions to the city's hottest jazz ensembles. ✉ *1929 Broadway, Vanderbilt* ☎ *615/329-4565* 🌐 *www.unioncommon.com*.

12 | Franklin

GO FOR

Civil War history

Quaint downtown

Cute shops

Sightseeing ★★★★☆ | Shopping ★★★★★ | Dining ★★★★★ | Nightlife ★★★☆☆

Pull off the interstate 20 miles south of Nashville, and a simple sign will welcome you to the "number one small town in Tennessee." Strictly speaking, Franklin, Tennessee, is closer to a city than a small town—more than 78,000 people now live in Franklin, which is more than six times the number of people who lived there as recently as 1980—but through all its growth, Franklin hasn't forgotten its small-town manners. From its founding in 1799 until the Civil War, Franklin was a rural but wealthy community of tobacco, hemp, and livestock farmers, as well as the many black Americans who were brought to Franklin as slaves. In 1864 the Civil War devastated Franklin, and when slavery was abolished, Franklin's plantation economy collapsed. In the years since, Franklin has experienced a slow climb back to prosperity. However, today it's one of the wealthiest cities in one of the wealthiest counties in the country. You can still find huge, rolling tracts of Tennessee greenery throughout Franklin, dotted with antebellum and Victorian homes and Civil War battlegrounds. Downtown Franklin is the quintessential picture of small-town charm, packed with shops, restaurants, and quaint cafés, all crowded into historic redbrick storefronts around narrow, lamp-lit streets. Franklin's history has been anything but simple, but spend an afternoon making small talk over a plate of fried pickles, and you're liable to feel like you've been transported to a simpler time.—*by Christy Lynch*

Sights

Carnton Plantation
This stunning antebellum plantation home was converted to a field hospital after the Battle of Franklin in 1864. Today, the plantation offers several different tours, including one on Thursdays that focuses on the individuals enslaved at Carnton Plantation and how emancipation changed their lives. Be sure to explore the grounds after your visit. In addition to the house, there are gardens, several outbuildings, and a Civil War cemetery. ✉ *1345 Eastern Flank Circle, Franklin* ☎ *615/794–0903* 🌐 *www.boft.org/carnton* 🎫 *$18 (adults), $8 (ages 6–15), free (5 and under)* ☞ *Last guided tour of the day begins at 4 pm.*

Carter House
On the morning of November 30, 1864, General Jacob D. Cox seized the Carter family's home and made it the Federal Army's headquarters

for the Battle of Franklin. Today you can tour this one-and-a-half-story brick house and hear how the Civil War changed the lives of one family in particular and the country at large. ✉ *1140 Columbia Ave., Franklin* ☎ *615/791–1861* 🌐 *www.boft.org/the-carter-house* 🎫 *$18 (adults), $8 (ages 6–15), free (5 and under)* ☞ *Last guided tour of the day begins at 4 pm.*

Fort Granger

Fort Granger was an earthwork fort created by the Union troops during the Civil War. Today, it's a park along the Harpeth River with a self-guided walking tour through the Franklin Battlefield. Start at the beginning of the path and follow the placards to learn the history of the Battle of Franklin. If you follow the path all the way to the end, it will lead you to Pinkerton Park. ✉ *113 Fort Granger Dr., Franklin* ☎ *615/794–2103* 🎫 *Free.*

Lotz House

Built in 1858, this grand house in downtown Franklin was home to a family of German immigrants during the years surrounding the Civil War. Even those who don't care for Civil War history will enjoy touring this house. It contains one of the best antique collections in Tennessee, as well as the art of Matilda Lotz, who became a world-renowned painter of animals after the war. ✉ *1111 Columbia Ave., Franklin* ☎ *615/790–7190* 🌐 *www.lotzhouse.com* 🎫 *$12 (adults), $10 (seniors 65+), $6 (ages 7–13), free (6 and under)* ⏲ *Closed on all holidays* ☞ *Last guided tour of the day begins 1 hr before closing.*

GETTING HERE

If you're staying in Nashville, you'll need a car for a day trip to Franklin. Renting a car or bringing your own is best; the rideshare fare will be pretty hefty, and there's no public transportation between Nashville and Franklin. However, once you reach Franklin's city center, it's easy to find street parking downtown, and most places will be walkable from there.

Pinkerton Park

This park has not one but two playgrounds for little ones to explore. For older kids, there are Ping-Pong tables, plenty of green space, and a paved 1-mile walking trail around the park's perimeter. There are also picnic tables, pavilions, and grills if the weather calls for barbecue. ✉ *405 Murfreesboro Rd., Franklin* ☎ *615/794–2103* 🎫 *Free.*

 Shopping

Carpe Diem

This small but mighty record store offers an impressive collection of vintage vinyls, antique doodads, and art. Run by the same folks as Kimbro's Pickin' Parlor next door, it definitely has a similar vibe: curated junk, gritty rock and roll, and down-home family lovin'. ✉ *212 S. Margin St., Franklin* ☎ *615/429–0157* 🌐 *www.carpediem212.com* ⏲ *Closed Sun. and Mon.*

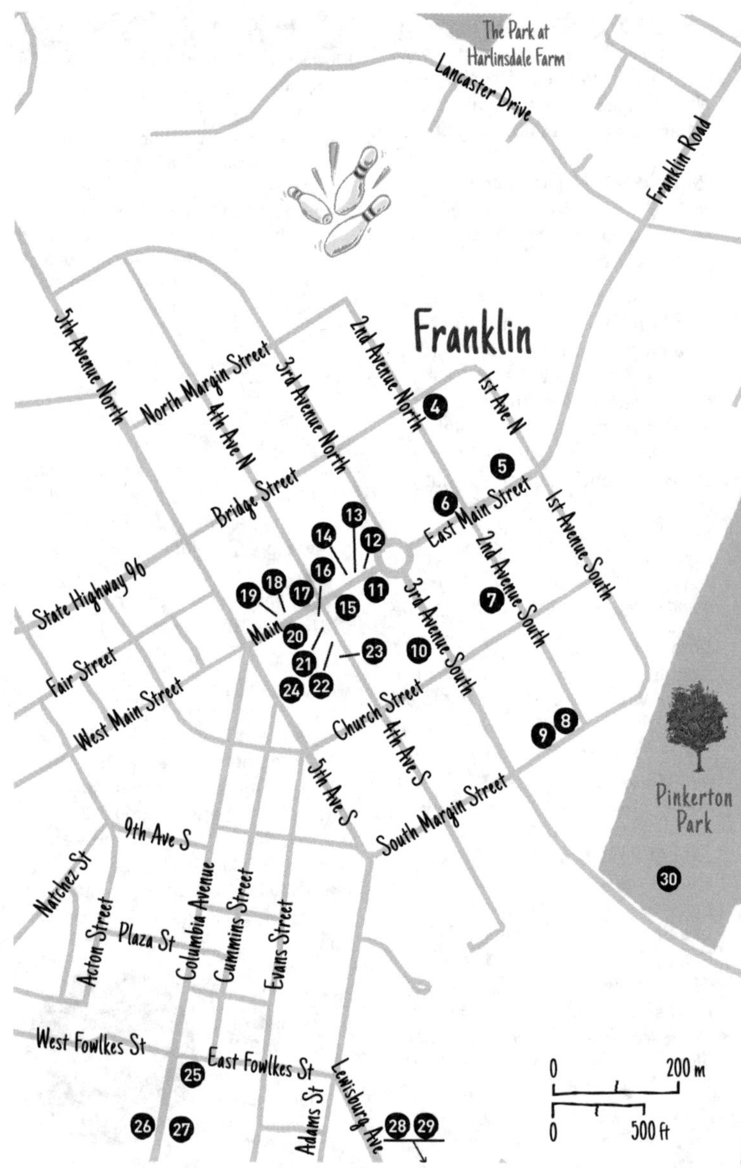
The Park at Harlinsdale Farm
Lancaster Drive
Franklin Road
Franklin
5th Avenue North
North Margin Street
3rd Avenue North
2nd Avenue North
1st Ave N
4th Ave N
Bridge Street
East Main Street
1st Avenue South
2nd Avenue South
State Highway 96
Main
3rd Avenue South
Fair Street
West Main Street
Church Street
4th Ave S
5th Ave S
South Margin Street
Pinkerton Park
9th Ave S
Natchez St
Acton Street
Plaza St
Columbia Avenue
Cummins Street
Evans Street
West Fowlkes St
East Fowlkes St
Lewisburg Ave
Adams St
4
5
6
7
8
9
10
11
12
13
14
15
16
17
18
19
20
21
22
23
24
25
26
27
28
29
30
0
200 m
0
500 ft

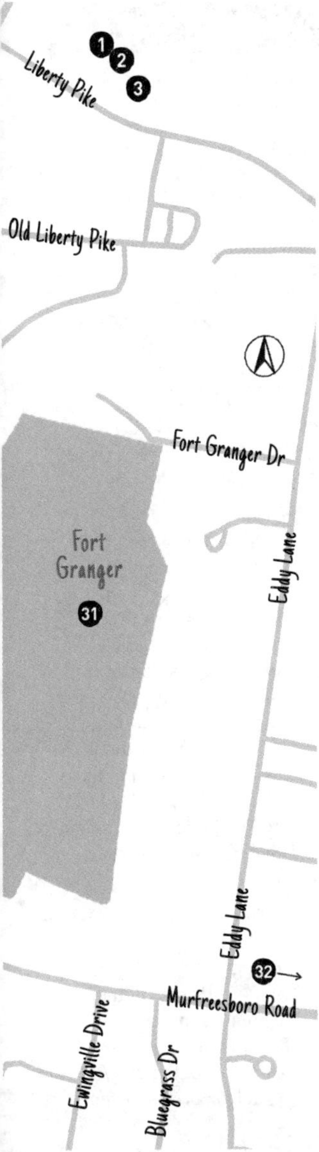

SIGHTS

Carnton Plantation .. 28
Carter House 26
Fort Granger 31
Lotz House 25
Pinkerton Park......... 30

SHOPPING

Carpe Diem 8
The Factory at Franklin.................. 2
Johnnie Q Jewelry ... 11
Landmark Booksellers 5
Music City Tea 32
Rare Prints Gallery 19
Savory Spice Shop ... 12
White's Mercantile... 15

COFFEE & QUICK BITES

Biscuit Love.............. 10
The Coffee House at Second and Bridge 4
Five Daughters Bakery 1
Frothy Monkey 24
Honest Coffee Roasters 3
Merridee's Breadbasket............. 22

DINING

Cork and Cow........... 21
55 South.................... 16
Gray's on Main 14
McCreary's Irish Pub.......................... 18
Puckett's Grocery and Restaurant 23
Red Pony................... 17

BARS & NIGHTLIFE

The Bunganut Pig 27
JJ's Wine Bar 6
Kimbro's Pickin Parlor 9
Mantra Artisan Ales.............. 29
O' Be Joyful 13

PERFORMING ARTS

The Franklin Theater 20
Pull-Tight Players Theater 7

The Factory at Franklin
You'll find boutiques, antiques, restaurants, a guitar shop, and a theater in this airy brick complex of late 1920s-era buildings. Once home to a stoveworks, it's now listed on the National Register of Historic Places. ✉ *230 Franklin Rd., Franklin* ☎ *615/791-1777* 🌐 *www.factoryat-franklin.com.*

Johnnie Q Jewelry
No, you haven't died and gone to earring heaven. You've just stepped into Johnnie Q Jewelry, a shop with so many beautiful pieces of handmade jewelry and vintage accessories, you may briefly feel transported to a higher sartorial plane. Featuring the designs of jewelry makers from across the United States and Canada (including five local designers), every piece is totally unique and certifiably eye-popping. ✉ *317 Main St., Franklin* ☎ *615/794-2763* 🌐 *www.johnnieq.com.*

Landmark Booksellers
There are so many rows of bookshelves filling out this snug bookstore, you'll feel like you're burrowing through tunnels of leather-bound volumes. Landmark Booksellers specializes in old, out-of-print, and rare books, but they have some new books, as well. You'll find plenty of Southern Americana here, and books that focus on regional history, culture, and literature. And all 35,000 books are nestled inside the oldest standing commercial building in Franklin (built in 1808). It's a bibliophile's dream. ✉ *114 E. Main St., Franklin* ☎ *615/791-6400* 🌐 *www.landmarkbooksellers.com.*

WORTH A TRIP

Arrington Vineyards: come for the wine, stay for the beautiful view of sloping Tennessee hills. For food, they have a small selection of cheeses, chocolates, and sausages to snack on, but you can bring your own food if you want something more. Wine tastings are available in the tasting lodge, or you can buy a couple of bottles and have a picnic on the lawn. On the weekends from April through October, there's live bluegrass and jazz music on-site.

Music City Tea
Shopping at this eclectic tea shop is probably the most fun you'll ever have picking out a package of oolong. You can taste as many teas as you'd like for free, and Jenny, the owner with a flair for theatrics, will even teach you how to prepare tea the traditional Chinese way. Don't leave without asking to see a demonstration of the "lazy American teapot." ✉ *1113 Murfreesboro Rd., Suite 405, Franklin* ☎ *615/775-8053* 🌐 *www.musiccitytea.com* 🕒 *Closed Sun.*

Rare Prints Gallery
For rare botanical prints, vintage maps, and lithographs dating back to the 1500s, Rare Prints Gallery is second to none. Don't be too intimidated by the art-gallery-meets-museum air of the place. From medieval lynx prints to *Vanity*

Fair covers from 1871, they have something for every price range. ✉ *420 Main St., Franklin* ☎ *615/472-1980* 🌐 *www.rareprintsgallery.com* ⏲ *Closed Mon.*

Savory Spice Shop

This spice shop will make you wish you had an excuse to buy five different types of cinnamon. They have more than 400 spices and blends in stock, and the best part is, you can taste-test them all—from Hawaiian black lava sea salt, to Hungarian sweet and spicy paprika, to whiskey barrel smoked sugar. ✉ *324 Main St., Franklin* ☎ *615/472-8980* 🌐 *www.savoryspiceshop.com.*

White's Mercantile

This folksy-chic boutique has the feel of an upscale general store. Owned and curated by country singer/songwriter Holly Williams (daughter of Hank Williams Jr.), every item reflects her style. There are decanter sets with deer and geese on them, candles scented like leather and tobacco, and flannel throw pillows fit for any frontiersman with taste. ✉ *345 Main St., Franklin* ☎ *615/721-8028* 🌐 *www.whitesmercantile.com.*

Coffee and Quick Bites

Biscuit Love

$ | Southern. What goes better with buttermilk biscuits than a historical Queen Anne Victorian home? This one, affectionately known as the Corn House (after the Corn family who lived there from 1920 to 1980), is home to some of the best Southern brunch around, from the traditional (biscuits and sausage gravy with a side of cheese grits) to the unconventional (a biscuit burger with pimento cheese and tomato jam). **Known for:** cheese grits; historic location; gourmet biscuits. *Average main: $11* ✉ *132 3rd Ave. S, Franklin* ☎ *615/905-0386* 🌐 *www.biscuitlove.com/franklin.*

The Coffee House at Second and Bridge

$ | Café. This coffeehouse is in a literal house, built in 1904 in downtown Franklin, and during a good mid-morning lull, you can curl up with a cinnamon toast crepe in one of the sitting rooms and listen to a record or read a book. The library room is an especially good spot to pass a rainy afternoon with hot soup and a grown-up grilled cheese sandwich. **Known for:** crepes; sandwiches; cozy vibe. *Average main: $9* ✉ *14 2nd Ave. N., Franklin* ☎ *615/465-6362* 🌐 *www.thecoffeehousefranklin.com.*

Five Daughters Bakery

$ | Bakery. Located inside the Factory, this dreamy bakery seems to glow with soft pink light. They specialize in donuts, but not just any old donuts—these are 100-layer croissant-donut hybrids, cream-filled and glazed in flavors like spiced honey cheesecake and maple bacon (they also have a wide selection of paleo and vegan donuts). **Known for:** 100-layer donuts; classic pastries; vegan and paleo donuts. *Average main: $5 ✉ 230 Franklin Rd., Suite 11j, Franklin ✣ Inside Bldg. 11 ☎ 615/933–9332 🌐 www.fivedaughtersbakery.com.*

Frothy Monkey

$ | Café. This coffeehouse opens first thing in the morning and stays open through breakfast, lunch, and dinner, and there's plenty of porch space to enjoy your rosemary honey latte outside; in the evening, they expand their drink menu to include craft beer and wine. The menu is Southern comfort food with a New South twist (like johnnycakes with house-pickled okra and bacon-onion marmalade), but coffee is still the main event at Frothy Monkey. All their coffee is locally roasted by their own roasting company, and you can buy it by the bag from the café. **Known for:** locally roasted coffee; craft beer; comfort food. *Average main: $11 ✉ 125 5th Ave. S, Franklin ☎ 615/600–4756 🌐 www.frothy-monkey.com/locations/downtown-franklin ☞ Happy hr weekdays 4–6; wine specials on Wed.*

Honest Coffee Roasters

$ | Café. Franklin's first coffee roasting company is an honest-to-goodness great place to get a cup of coffee. Located inside the Factory, Franklin's converted industrial shopping complex, it's also a great place to get an honest day's work done on your laptop, and in addition to their ethically sourced and roasted coffees and selection of teas, there's usually an assortment of croissants, scones, and donuts available. **Known for:** locally roasted coffee; excellent espresso; friendly service. *Average main: $5 ✉ 230 Franklin Rd., Suite 11a, Franklin ✣ Inside Bldg. 11 ☎ 615/807–1726 🌐 www.honest.coffee.*

Meridee's Breadbasket

$ | Bakery. As soon as you squeeze through the front door of Meridee's Breadbasket, you'll feel at home. The shelves are stocked with fresh baked bread, and the cabinets are full of peanut butter pie and butterscotch bars. There are quilts on the walls and baskets hanging from the ceiling, helping the jumble of tables to feel more neighborly than crowded, and the service is as charming as the setting: ask any employee which bread you should order with your chicken salad sandwich, and they'll discuss it with you for as long as you like. **Known for:** Viking bread; chicken salad; pastries. *Average main: $7 ✉ 110 4th Ave. S, Franklin ☎ 615/790–3755 🌐 www.merridees.com ⏲ Closed Sun. No dinner Mon.–Wed.*

Dining

Cork and Cow

$$$$ | Steakhouse. This steak house has major chops: if an exquisite cut of beef isn't epicurean enough for you, you can pair your steak with lobster, crab, scallops, or shrimp. And with a long, luxurious cocktail menu and plenty of aperitifs, desserts, and even a port flight, your meal can drag on all evening with no end to indulgences in sight. **Known for:** steak; cocktails; swanky vibe. *Average main: $50 ✉ 403 Main St., Franklin ☎ 615/538–6021 🌐 corkandcow.com.*

55 South

$$ | Cajun. Named for Interstate 55, which cuts through the Mississippi Delta toward New Orleans, this Gulf-inspired restaurant pulls out all the stops: gumbo, po'boys, jambalaya, shrimp and grits, oysters (char-grilled, fried, or in the shell), and even fried green tomato–shrimp rémoulade. Tables are first come, first served, but it's worth the wait—especially for weekend brunch: Their build-your-own-Bloody-Mary bar has all the fixings for the hair of just about any dog. And their daily cocktail menu, including gems like Honey Hush and the Garden District, drips with Southern twang and Southern flavor. **Known for:** boozy brunch; oysters; Cajun classics. *Average main: $15 ✉ 403 Main St., Franklin ☎ 615/538–6001 🌐 www.eat55.com/franklin.*

Gray's on Main

$$$ | Southern. Before Gray's signature neon sign signaled innovative cocktails and comfort food, it was the sign for the pharmacy that occupied that space for 72 years. When Gray's the restaurant moved into the building in 2012, they kept all the discarded memorabilia from the pharmacy and decorated the place with handwritten prescriptions and vintage pill bottles. **Known for:** innovative cocktails; historic building; upscale Southern dining. *Average main: $30 ✉ 332 Main St., Franklin ☎ 615/435–3603 🌐 www.graysonmain.com.*

McCreary's Irish Pub

$ | Irish. If you need some place snug to get out of the rain, stop into McCreary's for shepherd's pie and a pint of Harp. Their selection of seafood fare, like the Galway fish sandwich, will give you that Irish coastal feeling even as far inland as Tennessee. If you're feeling especially decadent, stop by between 9 and noon on the weekend and give the bread pudding French toast a try. **Known for:** fish-and-chips; shepherd's pie; Irish beer and whiskey. *Average main: $12 ✉ 414 Main St., Franklin ☎ 615/591–3197 🌐 www.mccrearyspub.com ☞ Breakfast weekends only.*

Puckett's Grocery and Restaurant

$$ | Southern. If SunDrop and fried chicken set your heart aflutter, this Southern grocery store/restaurant combo is not to be missed. The cherrywood smoker out back churns out piles of pork, chicken, and

FESTIVALS OF FRANKLIN

Franklin's rotating roster of festivals is essential to its small-town feeling. Multiple times a year, the downtown square is blocked off and invaded by artists, festivities, libations, and cheer. Here are some of the best festivals to check out if you're visiting at the right time.

Main Street Brewfest
On St. Patrick's Day weekend, come taste local, national, and international beers in downtown Franklin amid live Celtic music and a sea of green getups.

The Tennessee Renaissance Festival
Every weekend in May, you can drive just outside of Franklin to watch a jousting match, toast someone in chain mail, and tour Castle Gwynn.

Pilgrimage Music and Cultural Festival
The newest festival on Franklin's block is a two-day music fest that takes place on Harlinsdale Farm each September. It's young but growing in popularity. Past headliners have included Justin Timberlake, Hall and Oates, and Willie Nelson.

Pumpkinfest
Trick-or-treating, professional pumpkin carving, and a costume contest for every age. Revel in Tennessee's perfect fall weather with every incarnation of fried street food, live music, and a chili cook-off.

Dickens of a Christmas
Apple cider donuts, arts and crafts, and carolers in hoopskirts. This is middle Tennessee's largest outdoor Christmas festival, where Charles Dickens's characters come to life against a backdrop of Franklin's historic Victorian architecture.

brisket every day, and you can buy their signature barbecue rub and sauce at the register. On your way out, after you've polished off a slice of fruit cobbler with homemade ice cream, shop the produce section for local eggs, milk, and greens. There's live music every night of the week except Sunday. **Known for:** barbecue; fried green beans; live music. *Average main: $20 ✉ 120 4th Ave. S, Franklin ☎ 615/794–5527 🌐 www.puckettsgro.com/franklin ☞ No live music Sun.*

Red Pony
$$$ | Southern. This sophisticated eatery serves innovative Southern cuisine in an upscale environment, for a dining experience that's elegant without compromising on fun. The menu changes six times a year to keep up with the freshest ingredients, and their award-winning wine menu shouldn't be overlooked; there's bar seating on both the first and second floors, but for a table, a reservation is your best bet. **Known for:** Southern cuisine; wine; shrimp and grits. *Average main: $30 ✉ 408 Main St., Franklin ☎ 615/595–7669 🌐 www.redponyrestaurant.com ⏲ Closed Sun.*

Bars and Nightlife

The Bunganut Pig
Franklin's oldest bar is an English-style pub known by locals as simply "the Pig." Downstairs, the stained glass–adorned door leads you into a dark Victorian-style bar, complete with a Beefeater statue, fireplace, and stuffed boar's head. Upstairs is a bit more modern, with pool tables and darts, as well as a second bar. On a nice day, the café-style seating outside feels especially old-world. ✉ *1143 Columbia Ave., Franklin* ☎ *615/794–4777* 🌐 *www.bunganutpig-franklin.com.*

JJ's Wine Bar
This historic home-turned-wine bar in the heart of downtown Franklin is overflowing with charm, inside and out: with countless cozy hideaways within, and a wraparound porch with picturesque views of Main Street without. Add soft music and even softer lighting, and it's the perfect spot to share intimate conversation and good wine. The center hallway is lined with wine-dispensing machines that offer 1-ounce, 5-ounce, and 8-ounce pours of 28 different wines. There's also a full bar if you'd rather order a whole bottle of wine, small plates, or cocktails. ✉ *206 E. Main St., Franklin* ☎ *615/942–5033* 🌐 *www.jjswinebar.com* ☞ *Closed Sun. and Mon.*

Kimbro's Pickin' Parlor
Broken jukeboxes, dusty lamps, countless hand-scribbled mementos thumbtacked to the walls—and, of course, some of the best live music in Nashville, which is saying something. This legendary restaurant, bar, and music venue puts on a show every night of the week, and Sundays are open-stage. Just bring an instrument, and they'll rotate the players. For great food, local beer, and a genuine everybody-knows-your-name vibe, Kimbro's is one of a kind. ✉ *214 S. Margin St., Franklin* ☎ *615/599–2946* 🌐 *www.legendarykimbros.com* ☞ *Expect to pay a cover to watch the band.*

Mantra Artisan Ales
At this brewery's clean and simple taproom, the beer is center stage. With 28 beers on tap, their offerings are widely varied and masterfully executed—from tasty spins on traditional favorites, like the black saison, to outrageous and original takes, like the Mantra RIP, an IPA brewed with Carolina Reaper Chilies. (Take small sips, it's spicy!) ✉ *216 Noah Dr., Suite 140, Franklin* ☎ *615/628–8776* 🌐 *www.mantra-brewing.com.*

O' Be Joyful
This bar serves up essential American staples every night of the week: hamburgers, hot dogs, beer, and whiskey. They don't get too inventive with their menu, preferring instead to perfect timeless classics like a black-and-bleu burger with an old-fashioned. And with one of Franklin's largest whiskey collections, you'll never have to order the same Sazerac twice. ✉ *328 TN-6, Franklin* 🌐 *www.objfranklin.com.*

Performing Arts

The Franklin Theater

The Franklin Theater's iconic neon sign is the centerpiece of downtown Franklin. Opened in 1937 and refurbished in 2011, the theater now offers an ongoing lineup of concerts, live theater performances, and movies (mostly second-run and classics). You can purchase beer and wine at the concession stand, as well as "Showtime" chocolate bars, created exclusively for the Franklin Theater by local chocolatier Schakolad. ✉ *419 Main St., Franklin* ☎ *615/538–2075* 🌐 *www.franklintheatre.com.*

Pull-Tight Players Theater

The Pull-Tight Players formed in 1968 and set up shop in their current location in 1985. They produce six main-stage shows each year in their intimate theater on 2nd Avenue, which in years past has been everything from a church to a grocery store. Between the small size of the theater and the popularity of the productions, it's best to get tickets in advance. ✉ *112 2nd Ave. S, Franklin* ☎ *615/791–5007* 🌐 *www.pull-tight.com.*

13 | Greater Nashville

GO FOR

Nature encounters

International cuisine

City classics

Sightseeing ★★★★★ | Shopping ★★☆☆☆ | Dining ★★★★★ | Nightlife ★☆☆☆☆

If you leave the neon lights of lower Broadway behind and drive out past the city's forests of tall-skinnies, you'll reach Nashville's actual forests. The greater Nashville area is wild with Tennessee greenery, especially toward the Harpeth River that winds west of town. Whether you're exploring by canoe or by foot, it's the ideal setting for spotting river otters or white-tailed deer. Greater Nashville is also home to some of Nashville's most significant historical landmarks, from antebellum and Greek Revival mansions to country-music-glitz log cabins. But most importantly: the food. Nashville's immigrant population has nearly doubled in the last decade. Large populations of Mexican, Kurd, Vietnamese, Cambodian, Laotian, and Arab people now call Nashville home, and many of them have settled and opened businesses around the outskirts of town. Just drive up Nolensville Pike from Bell Road to Thompson Lane, or travel down Charlotte Pike just west of White Bridge. You can't go wrong no matter which dumpling, kebab, or torta you choose. While the heart of the city remains a revolving door of immaculately tiled coffee shops and velvet-draped speakeasies, the outer regions have been slower to evolve. This means more down-to-earth gems that have stood the test of time—and fewer bachelorette mobs to compete with at the bar.—*by Christy Lynch*

Sights

Adventureworks Old Forest Adventure Park
Take a treetop tour of Kingston Springs, Tennessee, through the old-growth forests west of Nashville. There are nine steel cable ziplines on this course, and each one lets you safely soar above the wooded ravines and blossoming valleys along the Harpeth River. The longest line is about 700 feet long, the highest is about 85 feet high, and the whole journey takes about 90 minutes to complete. You can also visit their second location in Whites Creek. ✉ *1300 Narrows of the Harpeth Rd., Kingston Springs* ☎ *615/297–2250* 🌐 *www.adventure-works.com/adventurepark-nashville-west* 🎫 *$59 (adults), $47 (ages 6–17).*

Belle Meade Plantation
The tall limestone pillars of Belle Meade Plantation are markers of a bygone era. Today, this historic mansion is a museum at the center of 30 acres of smooth green pastures west of Nashville. In addition to the Greek Revival–style mansion, the property includes a

winery and more than 10 outbuildings. General tours are available, or you can take a themed tour like the Journey to Jubilee, which tells the stories of the people who were enslaved at Belle Meade Plantation. A complimentary wine tasting is offered at the end of your tour, or you can book a private tasting separately. ✉ *5025 Harding Pike, Belle Meade* ☎ *615/356-0501* 🌐 *www.bellemeadeplantation.com* 🎫 *$24 (adults), $20 (ages 65+), $13 (ages 6–18), free (ages 5 and under)* ☞ *Last tour begins at 4 pm daily.*

Cheekwood Estate and Gardens
At the center of this sprawling 55-acre botanical garden is a Georgian-style limestone mansion-turned-art gallery, enclosed by clipped lawns, terraced gardens, and an ancient-looking reflection pool. In addition to the collection of paintings and photographs inside the mansion, the Carell Woodland Sculpture Trail takes you down a 0.9-mile path of outdoor art pieces. There are seasonal garden displays, as well—including 150,000 blooming tulip bulbs in the spring and 5,000 chrysanthemums in the fall—so there's always something new to enjoy no matter what time of year you visit. ✉ *1200 Forrest Park Dr., Bellevue* ☎ *615/356-8000* 🌐 *www.cheekwood.org* 🎫 *$20 (adults), $18 (ages 65+), $16 (students), $13 (ages 3–17), free (ages 2 and under)* 🕒 *Closed Mon.*

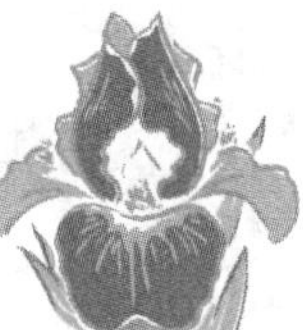

GETTING HERE

You'll need a car to reach the outer regions of Nashville. Though, if you don't have a car of your own, getting a rideshare is also a viable option. Thanks to the Briley Parkway and I-440 loops, even the most obscure locations in Nashville aren't more than 10 or 20 minutes away from the city center. Either way, it's best to make your journey during off-times, because commuter traffic in the morning and evening will really slow you down.

Dyer Observatory
Capping one of Nashville's highest points, the Dyer Observatory rises above Radnor Lake State Park with its imposing steel dome. Inside the dome is the Seyfert telescope, used for viewing the rings of Saturn and other astral wonders. On the second Friday of each month (March through November), the observatory hosts telescope nights for guests to stargaze and mingle with astronomers. Or, for a daytime visit, you can attend an open house between 9 am and noon on the first Tuesday of each month (March through November) to view the sun through a solar telescope and receive a tour from an astronomer. These are both ticketed events, but the cost is minimal (sometimes even free). Simply preregister online. ✉ *1000 Oman Dr., Oak Hill* ☎ *615/373-4897* 🌐 *www.dyer.vanderbilt.edu* 🕒 *Closed Dec.–Feb.* ☞ *Steep road can be dangerous in cold weather.*

Elephant Gallery

This art gallery and studio space in the Buchanan Arts District of North Nashville is irreverent, colorful, weird, and brilliant. The gallery presents both group and solo exhibitions in any style— even Garfield-themed or clown-themed styles. If you get the chance to attend a show here, you'll notice a distinct house party vibe, complete with box wine in the kitchen and bowls of chips. Recent shows have featured face painting and a pie bake-off. ✉ *1411 Buchanan St., North Nashville* ☎ *917/969–9755* 🌐 *www.elephantgallery.com* ⏲ *Closed Sun.–Mon.*

Foggy Bottom Canoe

The Harpeth River has mild rapids and major scenery. Just bring your bathing suit, and Foggy Bottom will provide canoes or kayaks, life vests, paddles, and transportation to and from the river. They offer a variety of tours, from 1½ miles to 11 miles long, and you get to decide how long you want your journey to last. Take all day if you want—pull onto the gravel shore, go swimming, pack lunch in a cooler, bring your dog. Just don't forget the sunscreen. ✉ *1270 Hwy. 70, Kingston Springs* ☎ *615/952–4062* 🌐 *www.foggybottomcanoe.com* ⏲ *Closed Nov.–Feb.*

Fontanel

The Mansion at Fontanel is a 33,000-square-foot log cabin in Whites Creek, Tennessee, filled with country music memorabilia, instruments, and stories. It was once home to country music star Barbara Mandrell, and her glitzy taste is unmistakable throughout. (There's even an indoor shooting range.) Guided tours of the mansion are offered daily, but that's only the beginning. The Fontanel estate also includes the Natchez Hills Winery tasting room, Prichard's rum and whiskey distillery, Café Fontanella, Adventureworks Zip Lines, a boutique hotel, more than 3 miles of wooded trails, and Vintage Creek, a clothing boutique and gift shop. ✉ *4125 Whites Creek Pike, Whites Creek* ☎ *615/724–1600* 🌐 *www.fontanel.com* 🎟 *$24 (adults), $22 (retired military, students, and educators, and ages 60+), $14 (ages 6–15), free (active military and ages 5 and under).*

The Hermitage

The home of former president Andrew Jackson sits at the center of more than 1,100 acres of farmland east of Nashville. Tours of the Greek Revival–style mansion are given daily by guides in full period dress, and you can explore outbuildings, gardens, the museum, and Andrew Jackson's final resting place at your own pace. If you follow the paved path around the full estate, it's about a mile-and-a-half walk. During April through October, weather permitting, horse-drawn wagon tours of the property are available. ✉ *4580 Rachels La., Hermitage* ☎ *615/889–2941* 🌐 *www.thehermitage.com* 🎟 *$20 (adults), $17 (ages 62+), $15 (ages 13–18), $10 (ages 6–12), $10 (veterans), free (active military and ages 5 and under).*

Nashville Zoo at Grassmere

Stretch your legs, pet a kangaroo, and fall in love with a red panda or two. This 188-acre farm-turned-zoo is home to more than 2,764 animals, with more joining the herd every year. For older children and adults, a tour of the historic Grassmere house and farm is a highlight. If you need a break from the Tennessee sun, follow the shady Bamboo Trail to visit the clouded leopards. Or, if it's raining, just bring your umbrella. The animals don't mind when it rains (they live outside, after all), and with all the fussy humans gone, you'll practically have the whole place to yourself. *3777 Nolensville Pike, Nolensville Pike 615/833-1534 www.nashvillezoo.org $17–$18 (adults), $12–$13 (ages 2–12), $15–$16 (ages 65+), free (ages 2 and under).*

Radnor Lake

This 1,339-acre state park offers 6 miles of trails spanning all difficulty levels, so visitors can enjoy an afternoon of leisurely bird-watching or take a strenuous hike. The most popular trail is the 2.6-mile Lake Trail, which circles the lake's circumference and provides great lookouts for viewing local wildlife, such as wild turkeys, white-tailed deer, owls, and blue herons. There's also an aviary, open to the public on Wednesdays and Saturdays, where injured birds of prey are rehabilitated and cared for. *1160 Otter Creek Rd., Oak Hill 615/373-3467 www.radnorlake.org Free.*

Shopping

McKay's Books

This two-story warehouse is the used-media mecca of the South. You can buy, sell, or trade everything from books to movies, CDs, records, games, electronics, and even instruments. If you're overwhelmed by the sheer number of aisles to explore, start with the bookshelf next to the stairs. That's where you'll find new releases that are up for grabs. *636 Old Hickory Blvd., Bellevue 615/353-2595 www.mckaybooks.com.*

Plaza Mariachi

Your nose will be the first to announce that you've arrived, with mouthwatering smells from around the world—Columbia, Mexico, India, the Mediterranean, and more. There's always a dazzling performance happening in the main atrium, like flamenco guitar, salsa dancing, or aerial arts. The rest of the plaza is a colorful marketplace of restaurants, coffee shops, bars, and shops that sell everything from clothes and jewelry to pottery and traditional South American dress. There's even a barbershop and a grocery store, so you can run your regular errands while you enjoy an international production. *3955 Nolensville Pike, Nolensville Pike 615/373-9292 www.plazamariachi.com.*

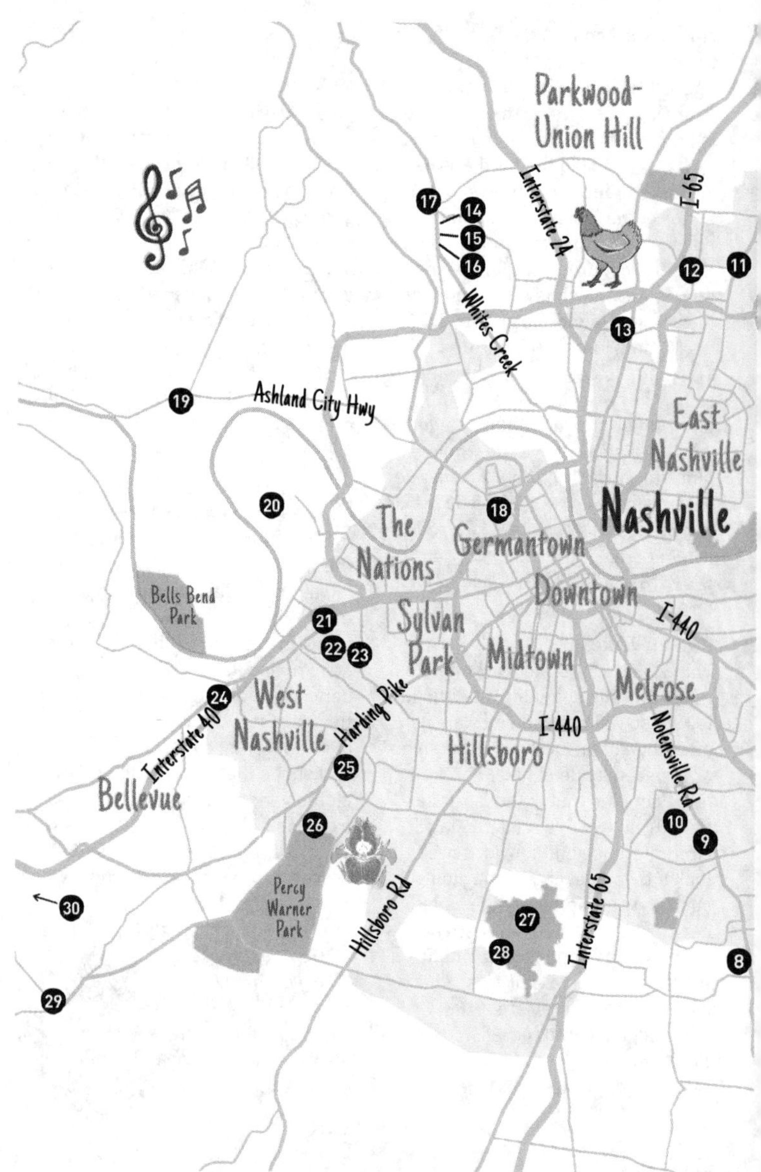

Parkwood-
Union Hill
Interstate 24
I-65
17
14
15
16
12
11
13
Whites Creek
19
Ashland City Hwy
East
Nashville
Nashville
20
18
The
Nations
Germantown
Downtown
Bells Bend
Park
21
Sylvan
Park
I-440
22
23
Midtown
Melrose
24
West
Nashville
Harding Pike
Interstate 40
I-440
Nolensville Rd
Hillsboro
25
Bellevue
10
9
26
Percy
Warner
Park
Hillsboro Rd
30
27
28
Interstate 65
8
29

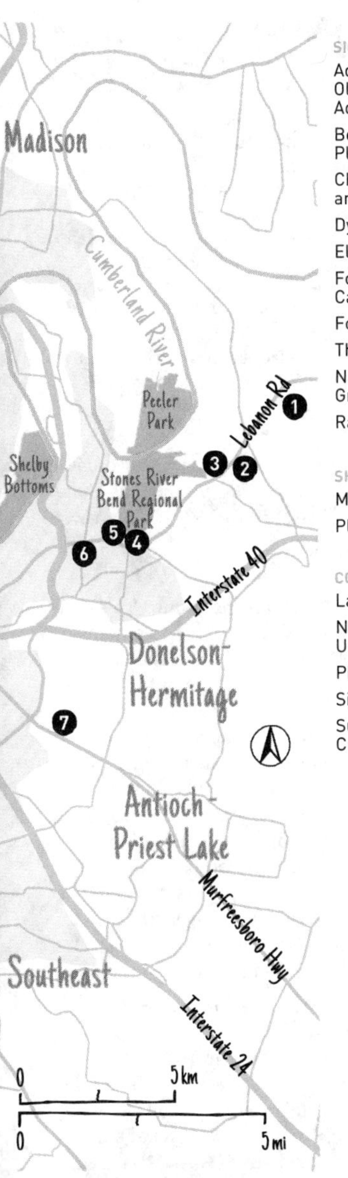

SIGHTS

Adventureworks Old Forest Adventure Park 14

Belle Meade Plantation 25

Cheekwood Estate and Gardens 26

Dyer Observatory 28

Elephant Gallery 18

Foggy Bottom Canoe 30

Fontanel 16

The Hermitage 1

Nashville Zoo at Grassmere 10

Radnor Lake 27

SHOPPING

McKay's Books 24

Plaza Mariachi 9

COFFEE & QUICK BITES

La Hispana Bakery .. 21

Nectar Urban Cantina 6

Phat Bites 5

Sidekicks Cafe 12

Subculture Urban Cuisine and Cafe 8

DINING

Loveless Cafe 29

Lucky Bamboo 23

McNamara's Irish Pub 4

Miss Saigon 22

Monell's At the Manor 7

Nadeen's Hermitage Haven 3

The Old School Farm to Table 19

Prince's Hot Chicken Shack South 13

Richard's Cafe 17

BARS & NIGHTLIFE

Dee's Country Cocktail Lounge 11

PERFORMING ARTS

Full Moon Cineplex 2

Oz Arts 20

The Woods at Fontanel Amphitheater 15

Coffee and Quick Bites

La Hispana Bakery
$ | Mexican. This Mexican bakery serves up fresh tres leches, bread pudding, cheesecake, and a host of other pastries so flaky you'll get almost as much on your shirt as in your mouth. Grab a Mexican Coca-Cola made to complete your sugary snack. **Known for:** Mexican sodas; friendly service; pastries. *Average main: $5 ✉ 6208 Charlotte Pike, Charlotte Pike ☎ 615/645–9723 ▭ No credit cards.*

Nectar Urban Cantina
$$ | Modern Mexican. Half café (pressed juices, coffee, and wraps) and half restaurant (tacos, burrito bowls, and a full bar), Nectar Urban Cantina is great whether you're in a hurry or have more time to kill. Inside an updated Tudor-style house, they offer fresh Mexican-inspired cuisine in a bright, casual space. If the weather's nice, check out their beer garden and outdoor margarita bar. **Known for:** tacos; juice; fried plantains. *Average main: $13 ✉ 206 McGavock Pike, Donelson ☎ 615/454–2277 🌐 www.nectarcantina.com.*

Phat Bites
$ | Deli. Maybe it's the graffitied walls, maybe it's the local bee pollen honey, but this crunchy-sandwich shop inside a converted garage is undeniably cool. Come any time, morning or night, and you'll find a goat cheese–smothered waffle, a hummus-stuffed veggie wrap, or a late-night cocktail that will suit your needs. **Known for:** hummus; funky atmosphere; sandwiches. *Average main: $8 ✉ 2730 Lebanon Pike, Suite B, Donelson ☎ 615/871–4055 🌐 www.phatbites.com.*

WORTH A TRIP: THE GREEN DRAGON PUB AND BREWERY

Tolkien fans, take heed! If you drive 30 minutes east of Nashville, you'll find a *Lord of the Rings*–themed bar in Murfreesboro that's definitely worth the journey there and back again. The owner, who can often be spotted in a silk vest and hairy hobbit feet slippers, is a major beer enthusiast. So, on top of the Middle Earth atmosphere, there's a long list of weird and wonderful brews to try. This pub is family-friendly and serves hand-crafted soups and sandwiches.

Sidekicks Cafe
$ | Southern. This country café in Madison, Tennessee, has a home-cooked appeal. Try a loaded biscuit for breakfast or a pimento cheese–and– bacon sandwich for lunch, and don't forget to check the cabinet for a daily selection of house-made pastries and desserts. By the time you leave, the staff will know you by name. **Known for:** Southern hospitality; chess squares; hash browns casserole. *Average main: $9 ✉ 1202 S. Graycroft Ave., Madison ☎ 615/300–8133 🌐 www.sidekickscafemadison.com ⏲ Closed Sun.*

Subculture Urban Cuisine and Cafe
$ | Modern American. This unassuming New American café takes on the world's street food one empanada, crepe, and Cubano at a time.

You can get their award-winning hot chicken in sandwich form, taco form, or (if you want to order off-menu) as hot chicken ramen. **Known for:** hot chicken; burgers; churrasco sandwich. *Average main: $10 ✉ 5737 Nolensville Pike, Nolensville Pike ✣ In the same shopping complex as Kroger ☎ 615/955–1223 🌐 www.subculture-cafe.com ⏲ Closed Sun.*

Dining

Loveless Café

$ | Southern. Southwest of Nashville on Highway 100, the Loveless Café serves up its famous scratch-made biscuits and country ham every day of the week. Long waits for a table are typical, so be prepared to do some shopping and play a round of cornhole while you wait. When the café opened in 1951, it was just chicken served at picnic tables on Lon and Annie Loveless's front porch. But over the years, the restaurant has expanded to include every iteration of Southern breakfast and supper. In 2004 the remainder of the on-site motel was converted into quaint country shops—chief among them the Hams & Jams Country Market, where you can get free coffee all day, Southern-inspired home goods and gifts, and barbecue to go. **Known for:** biscuits; country ham; fried chicken. *Average main: $12 ✉ 8400 Hwy. 100, Bellevue ☎ 615/646–9700 🌐 www.lovelesscafe.com.*

Lucky Bamboo

$ | Chinese. A bubbling koi pond, panda mural, and jungle of potted plants create a deceivingly kitschy setting for the most authentic Sichuan and Cantonese food in Nashville. You can't go wrong ordering a hot pot off the menu, but for something really special, come on the weekend from 11 am to 3 pm and order dim sum off the cart. Speaking of special, you can also order specials off the board at the front of the restaurant. Braised oxtail and dry pepper pig feet, anyone? **Known for:** dim sum; hot pot; sesame balls. *Average main: $10 ✉ 5855 Charlotte Pike, Suite B, Charlotte Pike ☎ 615/760–5930 🌐 www.luckybamboochinabistro.com.*

McNamara's Irish Pub

$$ | Irish. It's impossible to overstate how cozy this Irish pub is. There's live music every night of the week, but on Friday through Sunday, you can catch the owner himself performing traditional Irish tunes with his band, Nosey Flynn. After dinner, Finn McCool's Ice Cream Pie is an unbeatable treat, but you'll need at least four people to finish a slice. Or, if you're after something a little stronger, McNamara's serves every Irish whiskey you can get in Nashville. If there's a long wait downstairs, they also serve the full menu upstairs in the semi-secret sports bar. **Known for:** live music; steak-and-Guinness pie; full Irish breakfast. *Average main: $15 ✉ 2740 Old Lebanon Rd., Donelson ☎ 615/885–7262 🌐 www.mcnamarasirishpub.com ⏲ Closed Mon.*

Miss Saigon

$$ | Vietnamese. When the Far East comes to West Nashville, it means you get to have a pint of local beer with your bowl of filet mignon pho. Miss Saigon's selection of Vietnamese delights is unrivaled, but if you need help narrowing it down, the Bún Miss Saigon (their famous five-meat vermicelli) with a glass of homemade corn milk (yes, corn milk) is an unbeatable combination. **Known for:** vermicelli; pho; corn milk. *Average main: $13* ✉ *5849 Charlotte Pike, Charlotte Pike* ☎ *615/354–1351* 🌐 *www.miss-saigontn.com* 🕓 *Closed Tues.*

Monell's at the Manor

$$ | Southern. With its famous family-style dining and even more famous skillet-fried chicken, Southern hospitality is on full display at Monell's at the Manor. This restaurant calls Colemere Mansion home, a Southern Colonial mansion built in 1930, and they roll out a different meal every day of the week. Southern classics like roast beef, fried catfish, and chicken and dumplings are weekly staples, but it's the vegetables that really complete the experience. **Known for:** family-style dining; skillet-fried chicken; corn pudding. *Average main: $20* ✉ *1400 Murfreesboro Pike, Murfreesboro Pike* ☎ *615/365–1414* 🌐 *www.monellstn.com/at-the-manor.*

Nadeen's Hermitage Haven

$$ | Diner. For a neighborhood joint that takes diner fare to the next level, Nadeen's balance of folksy and classy won't disappoint. The rolls for their Philly cheesesteaks actually come from Philadelphia, and their biscuits are fresh every morning. **Known for:** poutine; fried pies; chicken and waffles. *Average main: $15* ✉ *3410 Lebanon Pike, Hermitage* ☎ *615/873–1184* 🌐 *nadeenshermitagehaven.business.site* 🕓 *Closed Mon.*

The Old School Farm to Table

$$$ | Modern American. This 1936 schoolhouse-turned-restaurant serves local, sustainable, hyper-seasonal food on a farm 10 miles north of Nashville. The farm's primary mission is to employ adults with intellectual disabilities, and the restaurant is a leading member of the Nashville Food Waste Initiative. Check their calendar for live music performances, and get a reservation if you can. **Known for:** brunch; seasonal menu and inventive cocktails; live music. *Average main: $25* ✉ *5022 Old Hydes Ferry Pike, Scottsboro* ☎ *615/336–0100* 🌐 *www.theoldschoolnashville.com* 🕓 *Closed Mon.–Wed.* ☞ *Reservations recommended.*

★ **Prince's Hot Chicken Shack South**

$ | Southern. Started in 1945 by James Thornton Prince and passed down to his great-niece André Prince Jeffries in the '80s, this is Nashville's most renowned hot chicken spot (the original location sadly closed its doors after a fire in late 2018). If

PARKS AND HIKING TRAILS

Nashville is enclosed by natural beauty on all sides. These are the parks where Nashville's wild green splendor is most vividly on display. (Watch out for snakes. This is Tennessee, after all.)

North of Town

Cedar Hill Park: A paved walking trail around a lake with plenty of ducks, turtles, and other animals to watch.

Beaman Park: Steep slopes, clear springs, diverse plant life, and more than 5 miles of hiking trails.

East of Town

Two Rivers Park: A pedestrian bridge, paved greenway trails, an 1859 antebellum mansion, and the happiest dog park in Nashville.

South of Town

Warner Parks: Percy Warner Park and Edwin Warner Park together make up 3,100 acres of forests, popular for their variety of gorgeous trails and curious creatures.

West of Town

Harpeth River State Park: five hiking trails, from easy to difficult, including the scenic Narrows of the Harpeth and Hidden Lake trails.

Bells Bend Park: 808 acres of former farmland, now an open green space for hiking and wildlife watching.

you're a beginner, try the four-piece tenders with white bread and pickles—don't be a hero; even the mild is plenty hot. There's limited seating, and the plastic tablecloths aren't out to impress anyone. Nonetheless, the food is nothing but impressive. Prince's was even named an American Classic by the James Beard Foundation Awards in 2013. **Known for:** hot chicken; seasoned fries; storied history. *Average main: $12* ✉ *5814 Nolensville Pike, Nolensville Pike* ☎ *615/810–9388* 🌐 *www.princeshotchicken.com* 🕓 *Closed Mon.*

Ri'chard's Cafe

$$ | Cajun. Drive out to beautiful Whites Creek for live music and authentic New Orleans favorites: po'boys, muffulettas, crawfish étouffé, and (of course) Abita beer. If it isn't too busy, Ri'chard himself will join the band for a couple of songs on guitar. This place offers laid-back fun for the whole family, and you'll need your whole family's help to finish all that fried okra. **Known for:** beignets; jambalaya; roast beef po'boy. *Average main: $15* ✉ *4420 Whites Creek Pike, Whites Creek* ☎ *615/299–9590* 🌐 *www.richardscafe.com* 🕓 *Closed Mon. and Tues.*

Bars and Nightlife

Dee's Country Cocktail Lounge

This dark, wood-paneled bar is a much cooler version of your parents' basement from the '70s. There's live country music most nights, including a bluegrass jam every Monday. And when there isn't a live band, the jukebox keeps the honky-tonk mood alive. It's worth the trek north of east Nashville for a round of darts, a game of pool, and a few classic cocktails. ✉ *102 E. Palestine Ave., Madison* ☎ *615/852-8827* 🌐 *www.deeslounge.com*.

 Performing Arts

Full Moon Cineplex

Horror, beer, and popcorn all under one roof—what more could you want? Full Moon Cineplex offers dinner and a movie every Friday and Saturday night, with a rotating lineup of classics and cult classics. The lobby is a wall-to-wall spectacle of vintage movie memorabilia: lunchboxes, action figures, movie posters—even a full replica of the house from *Beetlejuice*. The theater is also home to Lone Wolf Tattoo, so you can view and then permanently commemorate your favorite '80s horror movie all in one stop. ✉ *3445 Lebanon Pike, Hermitage* ☎ *615/321-3111* 🌐 *www.fullmooncineplex.com*.

Oz Arts

This converted cigar warehouse is now the prime destination for contemporary arts in Nashville. The grounds are dotted with outrageous sculptures, and the hallways are full of display cases with rotating exhibits of envelope-pushing visual art. But, of course, the primary function of Oz Arts is a venue for unique performances. From dance to theater to music to puppetry, nothing appears to be off-limits at Oz. If you crave something more than a tame ballet, let Oz inspire you with their modern lineup of boundary-crossing, discipline-bending art. ✉ *6172 Cockrill Bend Circle, West Nashville* ☎ *615/350-7200* 🌐 *www.ozartsnashville.org*.

The Woods at Fontanel Amphitheater

The Carl Black Chevy Woods Amphitheater is an outdoor music venue unlike any other in Nashville. Located on the property of the Fontanel Mansion and farm in Whites Creek, Tennessee, the stage is at the head of a private wooded glen, and the seating is spread out across the lawn that stretches throughout the rest of the clearing. Attending a concert here feels like hanging out in the woods with 4,499 of your closest friends. ✉ *4225 Whites Creek Pike, Whites Creek* ☎ *615/724-1531* 🌐 *www.fontanel.com/woods-at-fontanel*.

INDEX

A

B

C

F

G

H

Photo Credits

Chapter 4: OpCit/Flickr, [CC BY-ND 2.0] (64). **Chapter 5:** Matt Spicher (73). **Chapter 11:** legacy1995 / Shutterstock (147).

RESOURCES

With the exception of Franklin and Greater Nashville, which both require a car to visit, the neighborhoods covered in this book are accessible by bus, rideshare, foot, or bike from Downtown, which is located in the center of the circle that comprises the city. Join the downtown loop from I–40 if entering from the east or west, or I–65 if coming from the north or south to access downtown.

An all-day bus pass costs $3.25 for adults, $2.25 for ages 19 and younger, and $2 for senior citizens. More information on fares, schedules, and routes can be found at 🌐 *nashvillemta.org*. For information on getting to and around each neighborhood covered in our guide, refer to the beginning of each chapter.

The Music City Circuit (also operated by the Nashville MTA) is a free shuttle bus that travels along two routes: The Green Circuit travels between the Gulch and the Bicentennial Mall area and the Blue Circuit serves destinations between Riverfront Station and the Tennessee State University campus. The Music City Circuit will get you to Nashville's biggest downtown attractions like Bridgestone Arena, the Ryman, the Frist, and more. Neighborhoods are highly walkable and bikeable once you arrive.

There are also 33 B-Cycle stations throughout the city (🌐 *nashville.bcycle.com*), and you can bike from Hillsboro Village to Five Points in East Nashville for $1.50/hour (set up an account on your smart phone and pay with a credit card). Membership rates are also available for longer stays.

VISITOR INFORMATION

Up to date information can be found on Nashville's tourism board website, 🌐 *visitmusiccity.com*. There are several local magazines, papers, and websites for an in-depth look at the city's culture. The Bitter Southerner (🌐 *bittersoutherner.com*) is a design-forward website, email newsletter, and podcast that celebrates the rich culture and history of the American South through stories about music, food, and cocktails, in addition to fascinating and forward-thinking people and organizations. *TimeOut Nashville* as well as the city's community station WXNA (101.5 FM) are great resources for things to do and see.

NOTES

NOTES

NOTES

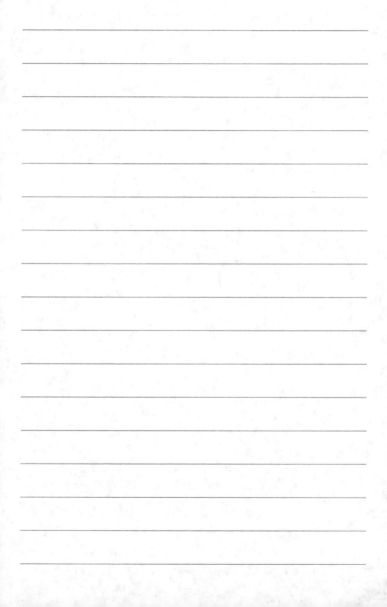

NOTES

NOTES

NOTES

NOTES

Fodor's INSIDE NASHVILLE

Editorial: Douglas Stallings, *Editorial Director;* Margaret Kelly, Jacinta O'Halloran, Amanda Sadlowski, *Senior Editors;* Kayla Becker, Alexis Kelly, Teddy Minford, Rachael Roth, *Editors;* Jeremy Tarr, *Fodors.com Editorial Director;* Rachael Levitt, *Fodors.com Managing Editor*

Design: Tina Malaney, *Design and Production Director;* Jessica Gonzalez, *Graphic Designer;* Mariana Tabares, *Design & Production Intern*

Production: Jennifer DePrima, *Editorial Production Manager;* Carrie Parker, *Senior Production Editor;* Elyse Rozelle, *Production Editor;* Jackson Pranica, *Editorial Production Assistant*

Maps: Rebecca Baer, *Senior Map Editor;* Mark Stroud (Moon Street Cartography) *Cartographer*

Photography: Jill Krueger, *Director of Photo;* Namrata Aggarwal, Ashok Kumar, Carl Yu, *Photo Editors;* Rebecca Rimmer, *Photo Intern*

Business & Operations: Chuck Hoover, *Chief Marketing Officer;* Robert Ames, *General Manager;* Stephen Horowitz, *Director of Business Development and Revenue Operations;* Tara McCrillis, *Director of Publishing Operations*

Public Relations and Marketing: Joe Ewaskiw, *Senior Director Communications & Public Relations;* Esther Su, *Senior Marketing Manager;* Ryan Garcia, Thomas Talarico, Miranda Villalobos, *Marketing Specialists*

Technology: Jon Atkinson, *Director of Technology;* Rudresh Teotia, *Lead Developer;* Jacob Ashpis, *Content Operations Manager*

Illustrator: Vincent Rega

Writers: Brittney McKenna, Hilli Levin, Destiny O. Birdsong, Laura Pochodylo, Jamie Sumner, Christy Lynch, MiChelle Jones, Chloe Stillwell

Editor: Rachael Roth

Production Editor: Elyse Rozelle

Designers: Tina Malaney, Chie Ushio

1st Edition

ISBN 978-1-64097-150-9

ISSN 2640-6349

Library of Congress Control Number 2018914623

SPECIAL SALES

This book is available at special discounts for bulk purchases for sales promotions or premiums. For more information, e-mail SpecialMarkets@fodors.com.

PRINTED IN THE UNITED STATES OF AMERICA

10 9 8 7 6 5 4 3 2 1

ABOUT OUR WRITERS & ILLUSTRATOR

Brittney McKenna is a freelance writer based in Nashville, and contributor for NPR, *Rolling Stone, American Songwriter,* and Pitchfork. Brittney wrote the East Nashville, Hillsboro Village, and Germantown chapters.

Hilli Levin is a native Tennessean who has lived in Nashville since 2009. She is a freelance writer, and an assistant editor at BookPage, and she's always ready to talk about her two greatest passions: books and travel. Hilli wrote the Gulch chapter.

Destiny O. Birdsong is a poet, fiction writer, and essayist whose work has either appeared or is forthcoming in *African American Review, The Cambridge Companion to Transnational American Literature, storySouth, The Feminist Wire,* and elsewhere. Destiny wrote our Midtown and Edgehill chapter, Free Things to Do, and Top Experiences.

Laura Pochodylo is a freelance web developer, digital marketer, and writer based in Nashville. Originally from Metro Detroit, she has lived in Donelson since 2014 and can be heard spinning vinyl weekly on Nashville's community radio station, WXNA (101.5 FM) with her husband Casey. Laura wrote Sylvan Park and the Nations, Melrose and Berry Hill, and Best Bars, and co-wrote our Downtown chapter.

Jamie Sumner is the author of the middle-grade novel, *Roll with It* (Atheneum/Simon & Schuster). She has written for the *New York Times,* the *Washington Post,* and others. She lives with her family in Nashville. Connect with her at 🌐 *jamie-sumner.com*. Jamie wrote What to Watch and Read.

Christy Lynch is a writer and editor living in Nashville, Tennessee. Read her work at NerdWallet, Livability, and elsewhere. Find her online at 🌐 *www.christy-lynch.*com and @christylynchpin. Christy wrote the Franklin and Greater Nashville chapters, as well as the Opryland guide.

MiChelle Jones has written for the *Nashville Scene, The Tennessean, Nashville Arts Magazine, The Dallas Morning News,* the *Wall Street Journal, Art in America, Variety,* and the *Pittsburgh Post-Gazette*. She wrote the Tennessee chapter of *Fodor's Essential USA*. MiChelle earned a master's degree in journalism from Northwestern University and undergraduate degrees from Carnegie Mellon University; she is also the recipient of two National Endowment for the Arts writing fellowships. She wrote the Wedgewood Houston and 12 South chapters.

Chloe Stillwell is an essayist and comedian living in Nashville. She has a Bachelor's in Creative Writing from the New School, and her cultural criticism has been featured in *Playboy*, *Spin* and *Bust Magazine*. Chloe co-wrote the Downtown chapter.

Vincent Rega is a multi-faceted artist, illustrator, and designer, born and bred in New York City. From murals, apparel lines, and album covers, to corporate signage, branding and packaging, his designs have been featured across a wide spectrum of platforms. Some of his past clients include M&Ms, MARS chocolate, Snapple, Disney, Sunkist, Dr. Pepper, Gillette, The Art of Shaving, Big Heart Pet Brands, and nonprofit organization 826NYC. Vincent illustrated all of *Inside Nashville*.